The Language of Experience

Pittsburgh Series in
Composition, Literacy, and Culture

DAVE BARTHOLOMAE *and*
JEAN FERGUSON CARR
Editors

The Language of Experience

Literate Practices and Social Change

Gwen Gorzelsky

UNIVERSITY OF PITTSBURGH PRESS

KH

Published by the University of Pittsburgh Press, Pittsburgh, Pa., 15260
Copyright © 2005, University of Pittsburgh Press
Manufactured in the United States of America
Printed on acid-free paper
10 9 8 7 6 5 4 3 2 1

Library of Congress Cataloging-in-Publication Data

Gorzelsky, Gwen.
   The language of experience : literate practices and social change / Gwen
Gorzelsky.
      p. cm. — (Pittsburgh series in composition, literacy, and culture)
   Includes bibliographical references and index.
   ISBN 0-8229-5874-0 (alk. paper)
   1. Literacy—Social aspects. 2. Literacy—Psychological aspects. 3. Reading.
4. Writing. 5. Learning. I. Title. II. Series.
   LC149.G67 2005
   302.2'244—dc22

                                       2004025539

2/16/06

For Trudy and Jim Batzel

Contents

Acknowledgments

Many people have contributed a great deal to this project, and I deeply appreciate their generosity and support. I especially thank Struggle's participants and my Struggle colleagues and friends, Joyce Baskins, Elenore Long, and Wayne Peck, for inviting me into their work. Taking part in Struggle was a gift in the best sense and a spur to grow. I am also grateful to Linda Flower for welcoming me into the Community Literacy Center and to the many project participants and staff with whom I worked.

Sincere thanks also to Jonathan Arac, Stephen Carr, Marianne Novy, and James Thompson for guidance, feedback, and encouragement. Special thanks to David Bartholomae for helping me to envision a different kind of project, to believe I could do it, and to see myself as a writer. I am grateful to Paul Kameen for a close and thoughtful reading of the manuscript and helpful revision advice. I thank Nancy Atkinson for consistently pushing me to think about my arguments' implications and for sustained friendship. Thanks to Linda Huff for helping me learn the theory and practice of ethnography.

I am grateful to Jean Carr, coeditor of the series in Composition, Literacy, and Culture, and to the outside reviewers who offered helpful feedback on earlier versions of the project. Thanks also to Kendra Boileau Stokes and Deborah Meade of the University of Pittsburgh Press for managing the project and for useful feedback, as well as to Trish Weisman for skillful editing. Also, I thank Gordon Wheeler for encouraging me to link Gestalt theory with composition studies and critical theory. My sincere thanks to David Rosenberg of the University of Pittsburgh's archives for professional help and personal friendship. I am grateful to my Composition Program colleagues at Wayne State University for intellectual stimulation, encouragement, and support.

I especially thank Rebecca Taylor Cohen and Gina Fitzmartin for introducing me to Gestalt theory and practice, for encouraging me to pursue this project, and for offering me a rare kind of friendship. I cannot express the debt I owe to Pamela Batzel for providing extensive feedback on drafts, for pushing me to think rigorously and write well, for conceiving the book's opening line, and for leading by example in encouraging me to see a situation from many sides and to address the empirical evidence. My sincere thanks, always. While I learned a great deal about promoting awareness from this project, I am deeply grateful to Sifu Robert Brown for teaching me the most effective way to expand awareness, which goes beyond any book's scope. Finally, more than I can say, thanks to Dennis Gorzelsky for inspiration, for incredibly generous friendship and support in everything, and for providing such a powerful example of growth.

I am grateful for the extensive institutional support I received for this project. I appreciate permission to use materials from the University of Pittsburgh's Beaver Valley Labor History Society archives. I am also grateful for an Andrew Mellow Predoctoral Fellowship awarded by the University of Pittsburgh and for the following grants awarded by Wayne State University: a University Research Grant, a Minority/Women Summer Grant, the Josephine Nevins Keal Fellowship, a Research Sabbatical, and a Humanities Center Faculty Fellowship. Each of these awards provided support that helped me complete an important stage of the project.

The Language of Experience

I

Conceiving Change: Models, Methods, and Literate Practices

THIS BOOK is about change. More specifically, it is about how literate practices can foster change, from self-revisions to collective social movements.[1] To understand this process, I study three different cases, two historical and one contemporary. Through these cases, I investigate how varied groups use literate practices to mobilize collective endeavors. In each, people draw on literate practices to define group goals, to catalyze support for those goals, and to design and implement strategies for pursuing them.

Two ethnographic chapters examine Struggle, a community literacy program that supports urban teens and parents. In Struggle, participants reflect on, articulate, and revise their life goals and plans for pursuing those goals. In the process, they strengthen key relationships and support systems. Two historical chapters analyze full-fledged social movements. One chapter discusses two radical religious and political movements of England's Civil Wars. The second explores the Pittsburgh region's 1930s unionizing movement. Each of these cases illuminates the way literate practices can foster social change in particular cultural, political, and economic circumstances.

I chose these disparate cases to examine how literate practices operate in different contexts. Three kinds of differences make these cases especially useful: differing emphases on individual versus group change as the focus for improving society, differing emphases on secular versus spiritual or religious grounds for change, and differing emphases on internal cohesion via cultural similarity versus greater political power via cultural diversity and numbers. These differences shape change efforts with a range of grounds, means, and ends. Thus charting the similarities and differences in the role literate practices play in each case provides two benefits. The cases' diversity gives commonalities greater significance than would more similar cases. This diversity also promotes understanding of how different contexts foster different roles for literate practices and produce differences in each group's size and efficacy. Those differences promote understanding of when, how, and to what ends literate practices can most effectively support change. Certainly, other cases could offer comparable diversity. But these three combined that diversity with particular relevance to my research context.

I first approached questions of personal and social change through an interest in Renaissance England's literature and culture, focusing on the period's widening material and cultural gap between rich and poor, its intensification of poverty, and its shift of power from local venues to the central government. Critical theory, from Foucault and Althusser to Spivak and Derrida, offered a way to use these historical events to better understand current relations of economic, cultural, and political power. I have been influenced by Foucault's understanding of discourses and power relations, Althusser's conception of ideology, Spivak's readings of Foucault and Marx, and Derrida's argument about how language inevitably differs from both referent and reception.[2] Despite their substantial differences, these arguments provided ways to understand and address a social system that promotes inequities and exploitation.

This interest prompted my turn toward composition and rhetoric. As I studied these subjects, I recognized that freshman composition exemplifies Foucault's arguments about how institutions and disciplinary practices help construct people's identities (or subject positions). I saw the link I had been seeking: the way to use critical theory not only to understand past instances of social change but also to promote current changes, both individual and collective. In developing my interest in collective change into a research project, I realized the importance of working not only with historical instances but also with a current empirical example. I was directed toward Pittsburgh's Community Literacy Center (CLC), cofounded by Linda Flower, who generously encouraged me to participate in and observe CLC programs so I could study how personal and social changes unfolded and what role literate practices played in those changes.

I began participating and observing at the CLC in early 1994, first informally and later as part of the staff. Initially, I took part in Inform, a program in which teens from city high schools worked with university mentors to produce documents and community conversations on issues central to their lives. They discussed such concerns as school policies on suspension, risk and respect, sexuality, gang violence, and teen-police relations.[3] From there, I moved to Hands-On Productions, a similar program in which teens and mentors wrote, acted, and produced videos on similar issues. In 1995, several CLC staff members invited me to join them in developing a new project. Struggle was designed to support adults and teens in renewing both their individual goals and their shared relationships; it involved adult-teen pairs rather than university mentors. I worked with Struggle until I left Pittsburgh in mid-1998.

I collected ethnographic data at various points in my participation at the CLC, but I eventually decided to focus my research on Struggle, not only because of its relevance to my interests but also because the collaboration and negotiation in the Struggle planning group offered as rich a data source as did our work with program participants. I audiotaped both our planning meetings and those Struggle sessions I facilitated. I also collected relevant documents, from the texts Struggle participants produced, program training materials, and brochures to our planning notes, grant proposals, and academic papers on Struggle. I took field notes not only on Struggle sessions and planning meetings but also on meetings with funding-agency representatives, public presentations of Struggle, and social gatherings attended by Struggle's planners and sometimes by participants (e.g., church services, baby showers, etc.). Further, I interviewed Struggle participants a year after they had completed the project, and I audiotaped these interviews. I transcribed audiotapes of both the interviews and Struggle sessions and planning meetings. The two ethnographic chapters are based in my field notes, transcripts, and collected documents. In selecting materials to use in both the ethnographic and historical chapters, I have been careful to include data that challenge the theory I used to interpret the book's three cases. I incorporate such negative cases into each chapter's analysis and into the larger argument made in chapter 7.

While working in Struggle, I drew on my earlier interest in Renaissance literature to learn about the context of two radical religious and political groups during England's Civil Wars. These groups, the Levellers and Diggers, emerged from the era's ferment of Protestant sects and used newly recognized interpretive freedom to construct scripturally based arguments for political and economic equality. I decided to focus on the Diggers' texts because they (unlike the Levellers) sought economic as well as political equality and actually formed small communities that temporarily pursued the way of life they advocated.

Near that time, I encountered the University of Pittsburgh's Beaver Valley Labor History Society (BVLHS) archives, a collection of materials related to the steel unionizing movement in western Pennsylvania. After surveying its range of union newspapers, pamphlets, posters, oral history project interviews, and similar materials, I focused on the *Union Press*, a local union newspaper first published in Aliquippa in the 1930s. I chose this journal because I was interested in Aliquippa residents' drive to seize civic control of their company town from the firm that dominated all aspects of local government from the town's founding in 1906 until November 1937. Chapter 6 depicts residents' successful use of literate practices to accomplish that redistribution of civic authority. In addition to examining the *Union Press*, it also draws on BVLHS transcripts of interviews conducted with union members as part of an oral history project, as well as on published sources.

During this process, I continued participating at the CLC, and that experience intensified my concerns about critical theory. I grew more aware of its seeming distance from concrete projects of social change, projects linking academics with critical theory's constituents. I heard occasional hallway references to Foucault's work with prisoners, Spivak's work with impoverished third-world women, and Derrida's involvement with marginalized groups, but I never saw such work discussed substantively in academic texts or other formal venues. And I saw little critical theory on how to promote change, work with concrete examples of collective grassroots projects, or support resistance to power. Instead, among readers I knew, critical theory seemed to encourage the presumption that change efforts are inevitably co-opted, blindly complicit, or eventually defeated. My Struggle participation underscored these concerns by highlighting the need for a sense of hope and agency often felt by critical theory's constituents.

I also began to encounter a range of literacy theory and research that offered different approaches to understanding change. For instance, work by Goody and Watt and by Ong provided heady, all-encompassing visions of how literacy transforms cognition. Later work by Heath, Ogbu, and Scribner and Cole produced more concrete evidence and nuanced arguments about how specific literate practices encourage particular kinds of cognition rather than transforming cognitive styles holistically. Ethnographic research on specific communities' literate practices by researchers such as Cushman (*The Struggle and the Tools*), Dyson, Farr, Lytle, and Purcell-Gates persuaded me both that such work does have broader implications and that each community's use of literate practices differs and must be studied in its own terms. Critiques by Berlin, Gee, Graff, and Resnick and Resnick echoed critical theorists' suspicion of institutions by demonstrating the historical function of schooling to socialize an underclass of low-wage workers. Yet their historically framed arguments also suggested that different contexts and social relations could use literacy instruction toward other ends. I encountered this suggestion explicitly in theories of community literacy developed from the CLC's own programs in pieces by Flower and by Peck, Flower, and Higgins.

Erickson's, Street's, and Szwed's arguments for pursuing ethnographies of education affirm that such research as the study of Struggle can contribute to more nuanced understandings of the various roles literate practices can play and the personal and social effects they can foster. Historical works by Burton, Gere, Miller, Royster, and others illustrate the perspective that can be gained by analyzing earlier examples of literate practices. They suggest that historical studies afford long-term perspectives and examples of other kinds of social relations, thus providing another key approach to studying literate practices. Like critical theory, such studies offer pictures of alternative social arrangements.

As I considered such work in relation to critical theory, I began to hear each kind of approach—empirical and theoretical—as amplifying different aspects of literate practices. Critical work emphasized alternate possibilities and illustrated how current conditions are shaped by larger practices and discourses with long, influential histories. It foregrounded the large-scale structures that shape identities and social practices. Empirical studies of current conditions seemed less able to grasp these structures. For instance, Heath, whose admirable work with Trackton's literate practices inspired me, also provided a caution by failing to see how her construction of her white working-class Roadville subjects played into discourses stereotyping working-class people (see Gorzelsky, "Letter"). Further, in their emphasis on what is, empirical studies often ignore what might be, the possibilities for bettering people's lives.[4] Yet my reading of empirical studies persuaded me that theoretical works often miss processes and the possibilities for intervening in them. They ignore how the complexities of individuals' felt experience (re)produce social reality. In revealing foundational structures, they miss the processes that shape those structures. In contrast, empirical studies miss the structures but reveal these processes.

Given my belief that language inevitably erases aspects of reality, I thought that even a synthesis of historical, critical, and empirical work couldn't provide positive knowledge. But my work in Struggle and my reading in literacy studies persuaded me that each approach contributed a partial knowledge. I concluded that a synthesis of the three can document both the structures and processes of social reality. It can present both existing and alternative social relations to consider how literate practices work to support change in varying contexts.

While reading work on literacy, I also encountered critical and experimental ethnography. I was strongly influenced by arguments such as Tyler's for composing ethnographies that foreground subjects' voices in dialogue with the ethnographer's to decrease the colonizing tendencies of traditional ethnography. Seeing this kind of work taken up by such researchers as those published in Mortensen and Kirsch's collection on qualitative studies of literacy, I decided to construct such dialogue in my text. My early drafts included more sections in my Struggle colleagues' voices. In asking them to respond to my depictions and to contribute their own, however, I came to feel I was imposing on their time and good will. Further, readers found some sections difficult to digest and tangential. Therefore, I balanced dialogue with cogency by including just two short excerpts composed by my Struggle colleagues.

Other work on critical ethnography influenced me as well, for example, Marcus and Fischer's call to situate ethnographic studies in the context of global political and economic relations, Clifford's emphasis on paying attention to the allegories undergirding our ethnographies, and Tyler's argument that ethnography can't directly represent reality but can—and should—evoke the possibility of a more equitable, just community. Unlike Willis, I don't systematically interpret my ethnographic subjects' relation to the larger economic or political systems.[5] But I consider how local uses of ideology, discourse, and change connect to both existing power relations and the question of systemic revision. Unlike Tyler, I believe ethnography can represent a partial—if always limited—depiction of reality. Still, I agree that part of its potential power (as in Mead's classic study of Samoa) is in evoking the possibility of more just and humane social relations.[6] I try to evoke such possibility in three ways: by combining my ethnographic representations with depictions of historical alternatives, by foregrounding the metaphors Struggle's participants and planners used to pursue change, and by emphasizing narrative, plot, characterization, and dialogue as well as description and analysis.

Further, following much critical ethnography, I include reflexive sections that depict my own changes. I do so both to provide another kind of data on change and to contribute to the book's underlying allegory of growth. Despite the dangers of presuming that change is organic or positive, I believe the allegory of growth through engagement with difference has powerful potential to encourage more peaceful, equitable social relations. Thus, like other recent ethnographers in composition and rhetoric (e.g., Cintron, Lindquist, and Schaafsma), I use explicitly rhetorical and literary strategies to make my text's form part of its argument and to accent my research subjects' voices. Still, cautioned by Newkirk's argument that qualitative researchers must eschew unrealistic success stories, I include failures, disconnections, and missed opportunities. In addressing both obstruction and growth, I try to ground a realistic hope.

Meanwhile, I discovered Gestalt theory through two friends who were doing postgraduate work at the Gestalt Institute of Cleveland. Because it emphasizes the importance of experiential (or phenomenological) knowledge, Gestalt helped address my concerns about critical theory's tendency to foster disconnection and pessimism by stressing the gulf between language and lived reality. Gestalt shifted my focus from language structures to the mesh between language use and experience. In the words of its foundational text, it helped me to see how literate practices emerge not strictly through language structures or content (such as discourses or ideologies) but through "habits of syntax and style" (Perls, Hefferline, and Goodman 321). Reading my ethnographic and historical data through Gestalt theory led me to see individual and social change not as struggles with ideology, uncritical thinking, discursive rules, or language structures but as problems of connecting language use with experience to revise awareness and perception. In the process, I've come to see this connection as central to change.

Working with Gestalt theory also helped define my stance on what kind of knowledge we can achieve and how. I still credit Foucault's argument in "Truth and Power" that disciplinary methods of constructing knowledge are closely tied to consolidating power. I also agree with Derrida that language cannot represent reality without distortion. I believe both are right about the power of discourses to shape what we say beyond our intentions or capacity to control the effects and implications of our words. I think Spivak, in "Can the Subaltern Speak?" and Althusser (despite their substantial differences) are right about the power of ideology to shape perception and experience. Yet unlike many readers of such work, I do not therefore conclude that representation has no connection with reality. While I agree that knowledge is partial, I believe we can use it to make our actions more effective and ethical, if never completely so.

Empirical, theoretical, and experiential approaches each produce such partial, provisional knowledge. Integrating the three is not like assembling puzzle pieces: it cannot produce a whole picture that offers us positive knowledge in the traditional sense. Still, by including multiple voices, it produces a richer representation with more—and more varied—ties to reality. While that reality is perhaps never fully knowable, we can achieve provisional, nongeneralizable knowledge to use in approaching new situations. For instance, as I argue in chapter 7, I do not believe we can produce a definitive, generalizable model of how literate practices support change because the process differs in each situation. But by examining patterns and differences in various cases, I construct a heuristic, a tool for analyzing how literate practices operate—and could be revised or extended—in a given context.

2

Contact Style

Since there is no nonmetaphoric language to oppose to
metaphors . . . one must . . . multiply antagonistic
metaphors.
JACQUES DERRIDA

Fundamentally an organism lives in its environment by
maintaining its difference and, more importantly, by
assimilating the environment to its difference.
PAUL GOODMAN

As for the Sage's presence in the world—he is one with it.
And with the world he merges his mind.
LAO-TZU

HANGE IS a slippery concept, hard to document and to explain.
To examine it, I turn to Gestalt psychological theory, an
approach based in early-twentieth-century experiments with
visual perception. Gestalt theory postulates that humans perceive both material and psychological phenomena in wholes or patterns,
rather than in fragmented units. In explaining perception, Gestalt emphasizes
the importance of the phenomenological, that is, of individuals' lived experiences and perceptions of reality. As one Gestalt theorist notes, such experiences are inherently private and can be represented, evoke empathy, and
suggest commonalities but cannot be shared (Zinker 96). I find this phenomenological focus useful in explaining how I changed as a result of my Struggle
participation. Using Gestalt, I analyze these changes as an example of the self-
revision that is often necessary for academics as we develop community-acad-
emy partnerships.

For many months after I began participating at the CLC, I felt hurt and
defensive when my colleagues expressed skepticism about academic discourses and institutions, especially critical discourses such as Marxism and post-

structuralism. I perceived their comments as rejections of investments that had played a key role in my development. Only well over a year into my work there did I begin to hear their skepticism as more than anti-intellectualism. Then I began hearing institutional oppositions and a frustration with leftist academic critiques that offered little or nothing to concrete projects of community work and social change.

A Gestalt reading would interpret this shift as a change in my perceptual processes. Rather than introjecting (or swallowing) my colleagues' comments as dismissals of my investments, I gradually learned a perceptual process of listening for broader institutional and interactional causes with less personal import. My initial perception arose from a solipsistic, insecure structure. My changed perceptual processes arose in part from changed proprioception, the perception of internal (rather than external) stimuli. Those proprioceptive changes provided a different structure for understanding my colleagues' skepticism. Gestalt theory holds that such perceptual shifts expand one's field of possible actions.

In this case, a broadened field of possible actions led me to redefine my academic work (and identity) in three ways. The first shifted the focus of my professional self-definition. When I began working at the CLC, I was strongly committed to strengthening the connections between composition and literary studies. As my work on this project unfolded, I came to see these subfields less as audiences to persuade than as sources of methods and content that can help me pursue questions (such as my questions about change) not bounded by field or subfield. That shift prompted me to take up Gestalt theory, despite the fact that I had encountered it through personal interest and had no academic training in its use.

The second change shifted the role of critique in my work. Before I joined the CLC, I wrote primarily in this mode. As my research progressed, I began weaving critique into historical and ethnographic frames. I did so for two reasons. These modes more readily encourage readers to act, while critique tends to promote a necessary—but not sufficient—self-scrutiny. By weaving critiques into these modes, I try to integrate both aims. Also, following Gestalt theorist Paul Goodman, I believe that different rhetorical forms can provide models for different processes of perception and proprioception. Thus by incorporating multiple forms (e.g., narrative, critique, and analysis), I encourage readers to use a range of perceptual frames in relation to my subject. Given Gestalt's argument that perceptual shifts expand one's potential field of actions, I hope these multiple forms can prompt such expansions for readers. Working with the mix of forms has shifted my own perception, encouraging me to experiment not only with different genres but also with different inter-actional approaches and investments of time and energy.

Those experiments led to the third shift in my academic work. I have begun to renegotiate the relationship between my own commitments (e.g., to a quasi-Marxist vision of social justice) and my colleagues' commitments, whether those colleagues are community activists, project participants, fellow academics, or students. I am learning not to relinquish my commitments but to pursue them with an intrinsic, equally deep respect for others' goals, such as people's efforts to develop their capacities for coping with a capitalist world. (After all, my academic endeavors serve that end, as well as furthering my personal and intellectual goals.) Similarly, I am taking a new approach to the problem of how discourses, institutions, and disciplinary practices shape people's identities, or subject positions. Through my Struggle work, I have heard nonprivileged learners' often-paralyzing sense of powerlessness. As a result, I have committed to developing pedagogical strategies designed to foster learn-ers' experiences of agency.

For example, in a change that parallels the shifts in my own writing prac-tices, I have moved from assigning critical papers toward assigning critique as part of other rhetorical forms that encourage students' sense of agency as writ-ers. In doing so, I am supporting students in developing skills they can use in the existing economic system as well as in experimenting—if they choose—with self-revisions. Because such self-revisions shift one's relations with others, institutions, and social groups, I see encouraging them as one of the most effective ways I, as a teacher, can support social change. In Gestalt terms, they foster reorganizations of experience, or changes in the way one experiences internal and external phenomena. Such changes are holistic in that they include cognitive interpretations, physiological responses, and emotional sen-sations. Gestalt holds that they revise one's perceptions of one's needs and of the environmental resources available for meeting those needs. By engaging in them with students or community partners, I support such perceptual shifts for everyone involved. Because such shifts change perceptions of environmen-tal resources—including the potential for coalition—they offer an organic way of moving toward a revised version of Marx's collectivity. Rather than seeking to impose philosophical principles or a theoretical program, this approach respects the cognitive, emotional, and visceral dimensions of people's experi-ence, honoring its phenomenological nature. Here the impetus toward social change revises social theory's approach by including all groups' provisional goals in collective negotiations that privilege respect for experience over ratio-nalist argument.

Such negotiations demand the kind of self-reorganization Gestalt theory explains. While these reorganizations can only occur voluntarily, they still entail risk and loss as they revise habitual perceptual frames, interactional styles, and behaviors. Of course, as individuals we often find such changes difficult. In conjunction with our personal resistances, larger social, cultural, and institutional factors inhibit the possibilities for change as well. Poststructuralist theory highlights some of these factors and offers approaches to addressing them.

Individual resistance to change is complicated by the stasis promoted by discourses and institutions. Together, these forms of stasis shape how knowledge, identities, and self-other relations are constructed. In "Limits and Openings of Marx in Derrida," Gayatri Spivak shows how the intersection of the three makes philosophical systems such as theoretical Marxism vulnerable to totalitarian uses. She does so by examining Marx's plan to mobilize workers' resistance to capitalism. Marx tries to show his target audience (members of the German Social Democratic Workers' Party) the double nature of work as a commodity whose surplus value, by definition, exceeds its use value. In Marx's argument, use value exists empirically prior to any exchange. But in defining use value, Marx can name it only in relation to exchange value. Thus it appears only after exchange and, in workers' lived experience, it equals (rather than exceeds) exchange value. Therefore, Spivak concludes, surplus value and capitalism's exploitation remain invisible. By presenting use value as an origin that can emerge only after its product, exchange value, appears, Marx prevents workers from understanding their experiences in its terms. Thus workers find little ground in Marx's theory for resisting capitalism.

Spivak describes Marx's approach as antihumanist because it displaces workers' experienced reality in favor of Marx's abstractions (use value and surplus value). She shows that by trying to persuade his audience on a strictly cognitive level, Marx excludes their phenomenological experience, the sensory and emotional grounds of their perception and thinking. Attempts to impose theoretical principles in the face of such conflicting experience solidify visions of social good into coercive institutions. One example is Stalin's attempt to collectivize Soviet farming by forcing Russian peasants to relocate to industrial centers or deporting them to labor camps. Thus Spivak's reading suggests that experienced reality cannot be readily replaced. Rather, efforts toward social transformation must negotiate with people's formulations of their experience.

Spivak examines the complexities of this negotiation, and the obstacles it poses for academics, in "Can the Subaltern Speak?" The essay explores how discourses and institutions constrain even well-intentioned efforts to produce scholarship that supports liberatory projects. While validating antisexist work among women facing race or class oppression, as well as research on their lives, Spivak warns that such work inevitably also constructs oppressed (or subaltern) subjects in imperialist terms, "mingling epistemic violence with the advancement of learning and civilization." As a result, despite such research, "the subaltern woman will be as mute as ever" (295). She concludes,

> In so fraught a field, it is not easy to ask the question of the consciousness of the subaltern woman; it is thus all the more necessary to remind pragmatic radicals that such a question is not an idealist red herring. . . . In seeking to learn to speak to (rather than listen to or speak for) the historically muted subject of the subaltern woman, the postcolonial intellectual *systematically* "unlearns" female privilege. This systematic unlearning involves learning to critique postcolonial discourse with the best tools it can provide and not simply substituting the lost figure of the colonized. (295)

Established discourses (such as academic discourses, from anthropology to history) and institutions (such as universities and publishers) offer scholarly researchers particular narratives and circulate those narratives through established channels. Because academics work within culturally sanctioned narratives and pursue refereed publication, we find ourselves constructing predictable depictions, such as that of the "victim of imperialist racism" or the "heroic subaltern revolutionary."[1] In Spivak's terms, we constitute subjects from the terms available in the imperialist repertoire.

Yet, as she suggests, subaltern subjects also construct themselves, inevitably, by using or responding to the discourses available. Thus they cannot articulate a subaltern perspective free of ideology any more than sympathetic intellectuals can. Spivak demonstrates this point dramatically in a critique of Foucault and Deleuze's failure to recognize how ideology can shape perception. In contrast with their claim that interest always finds itself where desire leads it, Spivak shows that ideology can lead people to desire against their own interests (274). She does so by examining the Hindu practice of widow-suicide as it evolved in response to British suppression.

In this practice, *sati*, widows immolated themselves on a deceased husband's funeral pyre. Spivak shows how the British criminalization of sati overwrote the Hindu patriarchy behind the practice. This erasure, she argues, suggests that Hindu widows practicing sati in defiance of British law acted through free will. Both British and Brahmin authorities used the notion to jus-tify their positions on sati. The British rationalized colonialist domination by arguing that they were saving Hindu women from coerced suicides, while Hindu nationalists (during and after the colonial period) authorized resistance to colonialism by depicting widow-suicides as nationalist heroines. Such women faced a choice between cultural marginalization and exploitation on the one hand and identifying with imagery of self-obliteration on the other. Thus in both British and Brahmin depictions, Hindu women are subjugated through the notion of free choice, which justifies patriarchal positions by eras-ing ideology's role in determining the women's actions. Spivak concludes that the women desire—and act—against their own interests (299). Thus she insists on ideology's power to shape not only empirical circumstances but lived experience (here, the widows' practice of self-immolation).

Because subalterns can and do adopt ideologies that undermine their interests, Spivak argues, academics pursuing social change cannot rely on merely transmitting subaltern voices. Even insurgent subalterns, she warns, should not be used as models (287), a persuasive argument, given the Hindu nationalists' use of sati as a rallying image. Empirical research (such as ethnog-raphy) focused on disempowered groups risks precisely this result. Spivak con-tends that the danger of examples, whether generated through such empirical research or through the deconstructive approach she uses, is that they risk freezing the specifics of a particular situation into an ideal of resistance (292). Instead, she argues, such examples can, at best, evoke alternatives to the roles dominant ideologies cast for subalterns. Spivak develops just such an example by presenting the case of a young Hindu woman who joined the movement opposing colonial occupation of India yet found herself unable to carry out her assigned task (an assassination). She decided to commit suicide instead. To ensure that others would not attribute her act to an illegitimate pregnancy, the young woman waited for her menses, thus reinscribing the traditional reason for female suicide into a political statement, much as sati was reinscribed. Thus while Spivak concludes that "the subaltern as female cannot be heard or read," she constructs precisely such a reading of one subaltern woman's actions (308).

She produces knowledge while showing that no form of knowledge is trustworthy. Theoretical knowledge (including knowledge generated through critique, such as Marx's formulation of surplus value) partially erases people's lived experience. Empirical investigations (including ethnographic investiga-tions) construct subjects' lived experience in terms of the culturally sanctioned narratives available in academic discourses. Phenomenological knowledge (including subalterns' self-knowledge) voices people's constructions of their own experience in terms of the ideologies available in the wider culture. All potential ways of knowing experience, our own or others', thus take shape through discourse and ideology. All rely on language, which abstracts us from felt reality through its erasures, thus alienating us from our experience. Spivak concludes that the best we can do is, as Derrida suggests, play different forms of knowledge against one another in an effort to highlight the gaps, constructions, and erasures each produces.[2]

I agree with Spivak's larger argument. Yet despite the inevitable gaps and erasures in our knowledge, we inevitably must use that knowledge to act as best we can on an ad hoc basis. Given her trenchant warnings, I believe one way to work toward ethical action is for intellectuals committed to social change to pursue Spivak's suggestion that we "learn to speak to (rather than listen to or speak for)" marginalized groups. Thus we can begin to unlearn our privilege. Collaborative projects that bring community members together with academics provide a useful forum for such exchanges. Because academic life and work are often quite distant from marginalized groups' lives, such forums are crucial in fostering these exchanges. They and the collaborations they serve demand that academics and community members negotiate to define common goals and methods for pursuing those goals.

As academics concerned about perpetuating ideology, we sometimes avoid such negotiations because we fear furthering goals we see as ideologically mystified, co-opted, or complicit with systemic exploitation. And indeed, Spivak's warning account of sati highlights the dangers of supporting subaltern goals that can lead to self-destructive ends. Yet if we believe we know better what is good for a marginalized group, we parallel the British officials who criminalized sati to establish their own colonialist domination. If we as academics insist on pursuing what we believe is best for marginalized groups in the face of their opposition, we bolster the systemic tendency to disenfranchise those groups, positioning them as unqualified to make responsible choices for themselves. We bolster the hierarchical status quo of privileged academic knowledge and class divisions. This approach encourages academics' tendency to take a fundamentally disrespectful stance toward marginalized groups' perceptions and goals.

I see this stance as particularly dangerous for our self-construction because we have so often been the agents used by socioeconomic and political systems to disenfranchise such groups. When we take it, we undercut subalterns' opportunities to make choices for themselves—ideologically mystified or not—and to shape their own experiences. Gestalt theory holds that such experiences are central to learning, growth, and change. By obstructing them, we obstruct such change. Thus while Spivak emphasizes the danger of supporting subalterns' potentially self-destructive ideologies, I believe her stress on unlearning our privileges (of class, discourse, and ideology) offers a productive alternative. My reading of Gestalt suggests such efforts require learning to listen to subalterns as part of learning to speak to them. But rather than listening so we can transmit their voices as the products of a "pure" subaltern consciousness, I suggest listening so we can negotiate with marginalized groups, thus potentially revising our consciousness as well as theirs.

Such negotiations may integrate support for individual efforts at class mobility with efforts to foster systemic changes, or they may take other approaches.[3] By pursuing them, academics can form common cause with the marginalized constituencies we hope to support and till the ground for the kinds of coalitions that generate personal and social change. As Spivak's work suggests, these coalitions cannot follow predefined models or principles. Rather, they must emerge from specific contexts and the interactions among particular groups. Nonetheless, such specific examples can be used to construct heuristics, or exploratory frames, for other groups seeking to undertake such negotiations. Further, they enact praxis, the integration of theory and practice that puts the various forms of knowledge in dialogue with one another and so softens stasis to allow growth.

Gestalt theorist Paul Goodman illustrates how language practices can foster either praxis and learning or alienation and stasis.[4] He develops this argument in the second volume of *Gestalt Therapy: Excitement and Growth in the Human Personality*, authored with Frederick Perls and Ralph E. Hefferline. Here Goodman, like Derrida, examines language as an abstraction that generates the danger of alienation.[5] But unlike Derrida, Goodman does not define alienation strictly in terms of language. Instead, he associates it with tool making and "other acts of abstraction" (314). He describes its consequences for both perception (sensing externally produced stimuli, e.g., another's touch) and proprioception (sensing internally produced stimuli, e.g., hunger): "There is abstracted from the undifferentiated felt-self a notion, image, behavior, and feeling of the 'self' that reflects the other persons" (313–14). Earlier in the volume, Goodman links these consequences to consciousness, explaining, "The notion of 'mind' as a unique isolated entity *sui generis* is not only genetically explicable but is in a sense an unavoidable illusion, *empirically given in average experience*" (263). In this move, Goodman calls into question both phenomenological and empirical knowledge. Like Spivak's critique of the two modes of knowing, Goodman's stance suggests they are mutually dependent.

Goodman demonstrates that the illusion of mind as primary, originating force is reified in social institutions and, as a result, affects the body. This is particularly true, he emphasizes, in (post)modern society's double stresses of internal repression and external threats:

> Conceive that instead of . . . the re-establishment of equilibrium [in the person as physiological organism] . . . there exists a chronic low-tension disequilibrium, a continual irk of danger and frustration, interspersed with occasional acute crises, and never fully relaxed.
>
> This is a dismal hypothesis, but it is unfortunately historical fact for most of us. Note that we speak of the double low-grade excess of danger *and* frustration, creating a chronic overcharge of both receptor and proprioceptor. . . . Both of the emergency functions, deliberate blotting-out [of stimuli internal to the body] and undeliberate hyper-activity are called into play, as follows . . . the attention is turned away from the proprioceptive demands and the sense of the body-as-part-of-the-self is diminished. The reason for this is that the proprioceptive excitations are the more controllable threat in the mutually aggravating troubles. Toward the more direct environmental threat, on the other hand, the attention is heightened to meet the danger, even when there is no danger. But what is given by such attentiveness is "alien," it is irrelevant to any felt awareness of oneself, for the proprioceptive has been diminished. . . . If the process is long continued, the state of deliberate alertness to danger becomes rather a state of muscular readiness than of sensory acceptance: a man stares, but does not thereby see any better, indeed soon he sees worse. And with all this, again, goes a habitual readiness to take flight, but without actually taking flight and releasing the muscular tension.
>
> To sum up, we have here the typical picture of neurosis: *under-aware proprioception and finally perception, and hypertonus of deliberateness and muscularity.* (263–65)

Thus Goodman depicts alienation as fundamentally linked to abstraction, including language. Yet he approaches the consequences of alienation as modifications that change the human organism's physiological capacities (e.g., for perceiving stimuli from both inside and outside the body).[6] Goodman's description suggests that such changes alter humans' very being: "The basic human nature is part given, as [the various schools of psychotherapy] assume, but in part, adjusting to the various therapies, it *creates itself;* and this creative adjustment in favorable circumstances is itself an essential of the basic human nature" (281). Thus for Goodman, abstractive processes intersect with sensory processes to produce experience, which formulates sensations into abstracted descriptions. In turn, those descriptions take part in the ongoing revision of "the basic human nature."

Physiologist Karl Pribram's holographic model of brain and memory clarifies how such physiological modifications result from perceptual changes.[7] Pribram argues in *Brain and Perception* that the brain stores memories as dismembered representations, deep structures that it reassembles into "an experienced 'memory'" when internal or external stimuli call up particular content (xxvii–xxviii). Because the dendritic pathways used in such shifting reassemblies can themselves shift, our perceptual apparatus continuously self-replicates and self-modifies. It is a psychophysiological and cognitive form that literally embodies praxis. Pribram defines praxis, in opposition to skill, as the process of "learning what to do" (153). He holds that the capacity for praxis is rooted in perception, and loss of proficiency in particular forms of praxis, or apraxia, results from loss of one's ability to perceive or experience parts of the self (e.g., an arm or a muscle group) or parts of the external world (149–55). Thus Pribram concludes that "apraxias result from a failure in 'centering' of the corporeal self: an awkwardness more pervasive than the impairment of skills" (155). Because our psychophysiological perceptual apparatus both self-replicates and self-modifies, Pribram argues that structure and process are actually the same phenomenon viewed at different scales. Like ocean waves seen from ten thousand feet above or from the shore, representations (perceptions) can appear as structured images or as processes that "exert considerable force" and "are seething with activity" (xxviii–ix). Thus our perceptions are not static images but the ongoing activity of our perceptual processes.

In tandem with Pribram's model, Goodman's work helps me redefine Derrida's and Spivak's problems of reification and alienation. It shifts their emphasis on the play of language to an emphasis on the intersection between sensory processes and language practices (as one form of abstraction). Reification and alienation take shape at that intersection. Because praxis depends on perception, it emerges there as well. Some bodily processes and habits reproduce truncated perception and proprioception. Thus they generate alienation or apraxia. To foster praxis instead, we must amplify proprioception of our visceral responses and our abstractions, which in turn expands perception. By amplifying these awarenesses, we support the interplay between the abstract and the sensory. In Derrida's and Spivak's terms, we put theoretical (abstract), empirical, and phenomenological knowledge in dialogue at the psychophysiological level (which includes the visceral and emotional as well as the cognitive). In the process, both our abstractions and our phenomenological experiences are opened to change. Thus increasing proprioception and perception melts reification into praxis.

This shift in focus prompted me to ask three central questions about change: (1) How does the articulation of sensory experience with language practices shape habits and perceptions? (2) How can we develop language practices that respect self and other yet support the risks of change at the psychophysiological level? (3) How could such practices encourage collective ·efforts toward equity and justice?

Through his work on rhetorical habits, Goodman clarifies how practices of language use constitute identity. While Derrida and Spivak examine how discourses define positions for people (and at the same time erase their phenomenological experience), Goodman shifts the focus from language itself to particular habits of using it. In doing so, he illuminates the construction of self:

> From one angle, it is useful to define "personality" as a structure of speech habits and consider it as a creative act of the second and third years; most thinking is subvocal speaking; basic beliefs are importantly habits of syntax and style; and almost all evaluation that does not spring directly from organic appetites is likely to be a set of rhetorical attitudes. . . . A child forming his personality by learning to speak is making a spectacular achievement. . . . We may think of the sequence (a) pre-verbal social relations of the organism, (b) the formation of a verbal personality in the organism/environment field, (c) the subsequent relations of this personality with the others. Clearly the right cultivation of speech is one that keeps this sequence flexibly open and creative throughout: habits that allow what is pre-verbal to flow freely and that can learn from the others and be altered. (*Gestalt Therapy* 321)

Here the practices of language use (or the uses of its forms) rather than its content produce the self, as suggested by Goodman's description of basic beliefs as habits of syntax and style and of evaluation as a set of rhetorical attitudes. This is particularly true given the connotations of function and effects attached to *rhetorical*. In this view, language is a medium in which self-other and self-social relations are formed. Its practices help train people's capacities for particular kinds of perception and for taking action on their perceptions. Thus Goodman's approach to understanding how language shapes identity and social relations contrasts with Derrida's and Spivak's.

While the latter focus on the process's theoretical dimensions, Goodman addresses its material (empirical and phenomenological) aspects as well. Even as adults, he suggests, people who encounter previously unfamiliar language practices can take up those practices and so alter their capacities for perception and thus for action.

Goodman calls the interface between person and environment the contact boundary, and he emphasizes the mutually constitutive relationship between organism and environment:

> Experience occurs primarily at the boundary between the organism and its environment, primarily the skin surface and the other organs of sensory and motor response. Experience is the function of this boundary, and psychologically what is real are the "whole" configurations of this functioning, some meaning being achieved, some action completed. The wholes of experience do not include "everything," but they are definite unified structures; and psychologically everything else, including the very notions of an organism or an environment is an abstraction or a possible construction or a potentiality occurring in this experience as a hint of some other experience. . . . You may experience it [the field of vision] with the sounds "out there": [but] their root of reality is at the boundary of contact, and at that boundary they are experienced in unified structures. . . . There is no single function of any animal that completes itself without objects and environment, whether one thinks of vegetative functions like nourishment and sexuality, or perceptual functions, or motor function, or feeling, or reasoning. . . . We try in a detailed way to consider *every* problem as occurring in a social-animal-physical field. From this point of view, for instance, historical and cultural factors cannot be considered as complicating or modifying conditions of a simpler biophysical situation, but are intrinsic in the way any problem is presented to us. . . . When we say "boundary" we think of a "boundary between"; but the contact-boundary, where experience occurs, does not *separate* the organism and its environment; rather it limits the organism, contains and protects it, and *at the same time* it touches the environment. That is . . . the contact-boundary—for example the sensitive skin—is not so much a part of the "organism" as it is essentially *the organ of a particular relation of the organism and the environment.* (*Gestalt Therapy* 227–29)

Thus, like neurobiologist Antonio Damasio, Goodman holds that perception is sensory, its reality defined not by the external object but by the contact between that object and our psychophysiological perceptual system. Like Pribram, Goodman contends that we perceive in unified wholes. Language practices' role in constructing identity takes place within these structuring factors. As a key medium for constituting relations between the self and other (organism and environment, in Goodman's terms), language could take the place of Goodman's example of the sensitive skin. That is, it forms one aspect of the contact boundary, which relates organism to environment and which is where experience occurs. Here, language plays a significant, but not wholly determining, role in shaping experience (or "reality"). Rather, experience forms in the circuitry joining sensory and other psychophysiological responses to internal and external stimuli with abstractive systems such as language. That circuitry generates perception and proprioception—experience.

In this view, alienation is inextricably bound to the capacity to abstract; it is not intrinsic to language per se or even to abstraction per se. Rather, alienation results from the curtailed proprioception and hyperfocused perceptions produced by particular kinds of language use. For instance, the habit of formulating experience in black-and-white terms may prompt the denial and projection that attend diminished self-awareness and a narrowed, anxious focus on external threats (in the form of other people). Such projection can take the form of racism or other prejudices (as Goodman notes), and it typically accompanies decreased awareness of the projected qualities (e.g., laziness, materialism, etc.) in oneself (*Gestalt Therapy* 214). Clearly, such alienation involves the reification of concepts one fears or refuses to recognize in one's own experience.

Goodman's definition of neurosis implies that some language practices work to reduce awareness of internal stimuli and many external stimuli, instead heightening awareness of specific external threats. Such language practices generate alienation and, with it, reification. In contrast, other language practices facilitate a connection between sensory processing of such internal stimuli and the abstractions of language. They more fully integrate sensation with abstraction and so encourage rather than suppress proprioception. In turn, that integration revises the organism's overall perception and experience, changing his process of generating meaning and completion, or wholes. In other words, rather than generating alienation, some language practices produce a richer, more nuanced interweave between sensation and abstraction. Thus they spark changed proprioceptions and perceptions. In turn, those changes prompt the person to take action that differs from her prior typical responses.[8] That revised action can potentially produce the experience of meaning and completion in place of frustration and blocked energy.

For instance, a man who typically complains, "My keys are lost again!"

might reformulate his experience by restructuring his sentence: "I've lost my keys again!" That rephrasing prompts a changed sense of his own role, which in turn increases proprioception of his mental absorption in things other than the present. This revised understanding prompts him to focus more on the task at hand and to restrict his consideration of problems to consciously chosen times. As a result, the man experiences increased agency—the meaning and completion of his capacity to understand and intervene in his own habits, which he had formerly seen as external and beyond his control. Even in such a mundane instance, the person involved changes in relation to his social environment because he more fully grasps his own agency and has decreased the tendency to see himself as the victim of external forces.[9]

Because they expand a person's capacities to relate to herself and her environment, such language practices are heuristic. Thus while language use always poses the risks of alienation and reification, it does not inherently produce those outcomes, as Derrida and Spivak argue. Instead, Goodman's work suggests that people tend to have marbled experiences of language use—some alienating, some meaningful and completing. Because the latter are heuristics, frames for exploring new relationships between self and environment, they foster people's capacities to act in and change their environments. Thus they alter those environments, particularly our social worlds.[10]

However, Goodman indicates the complexities of large-scale social change and the entrenched social response to such changes:

> We have here [in the loosening of Americans' sexual mores] an interesting example of unequal development, the advance in some respects toward self-regulation while maintaining, and even increasing, a neurotic deliberateness in other respects. How does society adjust itself to attain a new equilibrium in the unequal development, to prevent the revolutionary dynamism latent in any new freedom— for any freedom would be expected to release energy and lead to a heightened struggle. The effort of society is to isolate, compartment, and draw the teeth of the "threat from below." (*Gestalt Therapy* 336)

Here Goodman uses the description neurotic deliberateness to indicate what he and his coauthors define as retroflection—the process of turning inward an impulse originally directed outward. Such impulses might involve anger, sexuality, and so on. The problem with retroflection, in their view, is not strictly the restraint of the impulse. (They suggest the wisdom of not punching one's boss, despite any impulses to do so.) Rather, the problem is one of unaware self-restraint, in which the person restricts the impulse and simultaneously erases awareness of that impulse and often the feelings and interpersonal dynamics that produced it. As a result, the person carries an unfinished (or incomplete) situation, and the outgoing energy blocked by the retroflection generates an internal tug-of-war. Such internal warfare, according to Goodman and his coauthors, causes physical, social, and psychological problems, while unfinished situations drain the person's energies. She develops chronic anxiety—neurosis—about situations she has not learned to resolve effectively. In short, such incomplete situations indicate loss of learning, specifically learning how to assimilate (to) a particular kind of situation.

In contrast, self-regulation here indicates one's healthy use of environmentally available resources to meet felt needs as they arise. Goodman contrasts that approach with blocking awareness of needs one does not have the capacity to meet and with following rigid proscriptions about how to meet needs. He contends that the spontaneity involved in recognizing and using environmentally available resources to meet felt needs is crucial to learning, change, and growth—and to flexible self-other relations. Nonetheless, as he indicates, such self-regulation is inhibited by (post)modern society's larger structures (social, economic, political, discursive, etc.). Thus even personal growth is complicated by institutions that support the status quo and by individuals' ideologically structured blocks to perception and proprioception. Both personal and social change face substantial challenges.

Yet Goodman's work, and Gestalt theory more generally, offer tools for supporting both kinds of change. They can help us as compositionists to extend our existing practices of critical and constructivist pedagogy to more effectively undertake such work. Like Derrida and Spivak (and Goodman), critical and constructivist pedagogy theorists, as well as critical ethnographers in composition, have argued that language practices play a crucial role in forming identity and self-other relations. They attempt to intervene in subject formation to promote personal and social change. But there are key tensions between the two approaches. While constructivist pedagogy emphasizes the crucial role of the affective in encouraging students' intellectual engagement, it misses critical pedagogy's equally important emphasis on how systemic inequities form identities. Likewise, critical pedagogy misses affect's central role in cognition. Goodman's work integrates these emphases by exploring how psychophysiological processes are linked with reification in individuals and in larger social structures.

Key critical pedagogy theorists such as Ira Shor and James Berlin show the need to engage English studies students in the active use of language practices to examine and critique their social worlds. In particular, both theorists emphasize curricula that prompt students to explore how language practices construct their worlds and identities. Constructivist pedagogy theorists such as David Schaafsma stress that to engage students in learning reading and writing practices, educators must provide structures that encourage students to explore their own interests and concerns through the skills they are learning.

Carol Edelsky highlights both the overlapping goals in these approaches and the tension between them. Both approaches emphasize students' active intellectual engagement and critical thinking. Yet as Edelsky illustrates, their methods for pursuing those goals produce key tensions:

> By and large, what whole language [or constructivist] educators fail to reflect on sufficiently is the non-neutrality of curricular choices, the historical and cultured (media-sponsored, corporate interest-supporting) nature of individual interests. By and large, what critical educators fail to interrogate sufficiently is the dominant ideology of teaching as method (rather than, for example, teaching as material display of theoretical and philosophical—as well as ideological—orientations) and the origins and implications of the prevailing view of reading as word getting. (1–2)

Edelsky goes on to explain that the essays in her collection explore two key tensions between these approaches. One is constructivist pedagogy's investment in creating structures that allow students to have "a significant voice in their own learning" versus critical pedagogy's investment in "teachers playing out a critical perspective" (3). As an example, she notes the naïveté of thinking that students' interests are intrinsic rather than influenced by the media and corporate interests. At the same time, she points out, training in democracy requires that students get "a significant voice in determining the ideas on the table, the topics to be studied, the projects they will undertake, the tasks that should make up those projects" (4). Second, Edelsky notes the tension between the two approaches' views of language learning. Constructivist pedagogy understands reading and writing as both social practices and meaning-making practices. "That is, reading is not getting words but making sense," and it requires immersion in "situations of real language use, i.e., situations where language is being used for communicative purposes, not where the language event is primarily about teaching or evaluating students' language proficiency" (5). Noting that this perspective is not central to most critical pedagogy, Edelsky concludes that while constructivist educators may "struggl[e] to maintain a focus on systemic critique in the curriculum," critical educators "may struggle with how to avoid assignments whose purpose is primarily instruction in or evaluation of written language" (5). Thus Edelsky's formulation of the tensions between critical and constructivist pedagogies echoes Spivak's description of the tension between the pragmatic work of liberatory projects and confronting subalterns' own ideology. Like scholars researching subaltern others' subjectivities, teachers are in danger of constructing students' (ideal) consciousness and at the same time of supporting an empowerment that, practically and ideologically, bolsters an exploitative status quo.

Certainly Shor and Berlin both emphasize the need for students' active, critical engagement with their curriculum, and Shor particularly stresses that students must have a voice in shaping that curriculum. But unlike constructivists, neither Shor nor Berlin pursues the affective dimensions of language practices and language pedagogy. For both, critical thinking remains essentially a cognitive function. Thus they operate in a Cartesian conception of mind, or what Goodman calls "the notion of 'mind' as a unique isolated entity *sui generis*" (*Gestalt Therapy* 263). That is, despite their emphasis on critical analysis as a key component of democracy and the negotiation of self-other relations through language, these thinkers miss the crucial ways in which emotional and physiological processes fundamentally shape cognition. Thus they particularly risk constructing an ideal consciousness for students. On the other hand, as Edelsky shows, constructivist pedagogy does more to engage these emotional and physiological processes but fails to link them to the central issues of difference and socioeconomic and political inequities. It, in turn, risks empowering students in ways that support existing systemic exploitation.

Like Spivak, critical pedagogy has turned to an approach of greater reciprocity, a speaking to and an effort to unlearn privilege as a means of negotiating these tensions. Lu and Horner's work linking critical pedagogy with critical ethnography in "The Problematic of Experience: Redefining Critical Work in Ethnography and Pedagogy" specifies this project for composition studies. They argue that to enable the personal changes critical pedagogy implies for students, teachers and researchers must expect such changes from ourselves as well. Lu and Horner offer a method to recognize and transform pedagogical habits that enact authoritarian teacher-student relationships. Thus they begin to work at what Edelsky calls "the dominant ideology of teaching as method" (1) and to grapple with the affective dimensions of social and intellectual relationships. They show how we can use critical ethnography to critically analyze not only the student's experience, as in most critical pedagogy, but the teacher's as well. Thus, they argue, we can creatively use two tensions: research versus teaching and respecting students' existing experience versus seeking to change that experience. We can promote our collaborative change with students rather than our singular change of students. This effort at reciprocity moves us toward the psychophysiological dimensions of reification because it implicitly calls for teachers and researchers to increase awareness of the alienated, reified parts of ourselves.

Lu provides an admirable example of such critical self-analysis in "Redefining the Literate Self: The Politics of Critical Affirmation." In this essay, Lu lists key goals of an ideal literacy, which she defines as critical affirmation. These goals include ending oppression, grappling with one's experience of privilege, approaching others' histories and experiences respectfully, and affirming a common human yearning for individual agency while respecting the different circumstances that produce and constrain that yearning (173). To begin theorizing this literacy, Lu reviews the potential problems with using personal narratives to examine subjectivity and its social construction. For instance, she points to the dangers of using personal narratives to generate professional capital; of presuming that personal narratives unproblematically represent a true self; of rigidly categorizing people according to ethnicity, sexuality, and so on; and of disembodying the personal by "privileging theory over lived experience" (175).

After revising her own (initially negative) responses to several others' scholarly use of personal narratives, Lu explains, "To practice critical affirmation, I need to confront my privileged class and ethnic ranking within the Asian immigrant community" (190). She goes on to explore how she had consistently overlooked class privilege in her own self-representations, despite having developed teaching strategies for helping students to find and confront such oversights. To address that tendency, Lu examines "one of the visceral reactions [she has] inherited from the racism and class elitism of home." Specifically, she examines her aversion toward dress or coiffure that "'make you look like someone from Chinatown' or 'like a Korean grocery store owner!'" She describes her efforts to combat such prejudices in herself, explaining that the process is particularly difficult because such judgments are usually private and so unchallenged. "They are prone," she concludes, "to produce lapses in our literacy practices, creating what we often refer to as 'unfortunate oversights' in how we pursue the goals of critical affirmation" (191).

After detailing her efforts to revise these prejudices in her daily life—and the difficulties she encounters in those efforts—Lu concludes that if we hope to encourage students to do similar work, as critical pedagogy advocates, we must pursue this work ourselves:

> We cannot ask our students to trust us to help them confront the paradox of their privilege if we cannot trust ourselves to do so with equal rigor. It is absolutely necessary that we engage in such writing and rewriting, utilizing in our own literacy practices the expertise and knowledge we apply to the literacy practices of our students. . . . We have to combat teacher illiteracy stemming from our own paradox of privilege. We need self-education on how we read and write the personal when conducting critical exchanges. . . . One way of "hanging together" would be to practice ways of reading and writing, speaking and listening, in which one's authority comes from one's ability to confront one's own privileges rather than to merely confront the privileges of others. (193)

Lu's emphasis on teachers' and researchers' participation in critical pedagogy's project of self-scrutiny is a crucial contribution to the field. As she argues, composing personal narratives that enact such scrutiny is key to generating reciprocal relationships between teachers and students, researchers and subjects. It parallels Spivak's call for academics to unlearn our privilege. If we hope to encourage students (and others) to develop critical consciousness about self-other relations and systemic privilege, we must foster such reciprocity. Given critical pedagogy's emphasis on that goal, Lu effectively demonstrates that personal narratives of self-scrutiny are crucial to developing a successful critical pedagogy.

Her description of examining how her "visceral reactions" to some others can produce "unfortunate oversights"(191) evokes for me Goodman's emphasis on proprioceptive awareness. That is, Goodman's approach is precisely to cultivate awareness of such visceral reactions to expand not only one's self-understanding but also understanding of one's habitual self-other, self-environment relationships. He provides methods for pursuing the kind of readings of self and culture that Lu advocates. In short, Goodman offers a means of confronting one's own privileges by expanding visceral awareness and thus expanding environmental awareness as well.

As a result, Goodman's work, particularly in concert with Damasio's and Pribram's (*Brain and Perception*), extends Lu's project and provides an explicit means of integrating critical and constructivist pedagogies. It does so by enlarging constructivist pedagogy's emphasis on the affective to provide a more substantive understanding of how psychophysiological processes structure perception. Similarly, it extends critical pedagogy's emphasis on systemic critique by examining the psychophysiological roots of reification. Through this approach, Gestalt theory furthers the project described by Lu and Horner and undertaken by Lu. In its emphasis on expanding awareness and its specific means for cultivating that awareness, Gestalt provides a method for fostering the kind of work Lu's essay depicts. Thus it provides a method for Spivak's project as well, namely, unlearning academic privilege and learning to speak to others. Its methods enable educators and students, community members and academics to access the psychophysiological dimensions of perception—and thus of cognition. As a result, those methods offer specific means of transforming reification into deeper awareness and revised experience. Formerly rigid functions become spontaneous processes capable of ongoing adjustment to a changing environment. The challenge, then, is to examine how such transformations unfold and how to encourage them.

Goodman's work shows that by attending to our rhetorical and figurative habits, we can expand our awareness to initiate the kinds of experimental interactions that revise our selves and social relations. Spivak's and Lu's texts suggest that intellectuals, like others, must risk what Goodman calls the destructive moment. That is, to shift privilege, ideological understandings, and practices that support systemic exploitation, both groups must risk the change that Goodman says is inherent in contact. Like Damasio, Goodman stresses the role of visceral and sensory processes in shaping our reasoning and intellectual commitments. He draws on this understanding to describe how perceptions and thinking processes change:

> A basic error is not refuted—indeed a strong error, as St. Thomas said, is better than a weak truth—it can be altered only by changing the conditions of raw experience.
>
> Then, our method is as follows: we show that in the observer's conditions of experience he *must* hold the opinion, and then, by the play of awareness on the limiting conditions, we allow for the emergence of a better judgment (in him and in ourselves). . . . For we realize from the start that a strong error is already a creative act and must be *solving* an important problem for the one who holds it. (*Gestalt Therapy* 243)

Goodman invokes the example of the Cartesian mind/body split central to Western thought as an example of the kind of perceptual—cognitive—error that can be corrected only by changing awareness of the conditions of experience. He asks, "How, for so long and among so many bona fide and intelligent persons, did it come about that such a non-existent problem was felt as an important problem? For, as we have said, basic splits of this kind are never simple errors that may be corrected by adducing new evidence, but they are themselves *given* in the evidence of experience" (*Gestalt Therapy* 256). The key word, perhaps, is *felt*. This dualistic sense of self was felt—and thus perceived and thought—by Western thinkers. That is, these thinkers' felt experience of themselves (their own bodies and minds) involved a split rooted in limited proprioception. Goodman, of course, sees this diminished awareness as endemic in modern Western societies. Such experience is indeed felt, and this feeling (both sensory and emotional) structures perception. Thus the perception that results from diminished proprioception grounds the reasoning of those who experience it. In turn, they perceive their minds as separate from their bodies.

For Goodman, then, *awareness* doesn't mean the transmission of information but rather a reorganization of what he calls "the evidence of experience" (*Gestalt Therapy* 256). It requires a change in the circuitry linking sensory and emotional processes with abstraction. For instance, a person might pay attention to the emotional responses linked to a particular physical symptom, such as a headache. Through that attention, she might recognize that unexpressed anger triggered the headache, and she might increase her awareness of the anger and its cause, as well as of her psychophysiological response to it. Of course, in this case, that response involves withholding expression of the anger, in effect turning it back on herself in what Goodman calls retroflection. In this process, her experience of the headache fundamentally changes, as she recognizes her own participation in its genesis. She sees that she has choices about recognizing and coping with her own anger. After several such experiences, she may develop a larger-scale awareness of the integration of body and mind. That is, she may recognize that her emotional, physiological, and reasoning processes mutually shape one another and that they cannot, in practice, be separated.

As in the recognition of a headache's source, such changes shift one's potential for action in the environment. Goodman explains this process:

> What we are arguing, then, is not that these conceptions, Body, Mind, World, Will, Ideas are ordinary errors that may be corrected by rival hypotheses and verification; nor, again, that they are semantical misnomers. Rather, they are given in immediate experience of a cer-

tain kind and can lose their urgency and evidential weight only if the conditions of that experience are changed. . . .

> If a certain unrelaxed deliberateness is . . . altering the kind of fig-ure habitually presented in perception, it is from *these* perceptions as basic observations that one logically proceeds. Recourse to new "pro-tocols" will not easily or quickly alter the picture, for these again are perceived with the same habit. . . . Psychotherapy is not the learning of a true *theory* about oneself—for how to learn this against the evi-dence of one's senses? But it is a process of experimental life-situations that are venturesome as explorations of the dark and disconnected, yet are at the same time safe, so that the deliberate attitude may be relaxed. (*Gestalt Therapy* 266)

In this understanding, changing ideologies and reification is not a prob-lem of demystification, critical consciousness, or, indeed, philosophical work. None of those approaches, in Goodman's view, can affect ideological under-standings or reified conceptions. For him, demystification and critical con-sciousness are essentially impossible. Philosophical work functions only at the level of abstraction, and thus it cannot access perception, which is structured by sensory and emotional processes. That is, blocked perception and proprio-ception cannot be freed through rational argument. However, practices of lan-guage use—rhetorical forms—help to establish one's relations with oneself and with one's environment. Increasing awareness of how rhetorical forms shape these relationships reveals how they structure one's perceptions. Unlike rational argument, this recognition can change one's awareness and thus the conditions of one's experience.

Take, for instance, the man who recognizes that in describing his habit of losing his keys, he is establishing one or another kind of relationship with himself and his environment. In recognizing this process, as well as the men-tal absorption that prompts him to lose the keys, the man realizes that he has the option of changing his habits of reflecting and attending. His conditions of experience change because he has become aware of the mechanics of his habits and so gained the potential to intervene in those mechanics and change his habits. Thus his perception of his agency fundamentally changes because he in fact experiences himself as having greater capacity than he had previ-ously. In short, awareness of how his rhetorical habits shape his perception opens the possibility of revised perceptions and thus revised experiences of self and the world.

In this approach, interventions do not address content—as is usually the

case in philosophical (and other) arguments. Rather, they support attending
to one's rhetorical habits, recognizing potential alternatives, and experimenting with those alternatives. Such experiments can alter the sensory and emotional processes that shape perception; thus they can reshape perception itself
and, with it, one's potential range of actions. Early in "Can the Subaltern
Speak?" Spivak emphasizes "the necessity of the difficult task of counterhege-
monic ideological production" and calls for texts that can "serve as a counter-
possibility for the narrative sanctions granted to the colonial subject in the
dominant groups" (287). If such counterpossibilities are to arise, Goodman's
work suggests that they will not emerge from critical readings or theoretical
arguments alone. Rather, they also require interpersonal work in which conversants develop awareness of how their rhetorical habits produce particular
perceptions—particular reified, ideological ways of understanding the world.

To cultivate them, we can use Goodman's approach to undertake Lu's
project of self-scrutiny. That is, we can use our scholarship to examine our
own rhetorical habits, both in scholarly writing and in day-to-day interactions,
particularly pedagogical interactions. In doing so, we encourage reorganizations of our own awarenesses. As a result, we revise our experiences of ourselves and our environments. In such revisions, counternarratives
spontaneously arise. In other words, our expanded awareness not only of our
rhetorical habits but also of alternatives generates different formulations. As
Derrida and Spivak show, we do not have the direct, conscious control needed to fundamentally change the discourses that help shape our perceptions.
But Goodman's approach demonstrates that the means to ameliorate reification emerge not in discursive structures themselves but in our uses of discourses. That is, they take shape in the articulations of our sensory and
emotional processes as perceptions. Thus Derrida's stress on the rhetorical, figurative nature of language is indeed crucial. What Goodman's work offers is
the recognition that we can most productively attend to these aspects of language not at the level of discourse itself but instead at the level of individual
uses of discourse. That refocusing enables us to intervene in reification and
subject formation. Of course, using Goodman's work to extend Lu's project
means that we encourage real contact and the risks of change—loss and reorganization of the structures that formerly defined our selves.

Because that contact involves becoming aware of difference and finding
ways to work with that difference, it inherently promotes experimentation.
That experimentation in turn generates expanded awareness and thus revised
perception, proprioception, and action. Goodman contrasts a strictly discursive awareness with the awareness that results from real contact and produces
experimentation and change:

Note, however, that awareness is not a thought about the problem but is itself a creative integration of the problem. We can see, too, why usually "awareness" does not help, for usually it is not an aware gestalt at all, a *structured* content, but mere content, verbalizing or reminiscing, and as such it does not draw on the energy of present organic need and a present environmental help. . . . The process of creative adjustment to new material circumstances always involves a phase of aggression and destruction, for it is by approaching, laying hold of, and altering old structures that the unlike is made like. When a new configuration comes into being, both the old achieved habit of the contacting organism and the previous state of what is approached and contacted are destroyed in the interest of the new contact. Such destruction of the status quo may arouse fear, interruption and anxiety. . . . But the process is accompanied by the security of the new invention experimentally coming into being. Here as everywhere the only solution of a human problem is experimental invention. The anxiety is "tolerated" not by Spartan fortitude . . . but because the disturbing energy flows in the new figure. (*Gestalt Therapy* 232–33)

Again, Goodman emphasizes that conveying facts—the content of language—does not spark reorganizations of awareness because such communications operate strictly at the discursive level. Such awareness of understanding produces an understanding alienated from one's sensory and emotional processes. Thus it cannot be integrated into one's perceptual process and one's thinking. In contrast, genuine shifts in perception draw on the energy sparked by a sensually or emotionally felt need. In seeking environmentally available resources to meet the need, one initiates a "creative integration of the problem" with one's environment (232).

Take, for instance, the woman prone to headaches because she retroflects her anger. Having recognized her own role in producing the headaches, she may seek resources in her environment for dealing differently with her anger. She might, for example, watch co-workers to learn their strategies for tactfully communicating anger to a supervisor. In the process, she shifts her habit of retroflecting her anger by seeking and experimenting with strategies for expressing that anger. Here, language practices reorganize awareness because they move beyond the discursive level into connection with the woman's sensory and emotional processes. Her language practices change in relation to an internal stimulus (her anger) because by recognizing both the cause of her headaches and her role in producing them, she formulates the situation differently in describing it to herself. Her language practices change in relation to an external stimulus (the person toward whom she feels the anger) because she experiments with ways to express her response directly, rather than retroflecting it (and possibly expressing it passive aggressively without awareness). At the same time, as Goodman indicates, "the previous state of what is approached and contacted" is also "destroyed in the interest of the new contact" (*Gestalt Therapy* 233). In this case, the woman's prior intimidated relationship with her supervisor is destroyed in the interest of constructing a new relationship in which she risks the supervisor's displeasure (or even retribution) by raising her concern. Clearly, even such a small shift has social as well as individual consequences.

Thus addressing the problems of ideology and reification requires language practices that move beyond the discursive level to reorganize awareness by reshaping perception. Because perceptions help meet an individual's felt needs, altering them involves developing language practices that change one's awareness of both the experienced need and environmentally available solutions. Because ideology and reification are, fundamentally, questions of perception, we can shift them only by cultivating such language practices. In this approach, developing counterpossibilities for narrative sanctions and counternarratives themselves may draw on critique and discursive analysis. But fundamentally such counterpossibilities and counternarratives emerge spontaneously in the experimental process of new habits—often new practices of language use. The woman who experiments with ways of expressing anger to a supervisor constructs the possibilities for a narrative other than the sanctioned story of docile female worker. She initiates a counternarrative via her revised approach to the relationship with her supervisor.

Thus working toward social transformation requires such ongoing experiments with individual and collective experiences and interactions. Goodman's approach to that work addresses reification. For example, the woman who reified the abstract notion of subordination into retroflection—and a headache—has dissolved her embodiment of the idea. In the process, she has shifted her language practices in a way that discourages reification (and encourages praxis) by fostering sensory and emotional awareness. In the spirit of Spivak's and Lu's work, this approach elicits counternarratives by cultivating reorganizations of awareness in both marginalized and privileged people. That is, it urges both groups to reformulate their perceptions of organic needs within language and in relation to environmental resources for meeting those needs. This process promotes social change precisely because the previous state of what is approached and contacted is destroyed in the interest of the new contact. For instance, the relationship between employer and employee changes in the new contact that emerges during a unionizing effort.

Gestalt theory shows us how to use language practices to promote such holistic changes. These changes inherently involve risk and loss as the structures forming the self reorganize. Like Derrida, Goodman explores such loss by analyzing the uses and erasures of the past in the process of constituting the self and the other. Unlike Derrida, Goodman focuses on those uses and erasures as forms or functions. He considers how they structure day-to-day practices and links their forms to abstraction:

> Abstractions draw away from the more sensory and material particularity of the experience. . . . Habits, for instance, techniques or knowledge, are other fixed forms: they are assimilations to the more conservative organic structure.
>
> Many such fixed forms are healthy, mobilizable for the on-going process, for instance, a useful habit, an art, a particular memory that now serves for comparison with another particular to yield an abstraction. Some fixed forms are neurotic, such as "character," compulsive repetition.[11] But whether healthy or neurotic, *the past and every other fixity persist by the present functioning*: an abstraction persists when it proves itself in present speech, a technique when it is practiced, a neurotic characteristic when it reacts against a "dangerous" recurring urge.
>
> As soon as they are no longer of present use, the organism by its self-regulation sloughs off the fixed effects of the past; useless knowledge is forgotten, character dissolves. The rule works both ways: *it is not by inertia but by function that a form persists, and it is not by lapse of time but by lack of function that a form is forgotten.* (*Gestalt Therapy* 292)

Like Derrida, Goodman holds that using abstractions (such as language) to shape the self inevitably erases aspects of the past. But for Goodman, the past's power and significance lie not in the system of language per se but in how we use particular forms to shape current practices. Whether enacted by a person, institution, or larger social body, those practices exercise the force of the past. Here, understanding how the past shapes the present involves tracing the uses of both content and form as they structure an organism's ongoing process. Content entails "a particular memory that now serves for comparison . . . to yield an abstraction," while form consists of a useful habit, an art, or a compulsive repetition.

Such uses of content and form, according to Goodman, route the energies generated by organic needs into particular channels (the dendritic pathways Pribram describes). These channels constitute our habits or actively retain information for comparisons. Only these activations of content and form regenerate the abstractions that allow us to use the past. That is, as Goodman explains, information that seems unuseful and habits that no longer serve a purpose are erased. For instance, the woman who retroflected anger because she lacked effective strategies for communicating it tactfully loses the habit of retroflection when she develops such strategies. They better meet the need of coping with her anger, and her retroflective habit is no longer useful.

Through this understanding of how the past shapes subjectivity, later Gestalt theorists have developed approaches to learning how particular individuals actively use past habits or information to structure their identities. In *Gestalt Reconsidered*, Gordon Wheeler, one such theorist, explains how these uses of the past generate what he calls an individual's structured ground:

> The personal subjective past is part of the *structured ground,* which conditions the dynamic creation of the present figure. . . . The past is not regarded as strictly, directly causative, in quite the Freudian sense. . . . The *causes* of present behavior . . . must be sought in present dynamics. But like dreams, or fantasies, or mannerisms, or the structure of the interaction with the therapist, or "body language" itself— or even "techniques"—the past history of the patient is a clue, a way to understanding the subjective organization, or organized ground, of his present felt reality.[12] (76)

Wheeler's concept of structured ground builds on Gestalt's contrast between figure and ground. The term *figure* designates what is present in one's awareness, while *ground* indicates the background against which that awareness emerges. Together, figure and ground compose the whole of the organism's experience. Wheeler defines structured ground as the set of individual, family, local, institutional, and sociocultural information, forms, and practices that shape one's perceptual processes. Of course, those factors likewise shape one's habits—one's style of contacting oneself and one's environment. Wheeler explains that "these . . . are *structural features* of the personal ground, which must be considered in any 'gestalt analysis,' as much as or more than 'figure formation' itself—if only because these *structures of ground* are the *conditions* of figure formation, the prerequisites and determining factors in the particular *kind* of figures achieved in various situations" (118).

Holistic changes that can elicit counternarratives must link features of this structured ground with an alternative or expanded set of practices. Like Goodman, Wheeler shows that such processes must begin with people's phenomenological experiences of reality:

> Therapeutic change flows from *going to the contact that is possible*
> . . . the complex interpersonal intervention of joining-and-analyzing
> that contact process, *thereby destructuring it*, unblocks the rich and
> spontaneous possibility of a new and more satisfying creative adjust-
> ment, a new organization of self in the field. . . . Gestalt formation
> means a resolution of figure *and* ground, in terms of each other . . .
> ground resolution is itself highly structured and enduring over time
> and . . . our understanding of contact and of our clients is enhanced
> by direct attention to these ground structures. (145–46)

I read *therapeutic change* as the integration of new modes of perception, proprioception, and action into a person's existing structured ground—i.e., as learning. From this perspective, learning is fostered especially when a teacher works to understand how learners' internalized forms and content shape their perceptual processes and their field of available actions—that is, their contact styles. The teacher then uses that understanding to work with the moments of contact that occur in the interactional learning situation itself (whether college classroom or community literacy project).

Here, the instructor begins from the contact styles learners are using, and able to use, rather than trying to impose a different set. Yet at the same time, the instructor brings the forms and content of her own language practices—her contact style—into the interaction. Thus she facilitates Wheeler's joining-and-analyzing of the contact process, destructuring it, because the contact is encouraged rather than preempted by an effort to impose a form other than the one that emerges of itself. Such interactions might, for instance, evolve partly from the language of assigned texts or activities, but they would, by definition, engage participants in a present-centered interaction. In the process of destructuring that interaction—that is, of simultaneously working in and analyzing it as a contact process—the possibility of creative adjustment emerges.

Still, as Goodman and Wheeler note, the risk and loss that attend such reorganizations of self are real. Wheeler explains how the energy flow in that process prompts changes in both the individual and that person's environment:

> Finally, if all these various pitfalls [in achieving contact] are nego-
> tiated, and the "meeting" with the new is achieved, there comes the

moment where the self must "let go of the self," for the actual contact in the fullest sense to take place (p. 533). That is, the "something old" that must be destructured and reorganized is not only in the environment, but also *in the self.* In Piagetian terms, both assimilation *and* accommodation (the restructuring of the self) must take place (Piaget, 1947). At this point, the self must be "sure enough of itself" to risk itself, its own given, past organization, in the new encounter. If it cannot, the result is "egotism"—the clinging to the frozen *self as it was*, the inability to take the plunge, and risk change, loss, unfamiliarity. Spontaneity is lost, and an exaggerated, hypercautious deliberateness appears. . . . That is, for relationship, or community, or commitment to take place, there must be a *giving of the self* to that contact, to that new organization—an element of *loss* (of pure/Perlsian "autonomy")—for the new configuration to be able to arise. . . . Full satisfaction, full contact which nourishes the self and adds to it, cannot be achieved without a certain sacrifice of the purely autonomous self, narrowly conceived—a letting-go of the self-in-isolation, or the self-as-impulse, in favor of direct commitment to *organized structures of ground.*[13] (82–83)

Wheeler's description implies that real contact requires that all parties not only risk the experience of destructuring and reorganization but actually undergo it. In this approach, community workers and intellectuals, project participants and mentors, and students and teachers all need to undertake self-revision to generate community and commitment to collective efforts toward social change. The contrasting possibility, egotism, suggests a reified self, one frozen both in its own neurotic loop of noncontact and in preserving existing social structures and relationships. Growth requires contact: assimilation, destructuring, and reorganization—change within oneself. Wheeler's approach positions social transformation as grounded in such moments of contact. Thus to foster collective (institutional and structural) change, people must change personally. We must revise our organizations of perception, proprioception, and action because those organizations shape our relations with others, that is, with the people, things, and institutions that form our environment.

This understanding has profound implications for people interested in social change, community revitalization, and teaching and scholarship intended to improve people's lives. It implies that I, as a teacher and scholar committed to those efforts, must risk and undergo destructuring of my self, reorganization of my perceptual and proprioceptive processes, and revision of my habitual practices and contact style. Those changes will, in turn, alter my relationships with people, things, and institutions. More specifically, to make real contact with students, community activists, and community project participants, I must experience an integration of new modes of understanding and interaction in a process that will inevitably shift and erase some of my earlier practices.

Goodman shows that encouraging aesthetic language practices can cultivate such holistic self-reorganizations. He argues that only language practices that foster real contact prompt such changes. He defines those language practices as poetic and contends that they are central to developing viable ethics:

> No such analytic language [e.g., empirical, operational, and instrumental] can reach contactful speech itself, for contactful speech is partly creative of the actuality, and the creative use of words plastically destroys and remolds the words. . . . The norms and protocols of good speech cannot be analyzed to simple concrete things and drives—these are not concrete enough; they are given in concrete and often very complicated whole-structures. To put it bluntly, linguistic reform—the cure of empty symbols and verbalizing [or alienated language practices]—is possible only by learning the structure of poetry and humane letters, and finally by making poetry and making the common speech poetic.
>
> The matter has a philosophical importance far beyond linguistic reform. There is a continual search, precisely among empiricists and instrumentalists, for "naturalistic ethics," one that will involve no norms outside the on-going processes. But if the criteria of correct language are so chosen that the feelingful and creative aspects of speech do not lend to the "meaning," are "merely subjective," then no such ethics is possible in principle, for no evaluation invites assent on logical grounds. On the other hand, if it is once understood—as should be obvious—that feelings are not isolated impulses but structured evidence of reality, namely of the interaction of the organism/environment field, for which there is no other direct evidence except feeling; and further, that a complicated creative achieving is even stronger evidence of reality; then the rules of the language can be made so that every contactful speech is meaningful, and then evaluation can be logically grounded. (*Gestalt Therapy* 331–32)

Reminding us that human perception is fundamentally structured by our visceral and emotional processes, Goodman explains that when reasoning is separated from those processes, its evaluations cannot prompt us to give ethical assent. Thus efforts to construct a philosophy based in objectivist ethics inevitably fail because those efforts are cut off from primary aspects of our perceptual processes. As a result, they exclude the only source of human norm formation, namely, sensory-affective responses. Rather, Goodman argues, the nature of perception means that an ethical language must promote contact with those processes in ourselves and others. That is, because of this perceptual process, the only access to reality we have is through our own visceral and emotional responses, as those shape our cognition. Thus feeling is the only direct evidence of reality.

Objectivists' efforts to isolate concrete objects as the bases of accounts of reality cannot succeed because we inherently perceive those objects as parts of complicated whole structures, whose very presence we grasp through our visceral and emotional processes. Language practices that promote contact with the direct evidence of these processes can form the basis of an ethics. Further, language practices that enable a person to shift her perceptions of her environment, and thus her relation to it, provide even stronger evidence of reality. In other words, such language practices similarly promote contact with the visceral and emotional, our direct evidence of reality, which emerges from our interface with the environment.

According to Goodman, the kind of language practice that promotes such contact is poetic language. In contrasting poetic language practices with empirical, operational, and instrumental language, he emphasizes that only the former explicitly uses feeling in shaping its evaluations (given that the latter types deliberately attempt to exclude feelings from their evaluations). Thus Goodman argues that only poetic language can ground ethical language practices. He defines poetic language as partially creating reality and creatively using words to destroy and remold language. Thus once again, what makes the play in language use significant is the way it intersects with the play in people's psychophysiological processes. The process of destroying and remolding the words in poetic language enables that language practice to partly create the actuality—that is, the language user's contact with himself and his environment.

Thus for Goodman, the intrinsic value in poetic (or aesthetic) language practices is in their capacity to foster contact and, as a result, change.[14] From this perspective, instruction in aesthetic uses of language have value not intrinsically but because they help learners grasp the workings of aesthetic language practices so they can take up such practices themselves. The value of this lies not in whether they produce critically recognized literary works but in whether they learn to use aesthetic language practices to promote contact, change, and growth. It is precisely such results (complicated, creative achieving) that define the aesthetic for Goodman. In this view, the aesthetic is less an object than a relation between producer and environment.

To cultivate such contact-producing language practices, one must allow space for negotiation of goals and relationships, as suggested by critical pedagogy theorists such as Shor and Berlin. A preestablished, closed structure, in contrast, promotes blocked perception and proprioception and so diminishes (or even forecloses) contact. Gestalt therapy often uses experimental situations, and Wheeler argues for encouraging clients to negotiate the terms, goals, and methods of these experiments. His argument potentially extends critical and constructivist pedagogies' emphasis on students' engagement:

> The process of *contracting* for the experiment . . . is considerably more interesting, and potentially more valuable for study and "experiment," than the official, formal "experiment" itself. That is, the whole business of how the client organizes and experiences mutuality, power, understanding or misunderstanding, self-revelation, hope and resignation, assertion and influence and affection and eroticism and work and play and so on, *in the contracting and negotiating process itself,* with another person under the particular conditions of therapy, is a richer field of study than how he performs or experiences the experiment, so-called, itself. But all this may well be neglected as both parties turn their attention to the "task" . . . which has been interposed. . . . To go in the . . . direction of heavy reliance on therapist-directed activities and implicit formal authority, is to remove the one best safeguard the client has against bad or destructive therapy (and to vitiate his best experiment at the same time): namely his right and support to engage in mutual process, mutual feedback, to influence and resist and suggest and complain, as this intimate and delicate process unfolds—the very thing that was lacking, so often, in his own original, troubled experience of intimate dependency. (96–97)

While the classroom is not therapy and teachers are not therapists, both Gestalt and pedagogy seek to stimulate learning, that is, experimentation with new language practices and revised contact styles. As Goodman's work demonstrates, in concert with Pribram's and Damasio's, for learners to understand the power of various language practices, particularly what Goodman calls poetic language, they need to experience—rather than hear about—that power. Thus learners' work with such practices must involve them in complicated, creative achievements, namely, revised perceptions and proprioceptions that prompt experiments with revised actions and contact styles. Wheeler's recommendation implies that educators can foster such experiments by negotiating with learners for real, immediate stakes within the educational context. In turn, these experiments ground personal and social change.

Encouraging such change in academic and community educational endeavors does not translate directly to social revision. Yet practices learned in such environments can ripple outward, though not with predictable or controllable results. By fostering microcosms of equitable, negotiated social relations, educators can support—though not direct—broader change.[15] While acknowledging the significant forces aligned against such change, Goodman affirms its potential and encourages pursuing it. In particular, he notes social structures' capacities to compartmentalize and block the energies sparked by personal and group instances of growth. Yet three pages after he stresses society's tendency to "draw the teeth" of such energies (*Gestalt Therapy* 336), Goodman sounds another note. After emphasizing the dangers of reification facing any effort to cultivate growth, he uses the example of psychotherapy to articulate a means of countering such reification in one's own practices:

> The history of psychoanalysis itself is a study of how teeth are drawn by respectability. It is a perfect illustration of Max Weber's law of the Bureaucratization of the Prophetic. But this law is not inevitable; it is a consequence of unequal development and consequent anxiety, the need of the whole to adjust itself to the new force and to adjust the new force to itself. What must psychotherapy do to prevent this bureaucratizing respectability? Simply, *press on to the next resistance.* (*Gestalt Therapy* 339)

Like Wheeler's recommendation, Goodman's argument applies to writing instruction. Read in tandem with Lu and Horner's and Lu's work, it suggests academics should work to increase our contact with the resistances we encounter in our educational and research endeavors. In doing so, we expand our awareness of potential approaches to addressing these resistances. This approach positions work with individuals as a point of intersection between personal and social change. It reminds us that while such personal changes cannot guarantee social transformation, they encourage social revisions. At the same time, by honoring all parties' resistances, this approach counters the dangers of reification so fearfully enacted in many uses of Marxist theory. It increases our capacity to help people develop language practices that foster contact, awareness, and experiments with revised contact styles.

We begin this work by developing awareness of our own roles in the microsystems of our educational and research endeavors and in larger social and cultural systems. That awareness potentially opens us to change. The psychophysiological, cognitive, and aesthetic form of such holistic changes is the most concrete, most fundamental—and therefore most radical—version of unlearning intellectual privilege I can imagine. It extends Lu's approach to producing a more effective critical pedagogy. At the same time, it allows us to pursue Spivak's suggestion that intellectuals learn to speak to (rather than listen to or speak for) marginalized others. That change can generate mutual shifts in perceptual processes and so generate experiments with an expanded range of possible actions, experiments that shift social relations and the status of institutions. The revised psychophysiological processes and resulting experiments with new rhetorical forms and contact styles inherently generate the possibilities for counternarratives and so for personal and social change.

3

A Passion for the Possible

ITERATE PRACTICES can expand awareness of our contact styles, others' differences, and new possibilities for relating to one another and ourselves. Struggle's participants used the program's writing and discussion prompts to do such work by experimenting with new rhetorical moves that helped them navigate blocks to their goals. Struggle's planners crafted prompts designed to raise awareness of rhetorical moves, and our process for doing so reveals our rhetorical patterns for negotiating differences. In the personal change stimulated by my Struggle work, I reorganized the evidence of my experience, in Goodman's terms. All these stories highlight how Wheeler's process of joining-and-analyzing one's interactions and literate practices can reshape fundamental perceptions, rhetorical habits, and contact styles. The stories interweave to show how contact-producing language practices can spark the revised experiences that ground change. Because they explore change across the individual, family, and working group levels, they begin theorizing the relationship between personal revision and larger-scale change.

Defining Struggle

Following are excerpts from a funded grant proposal written by Wayne Campbell Peck, who conceived the program and reformulated it through several versions.[1] Wayne wrote this proposal to secure resources to expand Struggle from its focus on individuals and small groups to include a focus on community-based organizations as well. Because the following chapters deal exclusively with Struggle's individual and small-group component, I present only the relevant proposal sections.[2] These excerpts introduce Struggle in the voice of its chief designer and convey what I believe is the spirit animating both Wayne's vision of the program and our collective work in it.

Wayne C. Peck
*Excerpts from Struggle: A Community-Based, Technology-Supported Initiative
for Human Capacity Building and Community Renewal*
Pittsburgh, PA December 1997
Why Struggle?

In urban neighborhoods, authentic renewal begins as we work from our strengths rather than our brokenness. . . . The Struggle Project is committed to creating contexts in powerful ways to promote authentic renewal. Our aim is to produce an organic transformative process rooted in everyday experience capable of changing what is tired and worn into what is new and still possible.

Over the last eight years, we've been crafting a process of community learning through Pittsburgh's Community Literacy Center in partnership with Carnegie Mellon University. We've discovered that community learning is effective as it develops and sustains the capacity to solve problems, to cope with obstacles, to commit with others, to imagine new possibilities, to achieve what seemed impossible—to act, to trust, and to hope.

What Is Struggle?

Struggle is a community-learning initiative through which participants build lives centered in action and reflection. . . . Struggle supports broad cultural exchange grounded in community life and urban experience. We have evidence to show that Struggle enriches interior lives and leads to productive action by individuals and groups. In Struggle participants use language—oral and written—to compose their life stories and to develop their life plans. Through Struggle, participants articulate individual and community goals and work to align resources for realizing them.

Grounded in Renewed Relationships

[. . . O]ne of the most pressing challenges facing our country is to strengthen the affiliative bonds between children and supportive adults. Struggle works by strengthening participants' affiliative bonds by building stronger family and community relationships. It focuses on community and family alliances, whether between adults and adults, parents and children, or young people and mentors.

How Is Struggle Structured?

Struggle starts where people are. Its goal is to produce life stories that lead to life projects. It draws upon oral tradition and encourages people in naming their own experience and articulating their personal goals. The structure of Struggle's focus on the Individual begins with dinner and dinner-table conversation during which people swap stories, weave narratives and venture to dream. After laying the groundwork for trust and mutual support, participants then work in pairs to do life-planning.

In this phase, participants work through a set of prompts using multimedia composing tools. Prompts are derived from the following primary questions:

What am I going through? (i.e., my struggle)
What am I up against? (i.e., the barriers)
What am I up to in my life? (i.e., my goals)
What are the ways to be together in this? (i.e., my support system)

In responding to these questions, participants begin the process of Struggle. Participants realize their own agency for making life decisions. Using multimedia tools, participants express their experience, identify plans, and chart courses of action for achieving their goals. In the final step of this phase, participants produce and deliver a publication of their Struggle discovery.

In designing Struggle, Wayne drew on his twenty-some years as pastor of First Allegheny Presbyterian Church, an organization affiliated with Struggle's secular sponsor, the Community House. Founded in the early twentieth century as part of the Settlement House movement, Pittsburgh's Community House continued to serve its surrounding urban neighborhood with a mission emphasizing personal and community renewal; alliances across race, ethnicity, and class; and social justice. First Allegheny supported that mission. As both pastor and the Community House's executive director, Wayne had reenergized such endeavors, orienting the life of both organizations around them. He explored the role of literate practices in such work in his dissertation, "Community Advocacy: Composing for Action (Literacy)," which drew on both his community advocacy experience and cognitive rhetorical theory. But the PhD in rhetoric was not Wayne's first endeavor in postbaccalaureate education. He brought a Harvard Divinity School degree and his background as part of the region's upper crust of white industrial-magnate families into a long-term alliance with residents of Pittsburgh's North Side, home to both First Allegheny and the Community House.

Joyce Baskins, Wayne's closest collaborator and friend, was a lifelong North Side resident with deep roots in the community. She brought an African American's perspective to the planning team, as well as extensive experience in working with community members and groups to support families and rejuvenate the North Side. Her education included some community college courses and participation in a research project that explored the cognitive operations of writing and helped establish a partnership between the Community House and Carnegie Mellon University. That partnership became the CLC, a long-term collaboration that brought university resources into community-based educational projects. As a result of her work with these institutions, Joyce could move effortlessly across the discourses of community, church, university, and funding agencies.

Carnegie Mellon brought Elenore Long into the CLC to facilitate CLC educational programs and do PhD research. Ellie's deep commitment to the CLC's work led her from there into First Allegheny and Struggle. Having completed a dissertation on how university mentors learned the discourses needed to work with CLC teens, Ellie integrated cognitive rhetoric with a bent toward humanistic projects emphasizing holistic growth. (See her dissertation, "The Rhetoric of Literate Social Action.") She occasionally joked that her Scandinavian, Lutheran upbringing in the northwest rooted her in an understated style and reserved sensibility almost the polar opposite of the CLC's community discourse. Yet her striking physical, social, and intellectual grace enabled her to support that discourse, as well as the hybrid discourses the CLC encouraged. (For an explanation of hybrid discourses, see Peck, Flower, and Higgins, especially 212–13.)

Those hybrids took shape in part from the discourses community participants brought to projects like Struggle. While some CLC projects recruited in area schools and other sites, most of Struggle's participants arrived through personal connections and word of mouth. Many were First Allegheny members or acquaintances of active church members. Many were swayed by the powerful force of Joyce's welcoming personality, which beckoned the tentative into projects they might otherwise have avoided. Almost always, adult participants were actively seeking some kind of personal renewal. Many also sought ways to support the adolescent family members they brought with them to the project and to reestablish their relationships with the teens in new ground. The adolescents, while sometimes reserved, seemed attracted to Struggle's emphasis on life planning.

Most participants lived on the North Side, a formerly German neighborhood that by the early 1990s had a black majority of residents. Facing significant poverty, crime, unemployment, and gang activity, the neighborhood grappled with the difficulties of providing a safe environment for families. At a playground adjacent to the public housing across the street from the Community House, a drug-related shooting had scattered playing children, miraculously injuring none. Women who lived in the housing complex and sometimes frequented the Community House strove to keep dealers away from the playground area while not betraying to police the young peddlers who, they said, were "good children, our children." Racial tensions plagued the area, as economic decline promoted friction between long-time white residents and their African American neighbors.

Race relations took a different shape in Pittsburgh's Hill District, home to Diane and Ian, two of the Struggle participants central to my research.[3] A historically black area, the Hill was sometimes seen as inhospitable to white visitors. In fact, it seemed inhospitable to outsiders generally. When Joyce visited with a video camera to make a tape for a Struggle project planned for the area, young men quizzed her on what she was doing and why.[4] She warned Wayne not to visit the neighborhood without her, and he complied. Aptly named, the Hill's narrow roads balanced houses on scant terraces carved into its slopes. As in the North Side, residents faced significant rates of poverty, crime, unemployment, and gang activity.

The racial tensions in these two neighborhoods reflected deep-rooted problems in Pittsburgh as a whole. The police department was widely seen in the city's African American communities as fundamentally—and violently—racist. The national ethos on race relations in the early 1990s had, of course, been set by the Rodney King beating, the subsequent acquittal of the police officers involved, and the resulting Los Angeles riots. A comparable incident in Pittsburgh rubbed salt in local African Americans' wounds. In October 1995, an African American driver who exited his car in what seemed a routine traffic stop in a Pittsburgh suburb was asphyxiated when police officers pinned him to the ground. Three of the five white officers present were tried on charges of involuntary manslaughter; one was acquitted, while proceedings for the other two ended in mistrials. Some Pittsburghers protested in support of the motorist, while others supported the accused officers (see "Protesting the Protesters").

Not infrequently, such concerns were addressed explicitly in First Allegheny services and in CLC projects, as well as in Community House participants' everyday conversation. In one case, Joyce described her daughter and white daughter-in-law's encounter with police, during which Joyce's young, pregnant daughter was choked in front of her four-year-old son, while her sister-in-law, just over five feet tall and "barely ninety pounds dripping wet" was thrown to the ground. Joyce noted that such experiences were typical—and traumatic—for the city's African American residents and particularly likely to foster anger in child witnesses such as her grandson. In the years following the black motorist's death, some city residents began calling for federal investigations of Pittsburgh's police. The U.S. Department of Justice investigated, and in early 1997 the city bowed to federal pressure and signed a consent decree agreeing to five years of close police oversight by the department (see "City Bows to U.S. on Police Reforms"). These tensions, echoing those across the nation, augmented the neighborhood conditions of crime, poverty, unemployment, and gang violence that formed the life contexts of most Struggle participants.

In Struggle

July 29, 1996. We met in a space named with the Swahili word for unity, Umoja. Twelve of us sat around an oval dining table, its African-print table-cloth casting a warmth of gold, brown, and russet hues over the white walls and dark hardwood trim. Sheila suggested that Jody, her fifteen-year-old son, wanted to say grace before the meal. Whether or not he had expressed that wish, Jody complied with a quick prayer, and we began passing the dishes of our Kentucky Fried Chicken feast around the table.

Though she was the only female teen at the dinner, and thus in this Struggle project, Janine was talkative, chatting with the Community House's staff and joining any conversation that presented itself. Her Aunt Joanne, who had come to participate as Janine's adult partner, was, by contrast, noticeably quiet, saying almost nothing. Of the four adult-teen pairs participating in this project, Janine and Joanne were the only white duo, the reverse of the ratio among the Community House staff.

I caught snatches of conversations involving Sheila and Maureen, who lived in an apartment complex a few miles from the Community House, had sons close in age, and talked easily. Maureen informed us that she worked two twelve-step programs and had been clean and sober for some time. Of the three black mothers who were participating in the Struggle project with their teenaged sons, only Diane remained reserved throughout the meal. Quiet and unsmiling, she spoke in short, clipped phrases, focusing her energy on super-vising and attending to Ian, her thirteen-year-old son, the youngest partici-pant. Although she was seated, Diane leaned over him, prompting Ian on whether he would like a drink, which dish he should take next, whether he was getting enough to eat.

As Ellie cleared dishes from the table and Joyce and I distributed slices of cake, Wayne began describing the Struggle project. Its goal, he explained, was twofold. First, it supported people in articulating their life projects and plans for pursuing their dreams. This just meant charting a path for life, defining "what you're going through, what you're up against, and what you're up to in life," he said, listing the project's central questions. Next, Struggle sought to help people to draw on the supports already present in their lives and to renew their family and community relationships. Each teen-adult pair, he continued, would work together at an Apple PowerBook and, attended by a Struggle planner, would use writing, conversation, and reflection to do life-project planning. Though each teen had joined the project with an adult relative, for most of the Struggle sessions the teen would work with another, unrelated adult. This arrangement, Wayne said, was to provide a new adult mentor for the teen, to produce deeper self-understanding for everyone, and to afford a base for the teen and adult relative to come together in a new way at the project's conclusion. The four women listened quietly, nearly motionless as their eyes focused on Wayne.

As Wayne concluded this introduction, Ellie marshaled television, VCR, and tape to show the project's new training video. While it played, I watched the adults attend politely to explanations of Struggle's basics, from turning on the PowerBook to operating the mouse and the HyperCard program housing the project's writing prompts. Stealing glances at participants' faces, I wondered about their responses to the video's minidramatizations of helpful and less helpful ways of supporting a Struggle partner. The short clips humorously illustrate the pitfalls of preaching, testifying, and scare tactics. Subsequent segments advocate allowing silence for your partner to think, asking for clarification, and honoring your partner's goals.

Near the end of the session, Maureen asked if Struggle's questions and life-planning activities were for everyone, adults as well as kids. One of us from the Community House staff replied yes, of course, and I noticed her face brighten.

July 30, 1996. To open the day's session, Struggle participants and planners gathered in the Umoja Room, strategically located to the immediate right of the building's entrance, just off its spacious lobby. Wayne briefly sketched the work we would do that evening. Glancing at the adults, I noticed that Diane's professional outfit of red jacket, culottes, and gold-rimmed glasses contrasted with the more casual dress and manner of Sheila, Maureen, and Joanne. She sat with her arms folded across her chest, shoulders hunched, leaning slightly back in her chair, and listened to Wayne without smiling. As she made a few remarks, her tone rose and fell sharply, suggesting a concern bordering on suspicion.

As the group broke into the adult-teen pairs who would work together throughout the project, I explained to Diane that Ian, her son, would be just across the hall. Noting that he would be working with Maureen and me, I pointed out the room, hoping to allay any anxiety she felt.

Initiating Struggle

Along with the training video, the Struggle planning team used a training manual participants could revisit later. The materials covered in the manual follow the video closely in presenting Struggle's central practices. In Gestalt terms, Struggle used literacy to foster holistic change by strengthening the links between abstractions (such as rhetorical moves) and experience (such as self-perceptions).

After giving an overview of the Struggle program and explaining why the program used writing, the training manual introduces a CLC practice known as rivaling (for the definition of this term, see Peck, Flower, and Higgins 217). The manual notes that rivaling helps people generate new ideas through conversation, then emphasizes that it can support people to "break new ground or face a difficult problem." Questions like those posed by Struggle are open questions that do not have a single right answer, it says. As a result, considering different points of view can help people deal most productively with such questions.

Rivaling can go beyond conversation, however. The training manual continues, "As a writer, you can also learn to *rival* on your own by imagining strong rival hypotheses in your own head. Rivaling means coming up with alternative ways of reading a situation, *alternative ways of defining the problem, or alternative solutions*" (emphasis in original). Next the manual explains how to rival, suggesting that participants "start a conversation in your own mind" and then predict what selected people "would say about your open question." The introduction of rivaling concludes by saying that Struggle uses both conversational and internal rivaling and will help participants learn how to rival.

This introduction to rivaling emphasizes the importance of encountering new and different perspectives to reconsider one's key concerns. By stressing this method, the Struggle program highlights the significance of heightening awareness of alternative views. While this emphasis may appear primarily cognitive here, its links to the experiential emerge as the manual unfolds. Thus in its introduction of rivaling, the manual begins to till the soil for a version of Wheeler's destructuring, or joining-and-analyzing. As the manual suggests, Struggle's version of joining-and-analyzing presupposes that it can occur not only in direct exchanges but in internal projection and reconsideration of such exchanges.

After introducing rivaling, the manual presents a printed version of the unhelpful supporter strategies covered in the training video. Encouraging participants to avoid these potential pitfalls when working with their Struggle partners, the manual names and demonstrates each. The list includes blame and complaint, preaching, and scare tactics. Its accompanying examples use vivid language in everyday moments of tension between adults and teens. For instance, in one exchange, a teen complains that adults never listen and do not understand modern teens' problems, while in another, an adult uses platitudes to address a teen's concerns as a commentator notes the "generic testimonials" offered when adults "just turn their tape recorder on, and out comes this little speech."

By sensitizing Struggle participants to the use of clichés, the manual echoes Goodman's concern that hackneyed language preempts genuine contact. The training manual urges participants to avoid this language precisely to increase the potential for such contact, as illustrated in a teen narrator's conclusion, "There's nothing wrong with any of these encouraging comments, but they're empty if adults aren't responding to something specific that a teen has said. The issue is 'can we talk with each other rather than talk at each other?'" In fact, the manual's description of these interactional pitfalls explicitly tries to expand participants' awareness of their rhetorical moves, those moves' possible effects, and potential alternatives. This echoes Goodman's emphasis on rhetorical habits and how those habits construct people's contact styles and personalities. Thus the manual's description of rhetorical pitfalls sets the stage for participants to develop greater awareness of their own contact styles and of the results those styles tend to generate in their interactions and thus their relationships. As Goodman and Wheeler indicate, such awareness can prompt people to experiment with revising their contact styles when they see interactional patterns they would like to change.

The training manual further develops a structure to support such work in a section on Struggle's key image, "a table surrounded by four important people in your life." These people are in dialogue with the participant about issues she defines as central concerns in her life. They can include people "in your life now, or [who] may have been in your life in the past—a friend who moved to another state, or a deceased grandparent, for instance." Further, those seated at the table might be people actually in the participant's life or well-known role models. "The goal is to gather together people who can help you form opinions about your life project and who support you."

This image develops a structure to support Struggle's version of joining-and-analyzing by providing a concrete picture people can use to visualize the abstract work described in the section on rivaling. The image works in the spirit of the Gestalt experiment. In such experiments, clients often initiate dialogues with a key other who is not present. They explain what, based on experience, they believe the other person would say and script their own typical responses. After paying attention to the rhetorical moves and other relevant features of the contact style used in the interaction, clients may try out a revised set of rhetorical moves, thus experimenting with the bases of a revised contact style. Struggle's image of a table of supporters echoes the structure of such experiments by asking participants to imagine what key others in their life would say about an issue crucial to the participant. This approach adds another building block to the foundation supporting Struggle's version of an internalized joining-and-analyzing. Such internalized joining-and-analyzing, facilitated by Struggle's writing practices, encourages the kind of awareness and experimentation Wheeler describes as the goal of the joining-and-analyzing process.

A sample dialogue reproduced from the video and titled "How to Be a Good Supporter" concludes the training manual and exemplifies key rhetorical strategies Struggle encourages and their rewards for participants. In this dialogue, a teen writer and adult supporter pursue a Struggle conversation, while a narrator glosses the exchange much as a sports commentator might. After the narrator introduces the conversants, the adult supporter asks the teen, "What do you mean when you say that you want to end up working behind a desk, on the top floor of the U.S. Steel Building, and to be in charge of a lot of people? There are three images here: the desk, the Steel Building, in charge of lots of people. Why is each of those images important to you? What do they symbolize for you?" When the teen, LaVonne, is silent, the adult supporter sits back and waits quietly, while the narrator comments, "Notice the move on the supporter's part. She leaves the ball on the tee 'til LaVonne's ready to tee off. There's no coercion here, nor is the supporter trying to put words into LaVonne's mouth."

This section of the dialogue models rhetorical moves that can support a Struggle writer and then explicates those moves. The adult supporter's question elicits further clarification of what Gestalt theory calls the writer's figure. That is, the question asks the teen to define—for herself as well as her adult partner—what is important to her about her image. Thus it asks her to clarify the nature of her goals. This prompts her to heighten her proprioceptive awareness. The adult supporter's posture of waiting when the teen remains silent works, as the narrator indicates, to make a space that encourages the writer to articulate those goals more fully as her awareness unfolds. The combination of the posture and the commentator's explication models patience and openness as rhetorical moves Struggle participants could use to effectively support their partners. The sequence implies that such moves might be key steps in the process of supporting a partner in augmenting her self-awareness.

The dialogue continues with the teen's eventual response that her image symbolizes success, arrival, and being "in control of my life." The narrator comments that the adult supporter notices the teen writer's equation of control over her life with power and money. Reminding readers of the CLC's rivaling strategy, he notes its usefulness in presenting "a challenging alternative" and in "urging your writer to break new ground or face a difficult problem." The adult supporter asks the teen, "What things in your life, or things that you already do, make you feel that you have control in your life?" The teen responds that she enjoys growing plants, and the narrator says the conversation has been productive, concluding, "Through their STRUGGLE, wider horizons and possibilities open up."

In this section of the sample dialogue, the Struggle training manual takes the CLC's cognitive strategy of rivaling and moves it into a life-planning context that extends the strategy's operation from the cognitive realm into the experiential. It asks the writer to consider other concrete dimensions of her personal life to prompt her toward a different perception of an issue she defines as personally significant. By asking her to draw on another facet of her concrete experience, the approach encourages her to reorganize her abstractions from the ground up (from her experience) rather than to shift her perception based on an abstract discussion of how she does have power and control in her life. This approach asks her to contact and juxtapose different aspects of her experience to change her awareness of the conditions limiting one aspect (a felt lack of control). This prompts her to reorganize the interpretation she makes of that aspect. Thus it uses abstraction implicitly (in the adult supporter's interpretation of the situation and formulation of an effective question) rather than explicitly (as the content of the conversation). Here abstraction serves as a tool to help the writer contact various aspects of her experience and put those aspects in dialogue with one another. Shifts in perception occur at this experiential level, not at the abstract level. This process requires the writer's active, holistic involvement. In Gestalt terms, it urges the writer to reorganize the evidence of her experience. She then feels the significance of this experience in a new way, rather than just hearing another person's view or articulating alternatives abstracted (alienated) from her felt sense of life.

This use of the rivaling strategy to encourage a partner's reorganization of her own experience contributes a key step to Struggle's revised joining-and-analyzing process. First, it helps the writer recognize the effects of her initial rhetorical formulation of being in control of her life. Specifically, the supporter's question implies that the writer's formulation said she is not in control of her life because she does not yet have any of her symbols of that control. Thus it limits the conditions of her experience, excluding awareness of areas where she does have control. In the same move, the question suggests the writer consider alternative definitions of what it means to be in control of her life. By asking the writer what she already does that makes her feel in control, the question offers her a chance to experience herself as having some control in her existing circumstances and to see that experience as a base for constructing the future she desires. In answering the question, the writer begins to reorganize her experience.

The exchange between writer and supporter does not explicitly analyze the rhetorical moves in their conversation, but readers of the training manual saw such analysis in the narrator's comments. Participants' Struggle conversations happened in the context of this attention to rhetorical moves and their effects, an attention that permeates the training manual. Its analyses taught participants to notice such moves and their implications. Like the sample conversation, actual Struggle conversations often focused on the content of the writer's concerns. But in both, rhetorical moves and their implications operated as an important subtext. Thus the sample dialogue fleshes out Struggle's revised, more implicit version of Wheeler's joining-and-analyzing. It thus links the abstractions of rhetorical moves with the experience of self-awareness to encourage holistic change.

By introducing Struggle's strategies for increasing contact, the training manual tills the ground for the kinds of work participants would do as they began responding to the program's HyperCard prompts. Designed to elicit conversation, reflection, and writing, these prompts build on the training manual's work, urging participants to expand proprioception by recognizing how their rhetorical habits shape their experiences. The prompts use a Gestalt-style experimental approach that encourages participants to recognize the conditions limiting their experiences. That recognition positions participants to reorganize those experiences and shift their perceptions. By developing the revised joining-and-analyzing begun in the training manual, the prompts help participants undertake such reorganizations.

After a brief refresher introduction to the Struggle program, the first prompt asks participants, "What do you plan to get out of the STRUGGLE project?" In Gestalt terms, it opens the program's central interaction by requesting that participants turn inward. It encourages participants to augment their self-awareness by defining a clear figure, a goal or desire they hope to meet through the program. This move invites participants to negotiate their agendas with planners' by suggesting they ground their work in their own goals.

The second prompt follows an explanation of Struggle's central metaphor of a table surrounded by four supporters. This prompt initiates the Gestalt-style experiment enacted through the program's series of prompts. It asks,

"What are your impressions of the first person you chose to sit at your table? Tell about their goals and dreams. What have they achieved? What do they value? Why are they so special?" In contrast with the first prompt, the second asks participants to turn outward to an other they value and see as central to their lives. Yet it also encourages increased awareness, this time of the other's qualities and accomplishments and why the participant values them. Thus the prompt fulfills Gestalt theorist Joseph Zinker's recommendation that an experiment begin by affirming a system's strengths (210–11). It accesses those strengths by eliciting a description from the participant even though other people from the system are not present. By framing the request in positive terms, the prompt asks the participant to actively affirm his own primary system's strengths via his response. Like the training manual's sample dialogue, it works at the experiential, rather than the abstract, level. That is, the prompt does not initiate discussion of the participant's perception of his primary support systems; instead, it asks him to list concrete examples of one person's positive features. By initiating the participant's contact with these concrete examples, the prompt sets the stage for his experience of such affirmation, rather than for abstract discussion of a person's or system's positive qualities.

The third prompt follows closely on the second by asking, "What are the goals, dreams and values you share with the person you just described? How have you made them part of your own life?" Here the focus again turns inward, but it does so in a more complex move that encourages participants to heighten their awareness of how they relate to a key other. Specifically, the prompt sets the stage for participants' heightened proprioception of how they have internalized values and developed their structured grounds, including beliefs, attitudes, values, and habits of thought and action. This prepares participants to later undertake Struggle's revised joining-and-analyzing by asking them to bring into awareness introjects, Gestalt's term for values consciously espoused but not integrated into one's spontaneous unconscious thinking. By revealing such undigested material (whether beliefs, values, or habits), the prompt encourages participants to make choices about it, to consciously assimilate it rather than enacting attitudes and behaviors they have adopted unreflectively. Thus the prompt prepares participants to join-and-analyze an internal dialogue in which they imagine what a significant other would say.

The second and third prompts are repeated for each of the four people participants choose. After this focus on positive personal relationships with others, the fourth prompt points participants toward more difficult life interactions by asking, "What are you struggling through in your life right now?" Like the third prompt, the fourth directs participants' attention toward the interface between self and the world. It encourages proprioception by asking participants to increase awareness of a key area where this interface feels painful or problematic. This prompt also parallels the third because it too fulfills Zinker's recommendations for an experiment. First, it positions learners to define the problem or area for change. Second, it does so only after offering heightened awareness of learners' own strengths and of systemic supports, based on their responses to the third prompt (Zinker 89–113, especially 106–7).

The fifth prompt encourages participants to sharpen a figure of the problem or desired change. It asks, "What are you up against? What are the obstacles in your way? What are the barriers to achieving your dream?" This prompt enacts a key facet of Perls, Hefferline, and Goodman's conception of an experiment. Specifically, it encourages participants to heighten awareness of internal blocks by increasing their awareness of how they perceive the external and internal factors preventing them from achieving particular goals. Gestalt theorists hold that increasing contact with their own blocks to achieving a desired goal is a crucial step that learners must complete before they are ready (or able) to see alternative possibilities.

To further prepare participants for considering alternative possibilities, the sixth prompt returns them to their own goals, this time by encouraging them to make contact with a positive imagining of those goals. "What are you up to in your life?" it asks, before continuing, "What do you want to accomplish? What MUST you achieve in order to say you have reached your life goal and lived your dream?" After the fifth prompt's efforts to increase participants' awareness of the blocks to achieving their goals, the sixth prompt renews their energies for pursuing those goals and finding creative approaches to circumventing their blocks. By asking participants to project their desires and ideal identity in concrete terms, the prompt urges them to sharpen their figures of those desires and that ideal self. Gestalt theory holds that sharpening a figure mobilizes energy to address difficulties by drawing on environmentally available supports to craft an effective solution.

The seventh prompt encourages recognizing and using such supports. It first asks, "Who can support you in your struggle?" then inquires, "How does this person help you see new paths, new possibilities? What would this person say back to you?" Thus it directs participants toward awareness of others as concrete resources, as potential partners and interlocutors. This builds on the third prompt, which asks participants to name four people to seat at an imagined table of supporters. In some cases, when a participant perceived another person as a block to achieving her goals, this awareness could involve a shift from seeing the other primarily as a problem to seeing the person as a potential supporter. For instance, a teen who saw his mother primarily as an authority who prevented him from doing what he chose could make contact with the ways she did—or could—support him to pursue some of his goals (without negating his perception that she sometimes obstructed his desires).

Further, the prompt's last question explicitly invites participants to enact Struggle's revised joining-and-analyzing. First, it urges the participant to initiate an internal dialogue that her Struggle partner and facilitator will rival to help her assimilate the material offered by her imagined interlocutor. When the participant articulates this dialogue, partner and facilitator ask how she might use her imagined interlocutor's comments. They encourage her to address the dialogue's problematic or undermining aspects by experimenting with new rhetorical strategies and their contact styles. By experiencing the possibilities for alternative responses, the participant has the opportunity to sort through what she wants to take from the projected interaction and what she chooses not to internalize. Through this assimilation process, she can reorganize her experience of the other person by accepting support without internalizing unhelpful feedback.

The final Struggle prompt invites participants to synthesize their work with the earlier prompts into a holistic life vision. It asks them to draw a map of their lives to show key past experiences (positive and negative), current location, and future paths. Then it asks them to interpret the map. This combination again encourages participants to ground their perceptions in concrete aspects of their experience before moving toward reformulating their abstractions. In drawing the map, participants produced graphic images and connections among those images. Like language, these graphics were abstractions, but like imagery in language, they operated at a far more concrete level than do abstracted concepts such as power, success, and being in control. By inscribing such images to make their maps, participants increased their contact with the various aspects of their past experience, the difficulties facing them, the potential resources for navigating those difficulties, and the goals and ideals they hoped to reach in the process. Thus map making increased participants' contact with how these facets of their experience relate to one another. By interpreting the map, participants could reorganize these facets into a new holistic perception of self, environment (including significant others), and relationship. Thus they gained the opportunity to revise their felt experiences of relationship.

As a series, Struggle's prompts use the rhetorical awareness advocated in the training manual to encourage participants to increase their contact with key elements of their experience. While not based in Gestalt theory, the prompts nonetheless structure this contact along the lines used in Gestalt experiments. Thus they position participants to mobilize their energies to negotiate difficulties by recognizing environmentally available supports. Further, the prompts interact with the Struggle participant's partner and supporter, who draw on the program's rhetorical strategies to initiate Struggle's version of joining-and-analyzing. Thus they help the participant experiment with alternative contact styles to more effectively assimilate and use available supports. As a series, they employ rhetorical strategies to heighten experiential awareness and so promote change.

Contesting Struggle

January 26, 1996. Joyce, Ellie, Wayne, and I had planted ourselves at the Umoja Room's table and now wrestled with plans to revise Struggle's Hyper-Card stack, the multimedia program housing the project's writing prompts and activities. In the past year and a half, we had done two trial Struggle projects with participants. In the meantime, a local foundation had agreed to fund further work on the program's pilot phase with a small grant that would cover our next year or so of experimental projects. Accordingly, we had begun revising the program's prompts and supporting materials to prepare for an improved Struggle project we would administer later in the year. Thus we were poring over the narrator's opening lines.

"How about, 'I want to invite you to an opportunity to do some life-project planning?'" Wayne asked.[5]

"What about 'hello' or 'hi' or something?" countered Joyce pointedly, pausing rhythmically at each of the options. She noted that we needed to establish a more personal, less professional or academic opening to connect with participants. Her suggestion implied that we needed this ethos to ground our request for participants' intellectual investment in the project.

We incorporated Joyce's revision, and once we had hammered out the introduction, Ellie suggested we use photos and voice-overs of teens who had participated in a Struggle pilot project. We discussed which teens' photos to use, and Ellie suggested a plan for the next screen: "We see a picture of Shana and hear her voice saying 'What is life-project planning?' Now, I didn't get the gist . . ."

"No, no," Joyce interjected. "She asks first, 'What is a life project?'"

"OK?" Wayne replied haltingly, his voice rising into a question.

"Then she could say something like, 'And how do we plan it?'" I asked of Joyce.

"Yeah," she answered, "because we still don't know what a life project means."

I suggested that Shana could articulate her personal experience of finding out what a life project meant through her Struggle participation, and Joyce agreed. Ellie pointed out that we needed to show the breadth of the life-project idea, to illustrate its various possibilities. "We have to figure out a way to provide different representations," she explained.

I suggested an example of how Shana might explain the understanding she had developed through her Struggle participation. "That's a little wordy," Joyce replied. "I like 'For me it meant figuring out what I want to do with my life.' That is so great. 'Cause that's simple. It's what you want to do with your life," she said, weighing each word. "I mean, it's simple but it's not simple. It gives them an idea."

We continued working on the stack and soon reached the moment to introduce its central metaphor, the table of four advisers chosen by participants. At this point, Wayne suggested we script a call for participants to seat their advisers at the table.

"Imagine . . ." Joyce began.

"Invite people to the table . . ." Ellie offered simultaneously.

"They have to see the table first," said Joyce.

"OK. 'Imagine,'" Ellie replied.

"Imagine a table and invite . . ." Joyce continued.

Missing Joyce's effort to break the stack's presentation into more concrete images that offered concepts in manageable bites, I broke in. "It might be important for people to define what it is they want to change about themselves before they invite their advisers to the table. Only because I think that might get us the richer response instead of the flat kind of . . ." I trailed off, trying to formulate my notion.

"How are we going to get this into words?" Wayne asked. "The time to make changes is after the person introduces himself to the other people at the table. . . . I'm just trying to follow where you're going."

"What I would do, Gwen," said Ellie, "to make the change thing not confusing, is to wait 'til the person introduces him- or herself to the other people at the table and then to ask 'Who am I? What do I stand for?' And 'What changes do I want to make?' goes right then. Because otherwise people might feel like it's punitive, like the first thing they're being asked is what's not good enough, what they need to change about themselves."

"I don't . . ." I paused, finally beginning to grasp the implication of their objections. "It hadn't occurred to me that that might come across as punitive. I was trying to think of it as a 'What are your goals?' 'What are your dreams?' kind of question, but I am really taking in that it could sound punitive."

• • •

Our interaction as a planning team in the above conversation demonstrates a rhetorical pattern with significant implications for groups attempting to build coalitions to pursue change. This pattern involves our group's conversational strategies for negotiating members' conflicting agendas and approaches. For instance, in this excerpt, Joyce's agenda pushed us to connect in rhetorically and intellectually effective ways with Struggle's participants, who typically came from nonacademic backgrounds and whose education ranged from some high school to postsecondary degrees. Ellie's agenda asked us to design program materials that would broaden participants' conceptions of a life project. My agenda stressed tilling the ground for participants' self-revisions. As the exchange illustrates, Ellie's agenda conflicted with Joyce's emphasis on presenting new concepts in a rhetorically and intellectually effective format. Similarly, my agenda conflicted with the rest of the team's felt need to affirm participants' identity and values before asking them what changes they hoped to undertake.

The exchange illustrates a three-step pattern of negotiation the group used fairly consistently to deal with such conflicts. In the first step, one member indicates the conflicting agendas by responding to another member's suggestion, either by raising a question or directly posing an alternative. The question or alternative might explicitly raise a concern about the original suggestion, or it might leave that concern implicit (sometimes developing the implicit concern in the second step of negotiation). For instance, Joyce responded to Wayne's proposed opening and Ellie's suggested introduction to life-project planning not by raising explicit concerns about their ideas but by immediately posing her own alternatives. Similarly, Wayne and Ellie responded to my suggestion that we introduce the concept of personal change earlier in the program with a question and an alternative. Notably, in none of these cases did the people raising the concerns express them as a critique of the initial proposal.

In the second step of negotiation, the person raising the concern typically offered a rationale for that alternative. In her response to Wayne's opening, Joyce noted the need to connect with participants initially on a personal, rather than an academic, basis. In her response to Ellie's introduction of life-project planning, she explained that we needed to introduce the concept of a life project before we suggested planning it. In response to my suggestion that people define their desired changes before seating their advisers at Struggle's table, Ellie noted the need to avoid confusion and the possibility of a seemingly punitive demand for change.

In the third step, team members tried to incorporate the original suggestion (or a part of it) when that was feasible, or they tried to otherwise address the agenda of the person who had made the suggestion. For instance, after opening with Joyce's initial greeting to participants, we did include Wayne's invitation to do life-project planning. Similarly, when Joyce insisted people needed to imagine a table before they could invite people to it, she followed up by incorporating Ellie's phrasing into a revised suggestion. To address my agenda, Ellie emphasized that to effectively support participants' growth, we needed to affirm their identities before broaching the topic of change.

Thus our rhetorical pattern for negotiating conflicting agendas emphasized posing alternatives, explaining them, and addressing the agenda subordinated by the group's decision. Unlike academic rhetorical strategies for addressing differences, our pattern did not emphasize critique but either left it implicit or quickly subordinated it to posing and discussing alternatives. I believe this pattern emerged partly in response to two key exigencies facing us as a working group: we needed to develop effective prompts in limited time because we all had other pressing commitments, and we needed to build and support an effective working relationship. I think the same exigencies motivated our efforts to address one another's agendas even when group decisions subordinated those agendas. These exigencies apparently shaped the rhetorical pattern we developed for negotiating differences within their pressures. Together, exigencies and rhetorical pattern contributed substantially to our group's process of building coalition amidst our differences.

Gestalt theory reveals how our pattern fostered coalition. As a group, we already had a strong shared figure, namely, revising the prompts and training materials so we could run another version of Struggle later that year. We had mobilized our energies toward pursuing that figure by meeting to work on the revisions, and in this particular meeting we contacted the materials related to our goal (materials ranging from our prior drafts to one another's agendas). That contact involved assimilating differences, both in assessing how to better fit the prior drafts to our goals and in negotiating one another's agendas to reach group decisions. Our decision-making processes sometimes incorporated various agendas and sometimes revised our agendas toward a new shared figure (such as introducing the idea of change later in the Struggle program to better support participants). Thus our negotiation pattern mirrors Gestalt's cycle of experience.[6] Further, it uses Zinker's method for raising concerns by articulating them directly, but not punitively or critically, and by affirming all group members' contributions. These features of our negotiation pattern enabled us to address those differences so as to strengthen, rather than fragment, our collective focus. Thus our rhetorical pattern illustrates how a diverse group seeking to build coalition developed effective literate practices for doing so.

The depiction of our interaction also reveals how the Struggle program's architecture developed to support the implicit joining-and-analyzing its prompts foster. Notably, each difference in the conversation dealt with rhetorical moves and their potential effects on Struggle participants. Joyce's concerns about an appropriately personal introduction and a step-by-step explanation of new concepts, as well as Wayne and Ellie's concern about deferring work with change, all addressed the stance each rhetorical choice enacted (academic versus personal, overwhelming versus accessible, and affirming versus punitive). In considering those choices, we undertook Struggle's version of joining-and-analyzing. This process shaped Struggle's architecture to model an affirming, nonconfrontational support for engaging in holistically challenging endeavors. Thus Struggle's materials model the rhetorical practices they advocate.

Writing Struggle

Joanne, who attended Struggle with her niece Janine, produced a document that highlighted the power of Struggle's central metaphor, suggesting it fostered the kind of contact Goodman attributes to aesthetic language practices. In describing her father, Pete, Joanne explained how she saw him working to right mistakes he had made with his children when he was an active alcoholic. Noting that he had stopped drinking, she said the value she shared with him was "trying to set things right. I think I'm just like him, because I'm really hard headed about different things. He tries to tell me now, 'Give an inch. You don't have to be that hard headed.' I think there are points to things, and I really stick to them. And I'm not an easy—to certain people and things—I'm not that easy to forgive or forget." Comparing her tendencies with her father's past habits, she concluded, "No matter what you did, he wouldn't give an inch. And now he does. I've seen his wisdom and his change. And hopefully I'll be able to change on some issues." Joanne's response showed that the second and third prompts encouraged her to make contact with strengths within her primary support system and with awareness of how she had internalized habits she now wanted to change, just as a Gestalt analysis of the prompts suggests they should have.

Her description revealed that she began pursuing that change before joining the Struggle project. Making contact with the change during Struggle seemed to position her to continue such assimilation in other key relationships. When Joanne responded to Struggle's succeeding prompts by recounting what she was going through, up against, and up to, she worked extensively with her mixed feelings about trying to find a husband and start a family. As a woman approaching forty, she saw herself as possibly too old, and she noted concerns about finding the right man. She stressed her fear of risking a relationship with the wrong man and her mother's urging to go out and meet someone. When she responded to the prompt asking, "Who can support you in your struggle?" Joanne named her mother, Lil, the first person she had seated at her table. Explaining what Lil would say to her about this issue, Joanne commented, "She'd probably say that having a child at 40 is not too old, or after 40 or however. And, yes, being careful [about who you meet] is being smart. But she'd end it by saying, 'You have to go out and meet somebody. You just can't sit at home.'"

Next, Joanne explained how she would reply. "Back to Lil, I'd say: 'If you meet them in the bar, you've got to think they're in there for a reason, someone else's sloppy seconds.' I believe that there are other places to meet people, and you don't have to go out [to a bar or night club] and meet somebody. You can be walking down the street and meet somebody." Thus Struggle's table metaphor positioned Joanne to undertake a kind of Gestalt experiment, one in which she envisioned what a key other would say to her and then responded to that person. She began assimilating an introjected imperative by developing a response that better fit her felt experience of concern, as articulated in her Struggle document. Thus she experimented with an alternative response and revised her relationship to the unassimilated material.

Further, Joanne's explicit contact with her efforts to learn to "give an inch" and take a less hard-headed approach to life may have supported her self-revisions. As Joanne explained in an interview conducted about a year after she completed Struggle, to manage some health issues, she was striving to maintain calmness. Notably, her explanation stressed her desire to add more people to her Struggle table because she had other important role models who helped her learn how to foster calmness. Her explanation and description of one person she wanted to add demonstrated the power of the contact encouraged by the table metaphor.

• • •

Building Struggle

September 14, 1996. We began in the Umoja Room with bagels, pastries, coffee, and juice. In the first hour, Wayne explained First Allegheny Presbyterian's history as a church, focusing much of his talk around the fire that had gutted the original church structure, which had adjoined the Community House's building. Over a year before, Joyce, who served as a church elder, had invited me to attend a service. Now I was participating with five others in a half-day Saturday orientation, the penultimate step in joining First Allegheny.

Wayne's eyes glinted, and he smiled boyishly as he described the spectacle of the fire itself, recalling a Pentecost Sunday many years earlier. To symbolize Pentecostal tongues of fire, Wayne and others had hung long, colorful banners from the sanctuary's ceiling, draping them under high-wattage spotlights. The hot lights, turned on hours before the service, had transformed the symbolic fire into a real blaze that destroyed the huge old church and its great pipe organ, long without an organist to do it justice.

Wayne had watched the scene from the top of the adjacent Community House as the church floors caved in on one another in rapid succession, imploding in the fire's heat. Describing the conflagration as the "blessed fire," Wayne explained how it liberated the church's resources from maintaining the huge building and organ for a shrunken congregation, thus freeing them for use in church-community projects that rekindled the congregation's life.

Wayne's description of his own arrival at First Allegheny amplified the story of rebirth. He had been hired twenty-some years before as the church's pastor in this room, whose dropped ceilings and painted woodwork were later transformed into the gracious Umoja Room through Wayne's architectural passion. While visiting his hometown, Wayne had interviewed on a whim, never meaning to stay twenty years.

He was hired to build bridges between the all-white congregation of the long-established, conservative Presbyterian church and the surrounding neighborhood. The aging, dwindling congregation was allowing their church to die rather than reconstructing it as an interracial, intercultural group in the new North Side of the late twentieth century, an urban, racially and culturally diverse neighborhood housing many poor and working-poor residents. As a graduate of Harvard's Divinity School and of the 1960s battles for race and gender equity, Wayne undertook to graft ethnic and class diversity onto a quasi-democratic, isolationist tradition.

After Wayne's story, we adjourned to a lounge outside the church sanctuary, on the Community House's first floor. Once we seated ourselves in a comfortable circle of couches surrounding a coffee table, Wayne asked us what had drawn us toward First Allegheny. Joyce described working at the Community House, growing more involved with First Allegheny over several years, though she had still attended the North Side's African Methodist Episcopal (AME) church, as she had since childhood. In part, she said, the fire brought her to First Allegheny. Like Wayne, she hoped to integrate the elderly, white, racist congregation with its surrounding community to remake First Allegheny as an intercultural church. She noted the irony that she had sung only traditional hymns at the AME church and had begun singing gospel only after joining First Allegheny. Joyce wanted her children and grandchildren to grow up in a church that was more like the world, she explained. "The AME church didn't have any white folks," she noted. "Any Hispanics. But the world isn't like that. The world has black folks and white folks and Hispanics. Why don't we worship that way, together?"

In Struggle

August 6, 1996. Maureen had finished describing her son, Lloyd, as one of the people at her metaphorical Struggle table of advisers. When she prompted Ian, her adolescent partner, for feedback, he commented that Lloyd was her "backstepper," and she agreed. We both praised Ian's figure of speech. Maureen made eye contact whenever she addressed Ian, and sometimes during her replies I noticed his eyes brightening.

In turn, Ian described his father, whom he had added to his table. Listing shared pastimes, Ian noted that his father pursued them "when he gets a break from his job."

At this point, Maureen invoked an earlier depiction of Ian's grandmother as a confidante, asking "Can you talk with your dad like you can with your grandmother?"

"No," Ian replied, noting instead his father's assistance with household chores.

"In other words, you have a lot of ways like your father, and you and your father are more than just father and son, you're like the best of friends here," Maureen continued. "So your father, he's a person that you can share your deepest secrets with, huh? Could you talk to your father about your goals for life? To get some direct answers, suggestions?" Hearing Maureen impose her own expectations, her story of an ideal father-son relationship, onto Ian's account, I debated whether to intervene.

"Well, when he's off from work," answered Ian in a halting rhythm, his tone suggesting deep skepticism. "He works at the airport, and he's busy a lot of the time."

"So he's like the fun part of your life?" Maureen modified.

Hearing her apparent respect for Ian's skepticism, and her almost immediate recasting into his terms, I was glad I had waited. "Yeah," Ian agreed, confirming her new version. "'Cause we don't get to see each other that much because he's at the airport working." The two moved to the next Struggle questions about Ian's father, and after brief exchanges, Maureen commented that Ian's father seemed to be a very special person in his life. As a single parent, she noted, she hoped someday her son would have a father figure, too.

August 6, 1996. After the session, Ellie and I discussed the challenges of encouraging teens' Struggle writing. Lloyd, her teen writer, had committed himself to a life project of playing professional basketball. Despite Ellie's encouragement to supportively challenge Lloyd to expand his envisioned possibilities, Joanne, his adult supporter, responded with the pleased comment, "I'll love to see you in the pros!" Ellie's description echoed Wayne's comment on a similar situation in a previous Struggle project, in which five-foot, nine-inch William insisted his life goal was playing pro basketball. I had encountered similar responses from Struggle teens, and I empathized with Ellie's concern for encouraging change without squelching teens' dreams. In contrast with such categorical, culturally pre-scripted articulations, I recalled the complicated exchange between Ian and Maureen regarding his relationship with his father. I realized he explored dissonances in his depiction of his mother as well. "My mom is like a gate," he commented. "She can open it whenever I need to go forward, but she won't open it when I need to go backwards."

• • •

In describing his parents to Maureen, Ian used metaphor and similes to explore ambivalence and complexity in key relationships. Goodman argues that aesthetic language uses cultivate contact with experience, while formulaic language uses promote avoidance. Such avoidance appears to characterize the culturally pre-scripted life-plan descriptions Lloyd, William, and other Struggle teens presented. These descriptions bespoke limited contact with statistical realities about their chances for attaining the goals they had come to desire. This avoidance grows clearer in light of the misfit between many of the teens' physiques and their target careers. It is augmented in the polite, formulaic response Joanne offered Lloyd.

In contrast, Ian and his adult supporter employed aesthetic language to communicate complexity and ambivalence in key relationships. He used metaphors such as backstepper to characterize his adult supporter's relationships with people at her Struggle table, setting the stage for her to reciprocate.[7] When Maureen's initial hypothesis about Ian's father met with his skepticism, she revised her description of his role. Ian agreed and elaborated on the difficulties in the relationship (his father's limited availability). In the process, he demonstrated contact with the relationship's complexities, and the joint formulation of the portrayal pushed Maureen to examine her structured ground, namely her commitment to a culturally pre-scripted ideal of father-son relationships. In Goodman's terms, this portrayal was "partly creative of the actuality" (*Gestalt Therapy* 332) for two reasons. First, it validated Ian in characterizing his own experience, even in conversation with an adult. Second, it enabled him to prompt this adult to consider her own possibly unaware assumptions. Thus it encouraged contact between the two and proprioception for Maureen.

Ian's use of the gate as a simile for his mother furthered this exploration of ambivalence and complexity. As Gregory Bateson shows, metaphor reveals primary-process thinking about relationships.[8] Given Goodman's explanation of how aesthetic language uses foster contact, Ian undertook a Gestalt-style experiment by offering and explicating this simile for his mother. That is, he used the simile to make his felt sense of his experience explicit by finding an image and attendant language to convey the complexity of his feelings toward his mother. Notably, his simile and explication allowed him to do so in non-confrontational, noncritical language. Thus he found a rhetorical move that expressed his mixed feelings without attacking or criticizing and thus was less likely to spark conflict with his mother if presented to her in his final Struggle document. Such moves are crucial to constructing and sustaining strong, mutually supportive relationships, and Ian's use of this one perhaps presaged a more resilient relationship with his mother. Both Joyce's and my interpretations of their changing relationship suggest this reading. A Gestalt analysis of Ian's similes suggests that in this context, encouraging such literate practices promoted his contact with others and with his own experience, thus encouraging him to work productively with complexity and ambivalence.

Contesting Struggle

March 7, 1996. Wayne described how Bob, a father in his late forties or fifties used the Struggle project to write his son, Jay. In the text, Bob promised Jay he would stay sober this time. But at Christmas, six or nine months after his Struggle work, Bob broke his promise and went on the binge that killed him.

Wayne had been thinking about Bob and Jay's situation. Referring to a prior conversation about the Struggle project, he explained, "You know, when we were talking about this reimagining ourselves, reconstructing ourselves, we're talking about how does one use one's history. What's most important about Struggle is not the rightness or wrongness of the trajectory of the promise. We need to say to people, 'Don't look there; look at the way people are using it for their own ends.'" We discussed critical history and pedagogy, and Wayne noted that deterministic language could foster hopelessness and apathy by implying that people were destined to particular circumstances without the power to change those circumstances or their lives.

May 8, 1996. The early afternoon sun streamed through the bank of windows at the far end of the third-floor room where Ellie, Joyce, Wayne, and I sat around a small oak conference table designed by a local craftsman. As we mapped out plans for the new Struggle training video, Ellie suggested we incorporate a reference to "On the Pulse of the Morning," the poem Maya Angelou had read for the recent presidential inauguration and which we planned to include in the video's opening. Wayne responded enthusiastically, and she noted that the poem prompted readers "to see our lives as things that are under construction."

Months later, I recalled the conversation while watching another audiovisual Struggle presentation that included clips of Angelou reading the poem. I had just seen a *Harper's* review that lauded the new African American literary anthology including the poem but condemned the piece itself as mediocre. The reviewer derided Angelou as "a very weak poet" and a "new, mediagenic . . . lawn jockey," protesting that no African American intellectuals had "uttered a word of criticism about her willingness to play the part" (Passaro 72). But the handful of black and white adults and children watching the Struggle presentation listened raptly to Angelou. Seeing them, I thought the reviewer had missed how people's everyday responses revealed the effects of particular rhetorical strategies, literate practices, and cultural productions such as Angelou's poem and celebratory reading.

June 19, 1996. Sitting at the third-floor conference room's oak table, Joyce, Wayne, and I discussed our newly completed training video's homemade feel. Wayne noted an academic colleague's dissatisfaction with another CLC video also produced in-house, then commented, "We have to spend a lot of time getting to know what is possible and developing a passion for the possible."

As the conversation unfolded, we concluded that because the training video was a tool rather than our final product, its unprofessional tone reflected an appropriate distribution of our resources in favor of Struggle's Hyper-Card stack. As often, we discussed funding, and this time Wayne raised the point that Struggle might be pigeonholed if it established its independence from the CLC's more academic endeavors. He also expressed concern about translating the project's Christian philosophical bases into a secular program. Mentioning the possibility that we might do an explicitly Christian version of the program, he suggested we frame it by saying, "In our lives, we are called to a personal exodus. That theme goes all the way through biblical narratives and is picked up by the early New Testament."

"Is that where you got the path from?" Joyce asked, alluding to Struggle's logo, a simple black-and-white graphic in which the word Struggle was written to angle upwards at its right end, its "S" formed by a winding path emerging below the word and receding into the page above it.

"Yeah," Wayne replied.

"We could use that when we do the Christian and religious one," she continued, her pitch rising, her words quick and bright. "We could put that scripture on the front when we do our video tape, and then the path. Oh my God! I like that."

Wayne said he wanted Struggle to name life's promise, redemption and right relationship with others. As we discussed how to embed these ideas implicitly in the secular version of Struggle, Wayne suggested we "take the specific *teloi* [ends or goals] of different communities in evocative language. 'Keep your eyes on the prize.' You know, 'the prize' means many different things, but that's language for modern people of the black freedom struggle. It just happens to be out of Christian language at the same time."

Writing Struggle

Diane's Struggle document emphasizes the importance of the felt experience produced by language practices, illustrating that to understand their effects, we must supplement the study of discursive and ideological work with inquiry into people's phenomenological experiences. In response to the prompt, "What are you struggling through in your life right now?" Diane began by stressing her frustration with a sense of low motivation, self-esteem, and failure to lose weight and quit smoking, two desired goals. She quickly linked this frustration with what she defined as the larger issue. "The first thing is, I don't know how to give my life back to Christ. I did at one time. I am not saved. I am baptized. When I lived in Texas, I joined a church; I felt uplifted, motivated. I felt loved and gave it. Because of it, my life changed, and so did my family's. We moved back to Pittsburgh, and I haven't found this. And it is ninety percent my fault, and I want to start here."

Diane's definition of her struggle emphasized that she felt a relationship with God to be her greatest need and that she had previously experienced this relationship in a Christian church. Her description suggested this church was probably evangelical. Thus it represents a position academics often regard as associated with misogyny, homophobia, and patriarchal class, race, and gender relations. The association is often accurate, and these issues (as well as such churches' theological dogmatism) raise important concerns. Yet Diane's clearly articulated experience and deep investment illustrated how strongly she felt the significance of this religious affiliation. She enunciated a sharply defined figure: the desire to reestablish it. A Gestalt approach demands respect for her figure and the power of her experience, despite troubling associations with the affiliation she desires. A Gestalt reading does not discount those concerns, but it does require academics who want to support coalition building with people like Diane to negotiate our concerns with others' experiences and investments.

As this theme unfolds in Diane's document, it demonstrates the complex functions of formulaic and aesthetic language practices in diminishing or augmenting contact with experience. Her response to the prompt on what she is struggling through concluded with a clichéd statement that her family had become "lazy in our way of doing things." Her response to the prompt, "What are you up against?" immediately following, continued such formulas, when she declared, "Mind over matter. . . . I have let myself become weak," "Lately, I pass by challenges," and "I am not hard enough with myself or disciplined enough or seek the proper help." These culturally sanctioned, prepackaged explanations enacted rhetorical moves that reduced Diane's contact with the blocks to pursuing her desire, blocks she probably articulated when she described, at other points in her text, the mental and physical exhaustion that deterred her from seeking, investigating, and joining a church.

In contrast, Diane's account of joining her Texas church included an image that suggested increased contact with her figure. She said, "I knew we were blessed when the pastor asked us to bow our heads without discussing it, and close our eyes, and 'was there anyone who wanted to join the church to raise your hands.' Once he finished at the end of the benediction, he asked all those people who had hands up to please stand. My husband and I held up our hands together. That's what I want back in my life again." Drawn from concrete experience, this image embodied Diane's figure perhaps more fully and evocatively than any abstract description could, particularly because it integrated her goals of marital, familial, and religious alignment. Diane's document shows she used this image to heighten her contact with the divide between her desired experience and her current circumstances.

This image and Diane's use of the table metaphor helped her move past the judgments of laziness and lack of discipline through which she reduced contact with parts of her experience (such as tiredness). Interestingly, they did so by positioning Diane to articulate another set of clichés that, in this case, seemed to move her into greater contact with her experience and reconciliation between her desire and her blocks to pursuing it. In addressing the prompt that asked who could support her in her struggle and how that person could help her see new paths and possibilities, Diane explained what her mother would say. "Life is not as bad as you may think," she began, then described from her mother's perspective the experience of living for twelve years in three rooms, with husband and children, in her brother-in-law's house. Diane imagined her mother saying, "Understand things take time," "You need to learn to pace yourself and stop rushing to have it all," "You are too hard on yourself," and "Look at where you are and what you have accomplished."

In the projected dialogue, Diane then scripted her mother's reminders of positive character traits and productive things Diane was doing. The words Diane attributed to her mother in this dialogue often followed formulaic constructions, yet they heightened her contact with previously discounted experience not acknowledged in any other section of her Struggle text, namely, her own achievements. I believe the clichéd language increased contact in this case because it was linked both to Diane's powerful image for her figure of religious affiliation and to the concrete example of her mother's experience of overcoming difficult circumstances through patience. Thus I suggest a revision of Goodman's theory of aesthetic and clichéd language. On the basis of my Struggle observations, I think Goodman's explanation of those language practices' effects often applies. But in this context of strong aesthetic language and concrete images, formulaic language heightened contact. Diane's text reaffirms the need to examine the experiential effects of specific language uses rather than relying solely on generalizations, no matter how generative.

Building Struggle

September 14, 1996. After we described what drew us to First Allegheny, Wayne gathered us in the sanctuary to read the statement of faith we might make the following day. As a group, we would see how many interpretations we could generate, he explained. We sat around an antique wooden table with heavy, ornately carved legs and a sturdy top while Wayne distributed copies of the statement. Noting the church's representative democratic governance, Wayne said that he as minister could not make a decision without its session of elders and vice versa.

Stressing interpretation and discussion, Wayne began reading the statement aloud. After presenting the first three sentences, which focused on baptism, Wayne noted that First Allegheny strove to be inclusive by recognizing all baptisms, not only Presbyterian baptisms. Next, the statement asked potential church members to answer a set of questions with the document's pre-scripted responses.

"Who is your Lord?" he read, following immediately with the statement's response, "Jesus Christ." "This one is often a stumbling block for people," he said. "If I were working from a feminist perspective," he continued, "I'd certainly object to the master-slave relation invoked." He went on to describe not only the roots of that relation but the cultural associations of female servitude implicit in the term. Thus the emphasis on various interpretations, he explained, again welcoming all glosses.

After a participant said she did find this troublesome, noting she was not very "Christocentric," Wayne reemphasized interpretative freedom. While he spoke, the tendons on either side of my neck tightened as I considered the implications of assenting to this language. Regardless of my interpretation, my assent invited others' interpretations, which might invoke all the implications of Lord—from subjugation and moral policing to Christocentrism—that I found problematic. I asked Wayne what we gained from retaining the language, and he replied that it guaranteed our association with the Presbyterian Church, which provided an established church's structure and material resources (including the CLC building). Reflecting later on the conversation, I realized that as an academic, I faced a similar problem in aligning myself with the university, another institution I sometimes found troubling. To build the Struggle planning group's coalition, I decided to risk the cultural and political entanglement posed by the statement of faith.

In Struggle

August 8, 1996. After I read it aloud, Ian silently read the HyperCard prompt from the PowerBook's screen: "What are you going through in your life right now? What are you struggling through?"

"What am I struggling through?" he repeated. "History, as in, I'm struggling through," he said, answering the question.

"Even now, in the summer?" I asked, surprised, seeking a response that suggested issues more central in Ian's life.

"A little bit," he replied, "because my dad still takes me to the library. I have to read books. And I just don't like reading those history books. I don't like going back in the past thirty to forty years ago."

Maureen commented, first summarizing Ian's difficulty, then connecting it to her own struggles with math, which made her fear pursuing further education once she had finished the high school brush-up program she had undertaken.

"History is a good class," said Ian, "but I just don't find it very interesting."

"It's because history is so far back," Maureen replied. "It's not something that you relate to like President Clinton today. Or Martin Luther King, or Malcolm X. If they would put that in school you could probably get A's because it's caught up with the century. See, our history goes back, to George Washington, Lincoln, the great guys before we were born, and it's hard to relate to them. But we know what President Clinton's doing today; you want up-to-date history. I know that because of Lloyd," she continued, comparing Ian to her teenage son, who was two or three years older. "Lloyd has civics, and he hates it because he says it's not up-to-date."

"I have two hardest things," Ian commented, "that Egypt stuff, the ancient books; I don't even know if that's true. And Vietnam. I'm not too good about that."

Grappling with my presupposition that Ian would gain more from exploring a dilemma more central to his life, I noted his categorization of both ancient Egyptian history and the Vietnam War as esoteric. The irony was mine and not his: he did not remember a time when the word Vietnam was code for everything relevant. Later, I saw the double irony of my failure to see that Ian had chosen a dilemma central to his experience. When I asked whether the issue felt important in his life, Ian replied, "Yes, because you've got to pass school."

"It is so important," Maureen confirmed, "because the only way that you can survive life in this world is higher education."

"And most people who don't get an education," said Ian, "end up out on the street." Studying my notes ten months later, I realized that Ian, at thirteen, felt sharply the need for credentialing and school's crucial role therein. Yet he also felt a disjuncture between his courses' educational work and the central experiences in his daily life. His Struggle responses voiced this disjuncture and its opposing pulls. Alienated by schoolwork, Ian still felt he needed school's credentials.

August 15, 1996. Midway through the session, I addressed a PowerBook malfunction by reading an explanation of the program's final prompt to Ian and Maureen. "It asks you what are some critical decision points that you dealt with in the past and how did you deal with them," I explained. "What was important about them? And then, what do you think will be your critical decision points in the future, given what you've planned to do, and how will you be prepared for them, or how will you deal with them?"

"I don't think I'll do anything different," Ian responded. "I'll go to high school, probably play football there. Get a scholarship for college. I don't know what college I might go to. I went for a tour of Maryland College 'cause my cousin plays football there. They have all types of business and doctor degrees there. 'Cause if you wanna play football for the NFL, you still need something to fall back on. 'Cause you might not always make it in the NFL."

"That's really good," approved Maureen. "You're right about that. You want to be a sports player, but you've got the main option set in your mind that you want a degree. Because you're guaranteed a job if you got a degree. It's your ticket for a job. You're so right about that."

"'Cause most athletes don't have anything to fall back on," Ian continued, "to find a job and stuff. Back in the past, I didn't know what I was gonna do. 'Cause when you're young, you don't really think of nothing you can do when you grow up. Until I got to the age of ten, that's when I started thinking of what I was going to be. Then, I wanted to be a veterinarian 'cause I liked animals. And I liked watching football, so my dad is setting me up for a little league summer football camp. And that's how I got interested in playing football. That's how I decided what I was going to be.

"Big decisions will probably be college. I still don't know about college yet. 'Cause I might have to spend like eight years there. Football's only four, but a doctor degree's like eight years. So I don't know if I'd like to stay eight years. I might not play football; I might just be a veterinarian. That's going to be a hard decision. Because I want to play football 'cause I like the game."

• • •

Ian's rhetorical pattern in discussing education reveals a central ambiguity, which Gestalt theory explains as an internal conflict demanding creative resolution. Both his and Maureen's phrasings illustrate this ambiguity. For instance, in Maureen's comment about the main option in Ian's mind, main option could mean first choice or first runner-up if Ian's pro football career did not materialize. Similarly, Ian expressed uncertainty about staying in school long enough to become a doctor. In the next breath, he had suggested he might abandon football for veterinary training, but that intention conflicted with his ambivalence about eight years of higher education. Further, the phrasing "football's only four" suggests Ian saw football as an academic endeavor in its own right. Like Lloyd's and William's NBA dreams, Ian's ambivalence and ambiguity indicates foreclosed contact with the statistical realities about how many African Americans achieve careers in professional sports.

This ambiguity positions higher education as an option if a professional sports career does not materialize, rather than as a primary goal. While higher education is privileged by middle-class culture (and Struggle's facilitators), professional sports seem to be privileged not only by Ian and others his age but by the adults in the Struggle project as well, as suggested by the responses of both Ian's and Lloyd's adult supporters. Notably, Diane, Ian's mother, mentioned the possibility of his playing pro ball in her conversation with Ian during the final Struggle session. A Gestalt reading explains such ambivalence as a case of two competing figures, or goals. Here, it suggests the ambivalence may operate as part of participants' structured ground. Both Maureen and Ian emphasized prior experiences of failure and difficulty in schooling and resulting feelings of blocked energy in attempting to pursue particular educational goals (history for Ian and math for Maureen).

Work by education researcher John Ogbu furthers this reading of educational ambivalence as part of some Americans' structured ground. Ogbu argues that African Americans' attitudes toward schooling have been fundamentally shaped in the past few decades by their experiences of the job ceiling. His ethnographic research shows that black American children witness a tension between their parents' stated emphasis on educational achievement and those parents' experiences of unemployment, underemployment, and discrimination. "Thus the actual example of the lives of black parents can undercut their stated encouragements," he concludes. "A resulting paradox is that black students may express high educational aspirations coupled with low academic effort and perseverance and thus low school performance" (240).

Ogbu's conclusions illuminate the experiences of Struggle participants such as Ian, and a Gestalt analysis heightens this illumination. It shows that while sports success is intrinsically valued in the community represented by Struggle's participants, schooling is pragmatically valued because of its currency in mainstream society but not intrinsically valued. Thus the imperative to pursue higher education is an introject, a value consciously espoused but not integrated into community members' spontaneous, unconscious thinking. Introjects inherently compete with intrinsic values. The rhetorical pattern of Ian's comments on education demonstrates just such conflict. His remark, "I have to read books [on history]" stood against his follow-up point, "I just don't like reading those history books." Similarly, he had explained that his two greatest challenges were ancient Egyptian history and the history of the

Vietnam War. Yet he emphasized the importance of precisely this work toward his goal of succeeding in school. His adult supporter, Maureen, reinforced Ian's perceived double bind, echoing his contrast when she agreed about the difficulty of relating to historical figures but affirmed that higher education is key to survival in life.

A Gestalt analysis shows that because one of Ian's two competing figures is an introject, his internal conflict is more destructive. Gestalt explains that by pushing oneself past one's intrinsic resistance to pursue an introjected goal, one reduces contact with one's own unaware rejection of that goal. The greater the pressure to pursue the goal, the greater the reduction in contact. Reduced contact increases alienation. Thus pursuing an introjected goal in defiance of one's intrinsic values deepens alienation. A vicious cycle develops: greater alienation produces greater resistance, which generates greater pressure on oneself and more alienation. Thus the traditional advice to subordinate desire to duty only worsens the problem. The resulting internal conflict consumes substantial energy, minimizing the energy and attention available for pursuing any goal. It produces guilt, anxiety, and the sense of paralysis some Struggle participants, such as Diane, describe, and it reduces one's capacities for devising a creative resolution to the conflict. Addressing it demands not intensified discipline but contacting one's resistance to deal creatively with it.

Contesting Struggle

August 26, 1996. Discussing why so much critical theory avoids the problem of hope, Wayne and I noted the problem's inherent challenge. "Well, it pushes you to have to grapple with teleology and spirituality," I commented, thinking of the tension between a postmodern disavowal of any telos and Marxism's emphasis on a promised end.

"What if we began to look at Struggle as forming identities around the recovery of hope?" Wayne asked. I replied enthusiastically, describing recent interactions with a Struggle participant who was wrestling with despair, fighting to pursue further education despite strong crosscurrents. Wayne said, "If we could name that process, find a way of saying, 'I know that I have this passion, and I need resiliency, that buoyancy that hopes and looks forward.'" Wayne's goal, he explained, was to cut through the unrealistic, even groundless, hopes for unlikely goals such as sports and music stardom. Instead, he wanted to "give people philosophic grounds to believe in something other than despair, to hope, rather."

"I think it's really hard to say, 'I'm going to accept this negative situation, and yet I'm going to hope anyway,'" I said. "Because when you talk about philosophical grounds for hope, it seems to me that it's both intellectual and emotional. It's an intellectual move, but it's more than that; it's a sense of faith."

"I think that one of the reasons that you don't hear about hope," Wayne replied, "is that if we give in to it, that's seen as acting out of weakness."

"That's a misreading of hope," I answered.

September 12, 1996. Early in our weekly planning session, Wayne contrasted Struggle with Roads to Work, a new CLC project designed to link urban teens with employers seeking entry-level service workers. Struggle, Wayne insisted, stood as a different kind of project, one emphasizing relationships. "It's a cri de coeur; it's a theological, philosophical statement. It is not about professional life per se or vocational life." When I asked whether we might redefine professional or vocational preparation in new terms, Wayne pointed out that most job training was "such a dumbing down." In contrast, he continued, Struggle was "giving everyday people like you and me the chance to see their lives as having a destiny."

Our conversation turned to a presentation I had given recently on Struggle. Wayne asked what questions had arisen, and I described some academic colleagues' concern that we were equating people's representations with their actual experiences. Articulating a poststructuralist understanding of the break between language and experience, they had pushed me to consider that break in discussing Struggle participants' work. I had responded by explaining that I believed Struggle supported people to develop representations that connected with their experience.

Wayne reemphasized his vision of Struggle as an occasion for everyday people to think of their lives as having destinies. "I want to allow people who don't usually think of their lives as having destinies to do that," he explained. "You know, political figures with power have destinies; warriors with power have destinies; bankers have destinies. Shakespearean people have destinies. How come everyday people don't have destinies? Or how come they aren't seen as interesting? The destiny of being one hell of a teacher or the destiny of being one hell of a meat cutter," he continued. "Struggle is interrogating that mythic world of meaning that we construct around the self in order to not give in to despair and at the same time is about life as this Homeric journey," he concluded.

While I appreciated Wayne's emphasis on the humanist tradition, I felt concern that by pursuing this approach, Struggle might, like that tradition, discount the material and psychological experience of working-class and working-poor people. Mentally replaying the voices of my working-class family and sometime co-workers, I expressed doubt that a vision of being the best meat cutter one could be usually energized the people doing such work.

"Let me back up on that," Wayne continued. "I think you're right on that. And yet," he said, invoking his experience working in a family-owned mining company during his college summers, "what if I said coal miner? The most interesting, exciting job I've ever had is coal mining. I bet a lot of people would make that same response."

"I think there's a lot of really deadening work out there," I answered. I could not articulate the tightness in my chest, my keenly felt sense of the difference between working a summer job as the owner's son, assured an excellent university education and professional possibilities, and the entrapment I had felt working my way through college with pizza-shop and retail jobs, wondering if I would manage to climb from service work to something more satisfying. Interactions with family and acquaintances had taught me that, like others, working-class people have varied, highly individual experiences. But I remembered my father, imprisoned in the local steel mill by family responsibility and a one-industry regional economy, continually pursuing self-employment. I recalled my husband's string of numbing printing jobs and his co-workers and their conflicted relations with jobs they needed yet longed to escape. The voices of several women, low-level secretaries, my co-workers in another part-time college job at a local bank, joined the murmurs of cafeteria and bookstore co-workers, all trying to circumvent the everyday petty humiliations of a supervisor or patrons.

I could not enunciate the very different experience of work these voices evoked, my sense of the trap, at least for working-class people, in the existing economic arrangement. I could not describe the wedge this arrangement drove between work life's often-desensitizing boredom, its petty degradations, and the intellectual and emotional energy required to explore life's ontological and epistemological dimensions. I knew professionals who felt trapped and numbed by their jobs. But status, relative freedom, and remuneration offered a compensation often missing from working-class positions. My chest clenched, and I feared that projects like Struggle might offer little in the face of a system based on retaining such class differentiations.

Explaining that I wanted to respect both people's ambitions and the sometimes deadening facets of their experiences, I suggested, "You can't really do vocational training without addressing the big questions that Struggle raises." Attempting to join Wayne's questions of meaning with the social and political questions raised automatically by class positions, I continued, "How do you have hope in your life? And what are your day-to-day practices? It's easy to dismiss these things and not relate them to the vocational, but in fact they're central to the vocational, because the only thing that gets you and me out of bed in the morning is that we love what we're doing; we're invested in it. It's not just work that we have to go to; it's a bigger sense of ourselves and who we are."

"And being enjoined in a kind of passionate struggle for something," Wayne replied. "If people are reducing the quest to skill-based learning . . . We know that it's not just about skills but also about the myths that organize our working space where you can deconstruct some of what are perhaps hollow promises."

"And that you can have a self that's bigger and richer than being a meat cutter or a clerk at McDonald's," I said, still reaching unsuccessfully for language to evoke a process of self-revision that would combine individual refashioning with an investment in civic involvement and democratic participation.

November 21, 1996. After a short planning session, Ellie and I chatted about the previous month's get-together dinner with the Struggle participants who had completed the project in August. Everyone but Ian had attended. During the dinner, which reconvened participants a month or so after the project's completion, Diane had smilingly described Ian's changed behavior at home, his more cooperative, less contentious interaction with her. The change, she suggested, had arisen from his participation in Struggle. Joanne recounted her recent vacation in the country, while Maureen updated us on her schooling, and Sheila sketched the progress of her fledgling in-home clerical support business.

When we suggested that people might want to exchange phone numbers with a partner so that teens would have a long-term adult supporter and vice versa, people were enthusiastic. In the face of our ineffectual attempt to draw names, Maureen, Sheila, and Diane undertook the process, devising a plan to pair each adult with an unrelated teen. It was this moment Ellie now recalled. "I think the thing that thrilled me the most about that meeting," she explained, "was the way the discussion about keeping in touch went. Despite all of our efforts to organize things, and maybe because of them, they just took over."

• • •

A Gestalt reading of these interactions suggests that while the Struggle participants made real contact with one another, I short-circuited the budding contact between Wayne and me during our exchange. Struggle's participants demonstrated their contact by acting explicitly in concert to pursue a shared figure, namely, establishing longer-term relationships between adult supporters and teens. In contrast, after my initial attempt to express a difference with Wayne failed to communicate my position, I retroflected the expression because I felt defensive, unable to articulate my concerns productively and nonconfrontationally. Absorbed in my emotional response, I missed Wayne's gesture toward addressing those concerns when he suggested deconstructing the hollow promises of financial and professional success. We began to make real contact but then avoided that contact because I withdrew. Therefore we missed the chance to negotiate a richer, more substantive response to an issue that clearly mattered to both of us. Further, I carried unresolved tensions into future exchanges. Both circumstances affected the Struggle planning group's cohesion.

Writing Struggle

Janine's interpretation of the map that concluded her Struggle text illustrated how images and aesthetic language helped participants contact and work through the complex, contradictory aspects of their experience. Thus it amplified Ian's and Diane's uses of metaphor by showing how such aesthetic language uses helped participants reorganize their experience to construct new understandings of self, others, and the world.

Earlier portions of Janine's text described her struggles to stay in school and out of past habits of drinking and cutting classes. Janine wrote about moving in with her grandfather (and her Aunt Joanne, with whom she attended Struggle) after completing treatment for anxiety, depression, and substance abuse at St. Agnes, a local hospital. She explained her conflicted feelings about leaving her mother to move in with her grandfather. "With my grandfather, he is working and shows me that I have got to go to school and doesn't let me get into trouble. There are no liquor and cigarettes, whereas I used to drink and smoke with my Mom—used to do a lot of things that I shouldn't have done. . . . I love them both, and I want to be with them both, but I have to choose. I feel torn between two people I love, and it is an equal love."

When she participated in another CLC project, Janine wrote a skit about her experiences prior to and during her hospital stay, titled "Living My Mom's Life." The play depicted how she had cared for her younger siblings and managed the household while her mother struggled with depression and addiction. The play presented her stay at St. Agnes, the move to her grandfather's, and her involvement at the CLC as key steps toward living her own life. Still, her

Struggle document, composed after the skit, articulated her conflicted feelings about the circumstances, citing not only the emotional turmoil Janine felt because of the sharp tensions between her mother and grandfather but her sense, as well, that sometimes her grandfather was too restrictive.

Janine's map and narrative explanation suggested she used her Struggle writing to increase her contact with the conflicts within her experiences and to begin reorganizing her understanding of that experience. Her narrative later explained, "I come to middle school, and we come to a horseshoe bend, which is off to the side and we go halfway down that, and we have 'Raising Brothers.' It's a dead-end down that street, so we turn around and keep going down the bend, and we see 'Living My Mom's Life,' and there is only a cliff at the end of that street, so we have to walk all the way up the hill. At the top of the hill, we have 'Making Friends.' . . . From high school we have 'Coming Down to the CLC,' and when we reach the top of the hill, we go all the way over. . . . We have another hurdle to climb over, which is staying in school. Then we come to the broken bridge—drinking, smoking, and depression. We get a boat, swim across the river, and make it to St. Agnes. Then the last stop on our journey is moving to Grandpa's house."

Janine's description presented her experience through topographical images that produced kinesthetic metaphors for her experiences. These images conveyed her felt sense of the incidents they illustrated and thus highlighted those incidents' pain, exertion, and dangers. Perhaps Janine recontacted those feelings because she was struggling with the desire to return to her mother's, a decision she knew might lead her back into similar dangers. Notably, her metaphor of the broken bridge and the boat emphasized her recognition that she needed the support of others (from St. Agnes staff to CLC participants to her grandfather) to replace the coping methods she had developed to survive her former life with her mother. It suggested what a Gestalt analysis reveals: individual change benefits significantly from systems-level support.

Thus in addition to using metaphor to enunciate mixed feelings, as Ian did, and to sharpen a figure, as Diane did, participants used it to augment contact with the complexities of experience, as Janine did. Yet this process did not immediately resolve the mixed feelings complexity produces. In the months following Struggle, Janine returned to her mother's. Her document described the risks this decision posed: "I know if I go back [to living with my Mom], I will go back to the way I was, cutting school and doing nothing all day and making no real use of my life, whereas with my grandfather, I go to school every day, and my whole life has completely turned around." The kind of reorganization Janine undertook, one that reintegrates conflicted emotions in a new way, takes time to complete. The increased contact her document demonstrates supports the process but does not guarantee a smooth path. Janine's conflicting characterizations of her life with her grandfather suggest she had not yet developed a clear figure, that she was still in the process of assimilating new material in what Goodman calls a creative adjustment. Like Diane's Struggle work, Janine's assimilation seemed to move in stages and include returns to earlier behavior patterns.

Building Struggle

August 11, 1996. Describing a guest minister who would deliver the following week's sermon, Wayne mentioned the speaker's courage and commitment as the writer of a letter supporting the Presbyterian Church's ordination of lesbian and gay ministers. I glanced at Jess, a lesbian minister who regularly attended First Allegheny with her partner, Terry. Seeing her smile at Wayne's accolade, I scanned faces for Kim and Vera, another gay couple who were active members. Just before the presermon prayer, Wayne moved to the sanctuary's rear doors and pursed his lips in a slight, expectant grin, then announced that Officer Johnson, the young gay black policeman scheduled to read the day's prayer, was not present and that Wayne was asking Mrs. Baskins to do so instead.

Joyce smiled, murmuring, "That's OK," her tone daring Wayne to disorient her. She gripped the rear podium with both hands, bowed her head, and instructed us to do likewise. Then I realized that Joyce—who rehearsed nuances of articulation and timing to hone her arresting presence—would not have had time to compose a prayer, let alone practice. But she prayed long and fervently. She often raised her hand to her shoulder, drawing it back so her thumb and fingers met to display elegant, artistically manicured nails, then darting it forward abruptly to accentuate each of the prayer's central points.

She prayed for mercy for the city, referring specifically to a new teen curfew, widely perceived as an invitation to ratchet up police violence against black youth, and asked that disaster be avoided. A few weeks before, she had written a piece for the city newspaper, arguing for a proposed civilian review board to monitor the city's police, then accused in multiple lawsuits by the American Civil Liberties Union of pervasive racist violence. Later, the federal Department of Justice would step in, citing the city force's endemic problems and imposing new, department-mandated policies. The following May, the proposal for a civilian review board would go before city voters in a referendum that would win substantially. But that day, Joyce prayed primarily for our spiritual growth, saying that everything would follow from it. I heard congregation members, particularly African Americans, murmur approval and support.

June 8, 1997. Mingling with fellow congregation members before the service, I took pleasure in seeing people such as Jess and Terry, Molly (Wayne's wife), and Charles, none of whom I would likely meet during my Struggle work. Yet later, as the sermon commenced, I felt the usual tightening in the tendons on each side of my neck, this time quicker and sharper than usual. Arguing for the importance of right relationships with God, Wayne's sermon warned against privileging professional success or accumulated accomplishments. Recalling my Roman Catholic childhood's emphasis on abnegation, I rebelled internally against what I heard as a black-and-white ethic.

Still, I recognized that this sermon, like most, affected other listeners differently. Joyce often answered sermons' most intense moments with an audible "Preach!" and other African Americans responded similarly. In the circle First Allegheny used to close its services, congregants often thanked Wayne for a sermon that had lifted, inspired, or energized. But the person whose difference touched me most was Ellie. Once, she had explained how reading critical feminism and social theory had devastated her spiritual and intellectual reserves of hope. Listening, I realized that experiences that had energized me had affected her quite differently. Later, when she described returning to the Community House after an unfulfilling stint as a full-time professor at a local college, I gathered that First Allegheny had helped her rebuild those reserves.

In Struggle

August 20, 1996. After our celebratory dinner, the kickoff to this concluding session, Ian and Diane, like the program's other original adult-teen pairs, adjourned to present their documents to one another. As their supporter, I began by asking Ian whether he would like to share particular parts of his document with his mom. After a pause without response, I mentioned that in earlier discussions we had considered beginning with his description of his grandmother.

"So you put her at your table, hmmn?" Diane commented, her voice rising partially into a question but then flattening into a statement. After she read the relevant section of Ian's document, Diane read aloud some of her own text's sections on her son. In them, she defined who Ian was and their relationship, then commented on Ian's personality, describing it as threefold at this point. She used the categories teenager-child, teenager-teenager, and teenager–young man and cited examples of his grooming and behavior with chores and homework to illustrate how Ian's actions fit each category. She concluded by saying that Ian could be funny, "when you want to be."

When he did not assent to the characterization, she pressed him, and Ian muttered, "It's natural."

"It's natural," Diane repeated, half-smiling. "You don't do it all the time."

"When I'm in the mood," Ian replied.

"Right," she concluded, her voice dropping to accent the word. "You're funny when—you—want—to—be," she finished, extending the phrase to emphasize its final word. "And you can be very mean. When you want to be."

We returned to Ian's text. "And the map," he said, opening the document to its final page, which included the life map he had drawn earlier. Diane smiled, a bit tight lipped, as she surveyed the map, yet I thought she looked pleased. Meanwhile, Ian pointed out its features to her. The pictures next to stars, he explained, depicted where he would really be going, and those included high school, college, and further down the map's road, "money and success." The pictures without stars, he continued, were the dead ends, the paths of temptation that he avoided. He gestured toward the "drop zone," which seemed to symbolize not trying in school, dropping back. As he showed Diane these features, Ian explained that they were the paths he was not taking.

"But sometimes you take them, right?" she asked, her tone deepening. "Sometimes you get a little lost, and then somehow you get back on the path." She then described Ian's lapses into drop-zone behaviors, explaining that sometimes he would "fuss" about getting something done, put off chores, and finally do them halfheartedly. Ian squirmed, muscle movements playing across his face as he slid in and out of eye contact with his mother. "Remember how my dad had five girls and said that we all had to finish high school no matter what? Even if we had babies, even if we had families? But how we had no support? You have support."

"What's support?" Ian asked.

"Support is giving someone help to get through," Diane answered. "Support is . . . what do I do when you have trouble with a class, when you fall behind in school?" she asked, her voice slightly metallic.

"You go to the school," Ian replied.

"What else do I do?"

"You get the work," he answered.

"What else?"

In the following pause, Diane answered the question: "I sit with you; I stay until it's all done, if that's what it takes. What else?" Ian did not reply but moved nervously. "Do you get to do the things you like to do?"

"No," he said.

"What do I do if you don't do it right?"

"Make me do it again," Ian answered, turning his head away from Diane, focusing his eyes over the table at neither of us, his legs and arms moving rhythmically.

Before he had quite finished, Diane said, "I sit with you and make sure that you do it until it's done right. When I do that, that's support. I'm trying to give you what I didn't have. Because making sure that you do things right, supporting you to do the right thing is my responsibility as your mother." Diane pulled Ian's text toward her and commented with surprise in her voice, "So you do have college on there!"

"Yeah," Ian replied. She noticed that at his drawing of college Ian had labeled the choice he believed he might need to make between a career as a pro football player or as a veterinarian.

"Because you want to play this kind of football," Diane said, indicating the "pro" label, "I don't want you to play street football. I'm afraid you'll get hurt and not be able to play real football." They briefly discussed the danger of playing in a neighboring apartment building's yard for fear of damaging the flowers and being held responsible. As Diane spoke, Ian contorted his mouth and slid his eyes away from hers while fidgeting his hands and feet. Occasionally, he protested a comment, and Diane replied by explaining why his protest did not provide a sufficient rationale. Her explanations usually concluded with an "OK? Definitely," whose ascending pitch did not quite reach the soprano of a question before falling to the alto of a response. Once she had surveyed the rest of Ian's map, Diane turned to him and said, "There's one thing you forgot." She paused. "You forgot something. You forgot my house."

Ian pointed to the map's start and said, "It's there, at the beginning."

"No," Diane answered. "It should be at the end." She turned toward me and explained, "He's going to buy me a house when he grows up." As she looked at the final points on Ian's map, she turned back to him and continued, "We, your dad and me, we want you to go to college, to be successful and wealthy."

"What's wealthy?" Ian asked.

"Wealthy is this," Diane answered, indicating the map's final picture, which he had labeled "money and success."

"Oh," he replied.

"These are your goals for yourself, too," Diane continued. "We encourage them." She read him the rest of what she had written about him, then requested his agreement with each point. Twenty minutes of our half hour had passed. Diane said to Ian, "OK, I've talked a lot. It's your turn. You can criticize me now." When he did not respond but instead squirmed, half smiling and looking away, she said, "Go ahead. What did you say in your document?"

"I've already said everything," Ian answered, and went on to relist two or three comments, none of which criticized his mother. I ransacked my repertoire for a tactful way to encourage Ian to voice his experience without setting him up, but I came up empty handed. The thirty minutes slid by, and we returned to the Umoja Room to reunite with the others and conclude the program.

Afterward, Diane warmly offered to help us in any way she could, encouraging us to ask for her assistance. "Please call if I can help," she said. She had had many reservations, she explained, but ultimately was very pleased with Struggle.

• • •

The complex dynamics of this exchange and their implications grow clearer through a Gestalt analysis. These dynamics reveal several rhetorical patterns with conflicting implications for the contact between Diane and Ian. In one pattern, Diane asked leading questions such as, "What do I do when you fall behind in school?" "Do you get to do things you like to do?" and "What do I do if you don't do it right?" By pushing Ian to answer within her terms and answering herself when he failed to do so, Diane's moves privileged her interpretation rather than eliciting Ian's or negotiating their different perceptions. These rhetorical moves told Ian what to think, and their pattern minimized spaces for his interpretation. In this context, Ian responded with bodily messages suggesting he struggled with ambivalence about whether to make or avoid contact with his mother. For instance, by squirming, moving in and out of eye contact with Diane, and turning his head away from her, Ian indicated discomfort with her position and mixed feelings about whether or not he wanted to stay in the interaction. A Gestalt reading suggests Ian was retroflecting, or restraining impulses to respond in particular ways. When he moved his legs and arms rhythmically while Diane questioned him on how she supported his school efforts, Ian may have retroflected desires to walk away and to push away his mother's interpretation. Similarly, by contorting his mouth when Diane commented on the dangers of street football, Ian implied he was retroflecting a response.

A parent telling a child how he should see his circumstances is the classic

Gestalt condition for forming introjects, with their potential for paralysis and alienation. In light of Diane's directives, Ian's introjects about schooling appear in both familial and cultural contexts. When Diane explained away Ian's comments and concluded her explanations with "OK? Definitely," her rhetorical patterns foreclosed key moments of potential contact. By using such directive moves to tell Ian how to understand their relationship and its implications for his schooling, Diane took a stance that undermined her potential contact with Ian's responses to schooling and to her expression of caring.

Yet, even more significantly, Diane's rhetorical patterns demonstrated a commitment to making genuine contact as well. For instance, on seeing Ian's map, she noted his inclusion of college, she pointed out to Ian a convergence between his goals for himself and his parents' goals for him, and she implicitly acknowledged her critical stance by inviting him to criticize her. Ian avoided doing so. This response, with his earlier body language, suggested Ian wanted contact with his mother but did not have strategies for pursuing it without raising conflicts he felt unequipped to handle productively. Ian's experience suggested his difficulties in broaching differences with an interlocutor he perceived to have greater power. My failure to make contact with Wayne implied similar difficulties with respect to an interlocutor I perceived to have class privilege. Nonetheless, both Ian's and Diane's patterns illustrated a substantial commitment to making contact and to their relationship, despite the difficulties they encountered in bringing such contact to fruition in this exchange.

Contesting Struggle

January 17, 1997. Ellie, Wayne, Joyce, and I discussed how to prepare to meet with a local foundation's funding officer. A few weeks before, another foundation, which had funded pilot Struggle programs, agreed to provide a third of the monies needed to develop the project over the next three years. Now we planned to approach another foundation for the remainder. Noting that the funding officer knew of the proposed CLC project that would link teens with employers seeking entry-level service workers, Wayne warned, "So she may come reading us as Roads to Work," which, he said, was important but "not as important as roads to passion and project and possibility."

March 6, 1997. Ellie, Joyce, and I listened as Wayne explained that foundations planned to shift funding from older children and teens' programs to early childhood interventions. "You are gonna have to make a business choice based on opportunity about how to be invested," a senior funding officer had remarked. A chill grew in the room as Wayne spoke.

June 12, 1997. On meeting the young funding officer interested in Struggle, we had learned that her foundation supported computer-based education in community organizations. It funded Community Technology Centers (CTCs), neighborhood organizations equipped with computer technology and offering urban kids a safe space and computer literacy. But most CTCs remained empty: the technology was there, but the kids were not. Struggle obviously reached participants substantively, she noted, with its simple but powerful questions. She suggested we tailor them toward organizations, retooling Struggle to help CTCs to refocus and connect with their communities.

As Wayne covered poster-sized pages with notes, we considered how Struggle could help neighborhood organizations develop a new vision and set of practices, as well as individualized pedagogies that linked an organizational mission to the surrounding community's needs. This Struggle would help CTCs move from off-the-shelf computer games toward uses of computers and writing for locally defined community purposes and social actions. Wayne suggested we offer an urban retreat for groups that could benefit from more structured learning and discussion.

· · ·

A Gestalt analysis of Struggle's shift in goals complicates poststructuralist theories of co-optation. Such theories tend to position any convergence with mainstream thinking or funding sources as automatic evidence of co-optation. In Gestalt terms, the Struggle planning team made contact with the funding officer's proposal, recognizing the significant sacrifices of key goals (e.g., working directly with community members). Yet Wayne's suggestion of an urban retreat center took up her proposal and molded it to pursue other key goals (e.g., facilitating holistic change through experiences of real, supported contact). His suggestion articulated our group values with the foundation's pragmatic goals, exemplifying Gestalt's cycle of experience as a model of contact. Reading it through Gestalt's filter amplifies the move's growth-oriented, adaptive features rather than the co-optation heard through a poststructuralist filter.

Writing Struggle

Janine's Struggle text illustrated how Struggle's prompts encouraged people to experiment with new rhetorical habits that had significant implications for their identities. In responding to the prompt that asked what she was up to in life, Janine described efforts to resolve family tensions and free herself to consider how to finance college and her plans to become a nurse. When she continued to the next prompt, on who could support her in her struggle, she first named Mr. Fine, a teacher who had facilitated her entry into CLC programs and who was known to CLC staff for actively supporting students. Wayne, who facilitated Janine's Struggle work, asked how Mr. Fine might rival her nursing goal. She replied, "I can imagine him saying, 'Well, your intelligence just goes beyond that—you ought to use it to do teaching and to become a teacher.' I can imagine him saying, 'Janine, you can do what you want to do, and you can go further,' and 'Don't let your ears stop you. [Janine can communicate and handle daily tasks on her own but is partially deaf.] Keep on writing, and never stop writing poetry.' The normal stuff a teacher would say."

When Wayne asked what Janine made of Mr. Fine's words, she answered, "Mr. Fine knows about my problems. He has suggested that I could teach blind or deaf children to write poetry and read. Actually, I think that is pretty interesting—because it involves learning to understand and see what they can't see and understand and hear. So that is one alternative, teaching." Later, Wayne inquired why nursing was first on Janine's list of possible careers, and she replied, "Well, first, my family is in the medical field. And, second, I like helping people get better." She cited her experience at St. Agnes and how staff there made her feel she belonged.

Janine's account of Mr. Fine's response and her application of it in considering possible career paths illustrated Struggle's implicit version of joining-and-analyzing. With Wayne's prompting, Janine noted that her thinking had been shaped primarily by presumptions based on family experience. (Her Aunt Joanne and other family members worked as nurses' aides.) Thus, in Goodman's terms, she developed awareness of the conditions limiting her experience. Further, she applied Mr. Fine's rhetorical moves for discussing her talents to broaden her definition of what work she would enjoy. Thus Janine's Struggle writing prompted her to experiment with new rhetorical strategies in much the way Wheeler explains people do to undertake new contact styles. Here, Janine's use of the rhetorical move of focusing on her talents led her to greater proprioceptive contact with her own interests and their relationship to possible careers. This use suggested that Struggle's implicit joining-and-analyzing, like Wheeler's version, prompted people to experiment with revised rhetorical moves and contact styles.

Building Struggle

March 23, 1997. Though I lived a scant few miles away, I had never before visited the city's theological seminary, located across town from the Community House in another racially mixed neighborhood, whose local economy, I had gathered, drew largely on illegal exchanges. But on this chilly gray Palm Sunday morning, entering the seminary's parking lot amid expensive-looking cars and well-dressed worshippers, I remembered the cultural activities and significant community organizations the neighborhood also boasted. Glancing at the other people walking toward the seminary, I confirmed that, for the moment, I was the only white person in the environs.

Once I had made my way into the sanctuary where the second annual Palm Sunday Unity Day Service of the city's Caucus of Black Presbyterian Churches was to be held, I spotted a handful of other First Allegheny members. Smiling and beckoning me to a seat nearby, Joyce welcomed me with a hug and pointed out other First Allegheny faces across the room.

After a series of slow, poorly performed choral selections, Joyce and a few other attendees tried to liven the service by clapping loudly and demonstratively, encouraging others to follow suit. "These Presbyterians wouldn't say 'Hallelujah!' if you choked them," she murmured. I laughed softly. Remembering her AME background, I thought of E. P. Thompson's description of loud, energetic, and emotional Methodist revivals as central practices in English working-class people's self-definition, as they opposed themselves to frigid, straightlaced middle-class English Presbyterians (350–400, especially 380–2). I wondered how such class divisions and practices had intersected with black American churches' development and whether the sea of restrained, well-dressed Presbyterians surrounding us represented primarily the city's black middle class. I also wondered whether Joyce's active participation might be a good-humored challenge, a call to take up a very different set of African American religious practices.

When Wayne came forward to perform his part in the service, I smiled, not knowing whether he could see us but hoping to provide a friendly face while he acted as the only white officiator before a sizable crowd of strangers. In his short prayer, Wayne mentioned the newly passed amendment to the American Presbyterian Church's doctrine, the Book of Rules. This revision excluded gays and lesbians, divorced members, and unmarried cohabitators from local church leadership roles. A tiny congregation in the midst of a large, conservative, and powerful regional presbytery, First Allegheny had nonetheless actively fought the amendment. Now, Wayne prayed that we would all, despite the new rule, work for inclusion. Near the prayer's end, he invoked "God, Mother to us all." I was struck by his courage in preaching abroad what he did at home, particularly given his tenuous position and an audience that seemed likely to respond unsympathetically to both gestures. When I heard the call for inclusion, I felt the impulse to imitate Joyce's earlier exclamation and proclaim an audible "Amen!" but I felt awkward, thinking I was unlicensed to take up a tradition that was not mine, anxious that doing so might imply a white woman's disregard for the mores of this African American group. Later, I saw the irony of my failure of courage in the face of First Allegheny's efforts to build intercultural communication, to support members in taking up one another's traditions.

I realized after the service that I had locked my keys in the car, and Molly, Wayne's wife, arranged to take me to pick up a spare set. As we chatted about the Unity Day service, Molly mentioned that First Allegheny might not be invited the following year. "Because we're such a mixed church?" I asked, alluding to the congregation's ethnic and racial medley.

"Yeah," she replied. When I said I had trouble knowing how to respond to such positions, Molly waived her usual quiet reserve, saying emphatically, "It's shitty." I explained that while I was able to argue for including men in feminist endeavors, I had difficulty speaking for whites' inclusion here because I occupied a different position. "Yeah," she said, "but I think exclusion in any form is wrong." I remembered bell hooks's descriptions of American blacks' experiences of strain around whites (165–78) and the voices of women who had expressed a need for space away from men despite important alliances with them, but I did not find a way to articulate those positions quickly. I felt torn about the Unity Day service debate about whether to include First Allegheny. Still, seeing the service's cultural separatism, I appreciated First Allegheny's courage, its generative response to forces that converged to break the fragile graft of alliance before it could knit.

Presenting Struggle

Following are excerpts from a paper Joyce presented at the 1997 Conference on College Composition and Communication. Her account amplifies my colleagues' dialogue with me and helps explain the work Diane and Ian accomplished. My depictions focus on Ian's interaction with his supporter and involve Diane only in public Struggle occasions and in the concluding session when Ian and Diane presented their texts to one another. In contrast, Joyce's excerpts represent Diane's interactions with her own adolescent partner, Jody, during their Struggle work sessions. Further, the excerpts present Joyce's conclusions about that interaction and its long-term effects on Diane and her relationship with Ian. Together, Joyce's depiction and mine construct a dialogue about how a few participants used the summer 1996 Struggle project.

The excerpts comprise Joyce depicting Struggle, insofar as possible in an ethnography. With Gayatri Spivak, I believe no representation is wholly ethical ("Limits and Openings of Marx in Derrida"). Yet with critical ethnographers, I believe in the intellectual and moral value of striving to represent others ethically while acknowledging my efforts' limits.[9] Because I have crafted the surrounding text and excerpted parts of Joyce's paper, her depiction is mediated by my work's shape and concerns (and editing). Still, her voice echoes through these filters.

JOYCE A. BASKINS
*Excerpts From Revising Pasts/Projecting Futures: Real People Writing
What Really Matters*
[After invoking Frederick Douglass's statement that "there is no progress without struggle," Joyce introduces the Struggle project and the participants she plans to discuss, noting that in each case "an important conversation is renewed. But not always in the direction we might expect." Introducing Diane as a manager who routinely directed others and made critical decisions, Joyce suggests that Struggle demanded a different conversational style that challenged Diane.]

In this scenario, you'll see that Diane renewed a conversation with her son Ian while working to build a more mutual relationship with her teenage Struggle partner, Jody. . . . When it was Jody's turn to seat the people around his table, he included his father, his grandmothers, and his mom. But, once he got his mom around the table, I don't think he knew what to do with her, what to say about her or their relationship. He had so much to say about his Grandma Pat, for instance, "She's always there for me. She helps me out. I stay with her sometimes. She intercedes for me." All of these wonderful accolades. But when it came to responding to the Struggle prompts in terms of his mom, he drew silent. He was hesitant. I think he didn't want to be too critical of her in front of Diane. Remember, Diane is a stranger, virtually a stranger. Jody's silence posed a problem for Diane because, I think, Diane saw the silence as a problem for Jody.

The dilemma that Diane faced is this: is it more respectful to take the lead from the *silence* and let Jody skip over ta[l]king about his [m]om? Or is it my role as a supporter to respect the fact that he brought her up, and seated her at his table? (After all, he was the one who had broached the topic of his mom. So maybe it's my role to help him get the fullest out of the conversation, not to drop it.) But if so, how do I do that supporter role without playing the heavy?

So Diane would have to follow up Jody's short, blanket responses with questions like: "What do you mean by just saying 'We don't get along'?" Knowing how to follow up posed a challenge for Diane.

Her role in Struggle required that she listen to what Jody had to say. As a parent I know, and you may well be aware of this too, that when you're in a parenting role, sometimes you think you can get by without listening. You can hear your teenager talking, but there are times when you're not really listening. But in working with Jody, Diane has to listen because she's a supporter. Now, I should tell you that supporting is a strategy of Community Literacy. In Struggle, teens and adults take turns supporting one another in moving through the questions of the HyperCard stack. In our training session, we went into a good amount of detail describing the moves of a good supporter: the key principle of being a good supporter is that you find or invent whatever moves [are] necessary to ensure that your partner—working through the stack—is at that time the authority over his or her own responses; she or he has the floor. So the name of the game, in large part, is listening. She was learning to listen—to really listen—to a teenaged boy. Now, I don't want to suggest that a good parent isn't also a supporter. But in Struggle, helping adults make supportive, rather than authoritarian, moves is imperative.

Diane overtly struggled to be a good supporter for Jody. Early on, she was direct and asked even leading questions [such as], "Don't you think that your mother loves you?" Yet rather than hold to this pattern, she kept experimenting with ways of opening up the conversation so Jody could really say what was on his mind.

One thing she would do was to repeat Jody's responses. I think she did this so he could hear what he had said, but also so it would sink in for her.

Another move she made was to support Jody when he was supporting *her*. When it was her turn to answer the questions in the HyperCard stack, she would prompt Jody, "For instance, you could ask me about my relationship with my mother?" She also encouraged him to type, to use the keyboard, not to worry about his spelling. She was really patient and supportive. In addition, when answering a question in the HyperCard stack, she would make reference to things he had said in his answers, making connections between his life and hers. Showing there were similarities between their responses, even though he was a teenager and she an adult.

But what I found most interesting about Diane's interaction with Jody is this: when she would ask him questions and respond to him, she kept making reference to her own son, Ian. For instance, responding to something Jody said about negotiating street life, she commented, "Ian will be facing some of these same things in the next couple of years." Often, it was as if there were three people in the conversation, Diane, Jody, and her son. Now, Diane also has a young daughter, whom she didn't mention during any of the Struggle sessions. Apparently, she was drawing a parallel between the experiences of Jody and Ian, both young African-American males growing up in an urban neighborhood.

Toward the end of the project, while all the pairs were sharing a dinner together, Diane was excited about something that had happened between herself and Ian at home.[10] And she wanted to share this with the other pairs around the table. She said that it was so much easier to get along with Ian these days, there wasn't as much friction between the two of them. He was more willing to cooperate with her in their home, rather than positioning her as an authority figure to resist. And she was attributing this to the fact that Ian had worked through the Struggle program with a mentor. Which may be so. But I sat in on some of the sessions between her and Jody. I saw that the longer they worked together, the more patient she was with him, herself, and the process of beginning a different kind of conversation. I contend that it was Diane who had changed as well.

Joyce's analysis of Diane's Struggle work extends the interpretation I have begun. The leading questions she points out parallel the kinds of leading questions Diane used with Ian in their final Struggle conversation about his text. Yet Joyce's depiction shows how Diane began to experiment with new rhetorical strategies as well. For instance, by repeating Jody's responses, Diane both supported his proprioception and, as Joyce suggests, started training herself to make greater contact with his perceptions. Diane began learning an alternative to her habit of foreclosing contact with Ian by preempting his views with her own, as demonstrated in their final Struggle session. Similarly, she enhanced Jody's and her own attention to rhetorical moves when she modeled such moves for him by suggesting questions he could ask to support her writing process. By referring to what Jody had said, Diane tried out rhetorical moves for validating her partner's perspective and increasing her contact with it, again strategies that contrast with her moves for interacting with Ian. Finally, Diane's frequent comparisons between Jody and Ian suggest she realized the rhetorical strategies she had undertaken could work effectively with her son.

Of course, Diane's final Struggle conversation with Ian occurred after the conversations with Jody depicted in Joyce's text. So it could be argued that Diane had not internalized the new rhetorical moves by the end of the Struggle project. Such work takes time and practice, and it may be most difficult with family members, where old habits are most entrenched. But as Joyce's conclusion argues, Diane practiced these strategies after completing Struggle, and they prompted a shift in her relationship with Ian, just as Goodman suggests they should.

Reflecting Struggle

This ethnography is in part a rhetorical analysis, in that I examine various groups' conversational moves for increasing contact with one another's concerns and for negotiating decisions. But because I am developing greater awareness of my own rhetorical habits and of possible alternatives by writing it (awareness that grows each time I revisit the interactions), it also entails a reflexive joining-and-analyzing of my Struggle participation. Thus writing the ethnography increased my contact, experimentation, and growth. By depicting these reflexive moments, I explore some otherwise inaccessible subjective dimensions of change.

Through my Struggle work, I recognized critical theory and pedagogy as sets of rhetorical habits, contact styles. This recognition transcended a more distanced academic rhetorical analysis of critical theory. Through it, I realized holistically how those rhetorical patterns could affect others. Observations of Struggle participants' need for hope, my colleagues' emphasis on inspiring hope, and Wayne's warnings about the dangers of deterministic language showed me potential effects I simply had not seen before. Watching the struggles of Diane, Ian, Janine, and Joanne made real Wayne's admonition against arguments implying people had little agency and so were destined to unfulfilling circumstances. Through contact with such struggles, I realized how critical theory and pedagogy could potentially foster apathy, hopelessness, and despair.

Such responses to critical theory contrasted with my own, which highlighted alternatives to what I saw as judgmental ideologies of competition and meritocracy. My encounter with critical theory had reframed my understandings of self and family in liberating ways. Engaged in that experience, I had missed the possibility that others might encounter critical theory quite differently. Ellie's account of how it devastated her reserves of hope amplified my contact with both other possible experiences and the extent to which my own experience took root in emotional investment as much as in cognitive engagement. Recognizing this emotionally shaped, subjective response, I concluded I could not accept such arguments as Althusser's notion that critical reading could free me (or anyone) from ideology's blinders. I realized I needed to respect the affective dimensions and subjective validity of others' responses.

This felt need destructured my structured ground, in Wheeler's terms. It reorganized my experience. For instance, I came to see the need to respect and negotiate with students' responses to critical theory and pedagogy when teaching the kinds of textual and critical analyses I valued. Otherwise, I concluded, critical pedagogy risked the kinds of alienation and hostility documented by sympathetic critics such as Russell Durst, David Seitz, and Jennifer Seibel Trainor. Similarly, I still believe textual analyses of language practices' effects contribute key insights, but I now think it is crucial to supplement them by studying how people in specific contexts use such practices and to what ends. Seeing Struggle participants' responses to Angelou's "On the Pulse of the Morning" and to religious discourses I found constraining, I concluded that I need to amplify both critical readings and my own responses with study of others' experiences, particularly in considering discourses I find cognitively or affectively troubling. I no longer see ideological demystification or critique as viable approaches to social change. Instead, I decided such change requires negotiation of ideologies, discourses, and values.

This belief is holistic rather than cognitive. It changed the conditions of my experience, prompting me to feel the need to negotiate, to risk my abstract ideals in real contact, and to recognize specific situations requiring negotiation. For instance, I saw that to connect meaningfully with Struggle participants such as Ian and Diane, I needed to engage respectfully with their investments in Horatio Alger narratives. I had to risk prized abstract values such as promoting redistribution of resources via systemic change rather than individuals' advancement within the existing system. Such abstractions embody prefabricated speech, which contrasts with the plasticity and unpredictability of language practices that entail real contact. Because such contact demands that we relinquish unattainable ideals to pursue viable ends by working with available resources, it evokes Wayne's call to develop a passion for the possible.

I undertook such creative adjustment in learning to see Struggle participants' investments in individual success as resources for productive personal and social-change efforts. This experience and Wayne's concerns about successfully transmuting Struggle's religious principles into a secular program suggest that in this instance, contact between such incommensurable discourses emerged especially through figures such as Struggle's path, which meant different things not only to various participants and potential funders but to those of us planning Struggle. Such images energized each group, if in different ways. Thus they offered a fruitful location for exploring the assimilation process that grounds negotiation of difference and change.

This assimilation process poses risks to existing relationships as well as to one's sense of self. Through a Gestalt reading of my Struggle interactions, I have learned I need to develop strategies for respectfully differing with others, risking their disapproval or withdrawal. For instance, by retrospectively joining-and-analyzing the conversation in which I refrained from explaining my perceptions of work and class to Wayne, I recognized I needed to develop strategies for presenting such differences. Had I explained them, we might have pursued a more productive conversation with potentially useful implications for planning Struggle. Similarly, had I risked joining Joyce's "Amen!" during the Unity Day service, I could have urged the kind of cross-race coalition First Allegheny represented. By failing to do so, I avoided risking offense to my hosts but also avoided real contact with them. Luckily, in joining-and-analyzing my Struggle colleagues' strategies for negotiating differences, I saw rhetorical moves for doing such work. While my experiments with such moves still produce mixed results, they are gradually extending my skills.

This joining-and-analyzing also increased my awareness of when I might choose to withdraw from unproductive interactions. That is, I recognized my boundaries in negotiating difference. In reexamining my postservice conversation with Molly, I realized that while I did not want to argue against groups' rights to a separatist agenda, I did want to actively support coalition building. Rather than discounting the subjective validity of such groups' positions or spending my energies in working against, rather than for, a cause, I realized I wanted to focus on pursuing alliances with interested partners. This reorganization of my perception led me to see differently, to diminish my attention to groups with opposing agendas and augment my attention to possibility.

4

New Heavens and New Earth

PROMOTING POSSIBILITIES for coalition was central to two seventeenth-century English religious and political movements that used literate practices to encourage social and personal change. A Gestalt analysis of one group's texts reveals how the writers positioned audiences to see their experience in new ways and to experiment with rhetorical moves with the potential to revise their contact styles.

The Levellers and the Diggers (or True Levellers) both sought to change England's political and economic system and its integration of church and state. They were active during the mid-seventeenth-century Civil Wars, an era when tumultuous religious, political, and economic upheavals challenged and transformed many of English society's core beliefs, values, and practices. Because their arguments for economic and political equality are rooted in religious beliefs, the Diggers' writings must be understood in the larger context of societal changes and the flowering of new literate practices encouraged by the Protestant Reformation: reading, silently and aloud; lay biblical exegesis and use of those exegeses to interpret personal spiritual experiences; and discussion and debate of religious interpretations, often to extrapolate them into political and economic theory. In Gestalt terms, the histories of these practices illuminate the structured ground that shaped audiences' responses to the Digger texts. They also highlight audience actions linked to the texts, showing how the writing prompted some audiences to reorganize their experience.

Further, the Digger and Leveller histories raise issues for a larger theory of social change and literate practices. For instance, they depict each group's demise, illustrating Goodman's point about society's drive to "draw the teeth" of changes that threaten to reorganize the existing social order (*Gestalt Therapy* 336). Their failures reveal the difficulties faced by groups trying to initiate alternative practices within a larger society that—rightly—recognizes such changes as a threat to its established habits of behavior and perception. This is so even when, like the Diggers, the group renounces all forms of violence. The

Digger and Leveller histories illustrate how the need to negotiate with established powers split the incipient alliance between the groups. Still, their failures produced legacies with long-term historical significance, which suggests that the contact styles they fostered enabled some of their key ideals and practices to persist.

Levellers' Seeds

In October 1647, the Council of Parliament's Army met so the soldiers' democratically elected representatives (or Agitators) could debate the army's political aims with Lieutenant-General Oliver Cromwell and his officers. Held at Putney Church, the debates pitted soldiers' call for universal male suffrage against officers' fear that voting commoners would abolish private property in favor of common ownership.

This army, known as the New Model, had defeated King Charles I in England's Civil War. Charles attacked Parliament's forces in 1642 after years of tensions set him and his Anglican lords and bishops against the Puritan faction (Parliament, Presbyterian merchants, and Independent gentry). Led by Cromwell, the New Model soldiers held strong religious and political convictions that prompted all the cavalrymen and nearly half the foot soldiers to volunteer. Still, more than half the foot soldiers were conscripted laborers and poor men. Nonetheless, "it was quite usual for a corporal or private to preach, while his less gifted officers listened in silence" (Brailsford 148). The army "debated every problem of church and state . . . and . . . read the pamphlets that poured from the London presses, more especially the unlicensed presses [which printed materials not approved by government censors]" (Brailsford 150).

Many of the New Model men fell into one of the three dominant Puritan factions that had formed by 1646. These factions included the Presbyterians, London merchants who sought to impose their faith as the mandatory state religion and held a majority in Parliament; the Independents, who were strongest among the New Model's officer corps; and the members of radical Puritan sects, or sectarians, lower middling sorts[1]—tradesmen, laborers, and poorer people—many of whom fought as New Model soldiers. Often these sectarians, both soldiers and civilians, allied themselves with a group labeled Levellers by their opponents. The Levellers insisted that no matter how poor, any man could vote to elect his lawmakers. Most of the army radicals were Levellers.

Like the Independents (including their officers), the radical soldiers clashed with the Presbyterians over religious liberty. They came from the lower middling and poorer classes. Some were literate, but few had much formal education. Rejecting the Anglican and Presbyterian churches, which often condemned the poor as immoral, even irredeemable, they formed various religious sects. Despite important differences, these sects shared key practices. Rather than listening passively to a minister's sermon and following a church's dictates, sectarians discussed the Bible and the social ideas they gleaned from it. They questioned the preacher after his or her discourse (both women and men preached). Via discussion, they interpreted scripture to craft new political ideas. The New Model soldiers drew on such discussions to debate their officers.

Their demand for the vote signaled their frustration with mandatory participation in a state church they opposed and tithes to support its clergy, repression of their religious practices, heavy taxes, and laws applied unequally to the poor and gentry. To redress the soldiers' grievances, the Agitators wrote and circulated *The Case of the Armie truly stated* (Wolfe 196–222), which proposed religious freedom, universal male suffrage, and other reforms. When the Council of the Army opposed it, the Agitators revised it. At Putney, the debaters began by reading the entire revised text aloud to open discussion.

When the debates deadlocked over suffrage, the army's factions produced rival proposals in efforts to win the soldiers' agreement. The council called a rendezvous for soldiers to pledge agreement to the chosen text. Meanwhile, a council subcommittee worked with civilian Levellers to produce a proposal advocating wide suffrage, while Cromwell countered with another text. Each group sought soldiers' signatures at the rendezvous. Radical officers supporting the Leveller *Agreement of the People* wore copies in their hats, topped with the motto "England's Freedom; Soldier's Rights." But Cromwell's faction declared this sedition, and a field court martial tried three of the leaders and sentenced them to death. One, Private Richard Arnold, was shot there at Corkbush Field, at the head of his regiment. Martial law was reimposed; debate ended.

Diggers' Seeds

As the Putney Debates dissolved into mutiny and martial law, a group that would call itself the True Levellers, or Diggers, was about to break ground. By the late 1640s, Gerrard Winstanley, their future leader, was immersed in Puritan intellectual activism. This tumult of discussion, debate, preaching, and pamphleteering drew on a long-established English tradition of communist

Christianity. Its adherents believed land should be commonly owned and distinctions between rich and poor should be leveled, so their opponents derisively named them Levellers. Enemies of the army radicals applied the label to the soldiers, hoping to discredit them. The group that joined Winstanley a year and a half after Putney deliberately echoed the Leveller name to underline their belief in smoothing socioeconomic hierarchies. The leveling tradition was especially strong in Buckinghamshire County, just northwest of Greater London, home to many New Model soldiers and fertile ground for the Leveller movement. The tradition dates at least to 1381, when English peasants rebelled against the nobles in an effort to establish a society of equals under the king (Cohn 210–11). While the rebellion failed, it sparked similar revolts through and beyond the 1640s, revolts that used the rallying cries and images of their predecessors (Brailsford 443).

The frequency of revolts increased in the late sixteenth and early seventeenth centuries, as England faced socioeconomic changes sweeping through the societies surrounding the Atlantic. The shift toward large-scale profit economies prompted the gentry to replace commoners' subsistence farming with commercial farming. They enclosed common land formerly farmed by the majority of people, forcing those people from the land and instituting severe vagrancy and labor laws. Designed to prevent displaced commoners from supporting themselves as traveling tinkers, entertainers, or beggars, these laws attempted to force the former farmers and craftspeople into despised wage labor. Enforcement methods included whipping, branding, the severing of ears, and hanging (Linebaugh and Rediker 36–70).

England's commoners responded by rebelling intermittently throughout the sixteenth and early seventeenth centuries. Those displaced into lives as sailors, indentured servants, and laborers in the New World often attempted (sometimes successfully) to establish alternative communities supported by subsistence farming, hunting, and gathering on commonly owned land. Such communities evolved in the Caribbean and in sections of North America (Linebaugh and Rediker 104–43). England's dispossessed petitioned, undertook legal actions, and filled in ditches dug to plant enclosing hedges, while London apprentices rioted. When such efforts failed, peasants facing enclosure revolted (Petegorsky 69–70). The 1607 Midlands Revolt, the largest of the age, spread across the three neighboring counties of Warwickshire, Leicestershire, and Northamptonshire, the last of which borders the north side of Buckinghamshire.

Some of the radical Buckinghamshire peasants who took up England's leveling tradition corresponded, and perhaps met, with Gerrard Winstanley, who, with the True Levellers, would attempt to establish an alternative, self-sustaining community. Earlier, Winstanley had established himself as a master clothier with the freedom to trade in the city of London. But in the early 1640s, a slave trader named Matthew Backhouse defrauded Winstanley of £274. Seeking operating capital from other tradesmen, including Winstanley, Backhouse took cloth to trade in North Africa for slaves he would later sell in the New World. But Backhouse did not repay Winstanley, who lost his investment in the midst of the cloth industry's collapse (Linebaugh and Rediker 140). He went bankrupt, turned to parochial charity, and was forced to accept hospitality from friends in the county of Surrey, just southwest of London and just touching Buckinghamshire. There the former tradesman and son of a successful cloth merchant hired himself out as a cowherd.

T. Wilson Hayes points out that Winstanley's circumstances were representative. "The process Winstanley passes through—from the son of a freeholder to an apprentice in London to a self-employed cloth merchant to a tender of someone else's cows on the heath—typifies the plight of thousands of men during the 1640s" (Hayes 34). In Winstanley's case, these stresses led him on a pilgrimage out of the established church in which he had been baptized to investigate various faiths for himself. For a time he was a Baptist, and he probably began his own lay preaching while part of that sect. But by 1648 he had rejected the Baptists' emphasis on their religious rituals and begun to seek another way. George H. Sabine says that many seventeenth-century English people shared Winstanley's pilgrimage: "Winstanley's religious development was in some degree typical; many men and women in England were passing through a characteristic religious evolution which took them first out of the larger and more stable religious bodies, like the Anglicans or the Presbyterians, into Independency, then into some Baptist congregation, and ultimately beyond the limits of any organized community" (8).

Winstanley's pilgrimage brought him into a world of English peasants and lower sorts who had energetically taken up the Protestant tradition of reading and interpreting scripture for themselves. Hayes explains that by the 1630s some respectable ministers frequently declared that common people have "all the wit and knowledge necessary to understand and believe the gospel." The ministers' sanction encouraged small tradesmen and other commoners without formal education to preach and testify to one another rather than to rely on the authority of ordained ministers (Hayes 4). Some Puritans, such as the scholar John Everard, renounced their earlier academic training to argue that "poor beggerly fellows, *Tinkers* and *Cobblers* . . . would lead people out of the darkness imposed on them by the scholars and clergy" (qtd. in Hayes 90).

Such people condemned the established churches' self-proclaimed monopoly on interpreting scripture and judging personal and social behavior. Truth and the spirit of God would move through poor working people, they claimed, not through the idle, privileged, university-educated scholars and clergy.

But these "mechanick" preachers, as their opponents described them, threatened the established clergy and the well-to-do. As Petegorsky describes it, "Brewer and baker, cooper and cobbler, tinker and tailor, all inspired by the light of revelation that burned within them, mounted pulpit and platform to spread their message to their fellow-oppressed and downtrodden." But to the more orthodox, he explains, this practice was a most "offensive and dangerous sin" (66). Such opposition to the everyday preachers was not just snobbery. The mechanick preachers threatened the established social, political, and economic elites because questioning religious dogma meant questioning—even undermining—the social systems that dogma upheld. Petegorsky clarifies this threat: "The struggle for freedom of conscience during the Civil War is therefore nothing less than a struggle for freedom of speech and expression. Religious freedom implied the opportunity to question the assumptions of the existing social order" (56).

As an active seeker of God, Winstanley became a mechanick preacher in his own right. He joined those who were using interpretation, analysis, discussion, and debate to hammer their religious experiences into social and political visions. In the process, Winstanley emphasized that each person has the capacity and the right to interpret the Bible according to her or his own experiences. In his book *Truth lifting its Head above Scandals*, Winstanley includes a dedicatory letter "To the Scholars of Oxford and Cambridge, and to all that call themselves Ministers of the Gospel in City or Country." In the letter, he insists that they are not the only people empowered to interpret the Bible, "For the people, having the Scriptures, may judge by them as well as you" (qtd. in Berens 62). He argues that each individual's spiritual experiences are the basis of truth and the lens through which that person can legitimately interpret scripture. By calling his audience to know God "from the Power of Light shining within," Winstanley, like Goodman, advocates practices that cultivate contact with this experience.

Describing spiritual pilgrimages such as Winstanley's, Sabine explains, "Such experiences existed far and wide in seventeenth-century England. They were spread largely by sermons, either heard or read, and by conversation and discussion" (11). These sermons had extensive power and reach. Via the printing presses, they moved throughout England as pamphlets read silently, or aloud to those who could not read. They were discussed, interpreted, and debated by the mechanick preachers and their fellow sectarians. Sabine explains that "the pulpit and a popular press . . . rapidly spread both religious and political thought to a multitude of obscure and uneducated men" (22). Common people were newly wealthy in religious and political pamphlets and in interpretive practices. They formed communities passionately interested in using those practices to renew their society. Reading, interpretation, discussion, and theorizing were no longer the province of the university educated and elite.

Seeing the tumult of new religious ideas and practices, the Civil Wars' political upheaval, and the age's intensifying, spreading poverty, many people believed that the millennium was indeed at hand. Like Winstanley, many peasants, laborers, and small tradesmen responded by constructing scriptural interpretations that positioned them as God's agents in renewing the world and forwarding the prophesied millennium.

Authorization

Reading Digger texts through a Gestalt frame illustrates how they use rhetorical strategies to prompt audiences to make contact with aspects of their internal and external relationships, aspects possibly outside most audiences' awareness. By fostering contact with this unaware material, the texts encourage audiences to reorganize their experiences. As Goodman argues, such reorganizations spark experiments with new rhetorical moves, which can initiate revised contact styles. Digger texts support such experiments by modeling rhetorical strategies that construct revised relations with self and others; more flexible, inclusive contact styles; and agency in a dialectical relation to larger social forces. They encourage audiences to reconstruct their contact styles as a way of reconstructing their social world.

• • •

Digger texts position poorer audiences to expand proprioception of their internal spiritual experiences. They prompt these audiences toward greater awareness of how their spiritual attitudes shape their social and material circumstances. Finally, they model rhetorical moves audiences can use to experience their own spiritual authority and to mobilize it to propose changes to the sociopolitical and economic systems they inhabit. The texts accomplish this work through four rhetorical strategies: biblical exegesis; the telescoping of biblical history with ancient English history and contemporary events; analysis of social, political, and economic practices; and stories of personal and group experiences.

By combining the first two strategies, Digger texts use aesthetic language to promote contact, thus encouraging poorer audiences toward particular kinds of proprioception designed to prompt reorganizations of experience. Some Digger texts, especially Winstanley's, root their arguments for economic equality and shared resources in several culturally sanctioned discourses. The first and most powerful is biblical exegesis. This discourse was the most legitimate means of producing knowledge in seventeenth-century England, and Winstanley draws heavily on its legitimacy to ground his position. He cites dozens of biblical passages to show that God intends the earth to be the shared possession of all people, and he does so particularly in the Diggers' manifesto, *The True Levellers Standard Advanced: or, The state of community opened, and presented to the sons of men.* "It is shewed us, That all Prophecies, Visions, and Revelations of Scriptures, of Prophets, and Apostles, concerning the calling of the Jews, the Restauration of Israel; and making of that People the Inheritors of the whole Earth; doth all seat themselves in this Work of making the Earth a Common Treasury; as you may read [here he cites more than fifty Bible verses]" (qtd. in Sabine 260–61). Winstanley uses this technique throughout *The True Levellers Standard* and many of his other texts.

To ground his texts' arguments, he also uses allegorical readings of scripture, a practice employed by many sectarians. The aesthetic language of these allegorical readings encourages poorer audiences toward expanded proprioception. In *The New Law of Righteousnes*, written in January 1649, Winstanley appeals to the poor to form a community and till England's commons. Here he reads the Adam and Eve and Cain and Abel stories allegorically:

> Therefore certainly this *Adam*, or first man that is spoken of, is he that is within [each person], as I have spoke of, which kils or suppresses *Abel*, who is the anointing; I am sure I have found him the cause of my misery, and I can lay the blame on no man, but my self. The first power that appears and draws my body into disobedience.
>
> And this is he that is the causer of all your sorrow and tears, he is *Adam* within, it is your self, your very fleshly self, be angry at none but your self. The Self is the first *Adam* that fals from the Spirit; he is those branching powers in created flesh that leads you from your maker; therefore blame not *Adam* without you, but blame *Adam* the first man within you; he within hath disobeyed, and forsaken Reasons Law of Righteousnesse.

You are the man and woman that hath eaten the *forbidden fruit*, by delighting your self more in the objects of the Creation, then in the Spirit; for the Spirit is the seed, the Creation is the fruit. (qtd. in Sabine 210–11)

Winstanley uses this allegorical reading not only to take responsibility for his own spiritual and psychological distress but to exhort his readers to do the same. While *The New Law* as a whole explicitly addresses various groups of readers at different points, it opens by appealing to Winstanley's "Dear Brethren . . . the despised ones of the world" (qtd. in Sabine 149). Thus I read the quoted passage and much of the text as Winstanley's direct supplication to the poor. In this supplication, he uses the allegorical figure of Adam, symbol of the fallen, materialistic, self-interested aspects of human nature, to depict his own increased contact with choices that caused his own misery. He urges readers to make similar contact with their own choices and thus to take up attitudes of agency and responsibility. His interpretation of Genesis encourages readers to recognize their own complicity with exploitation and to adopt *The New Law*'s project of forming a new kind of community. Like his critique of imagination, Winstanley's rejection of the "Adam within" is a rejection of abstraction. More specifically, here Winstanley rejects reified ideas of good (such as individual wealth). He enacts the rejection of "fixed forms," as Goodman advocates, thus revising their attendant reified perceptions and habits. Like Goodman, Winstanley holds that such reifications of sensory (or fleshly) experience diminish contact with one's experience and larger awareness. As a result, they cause human suffering. Winstanley rejects neither sensory experience nor material good per se. Rather, he tries to redirect people's tendency to abstract such experiences and goods into reified values by using aesthetic language practices such as his allegorical readings to prompt contact with parts of experience he believes may be outside audiences' awareness.

In another allegorical reading, Winstanley depicts heaven and hell not as realms in their own right but as states of mind and heart within each person (Sabine 211–13). His reading was considered so radical that it was illegal to articulate. First, this view works to shift audiences' perceptions by removing the fear of eternal damnation used by many established Protestant churches to threaten the disorderly poor. Second, like the allegorical reading of the figure of Adam, it tries to expand audiences' contact with their range of available choices and to increase people's sense of agency, authority, and responsibility by putting torment and delight within their control rather than in the hands of an external power. Finally, it encourages broader perception of possibilities for satisfaction by locating material and spiritual fulfillment within corporeal life rather than in an afterlife. This dramatic repositioning encourages audiences to seek fulfillment in material action. At the same time, it discourages them from acquiescing to destructive material conditions in hopes of the world to come. In prompting audiences to revise their proprioception of their own choice making, Winstanley's allegories simultaneously urge a reorganized experience of people's relation to the social environment.

Like Struggle's training materials and prompts, Winstanley's texts encourage such reorganizations of experience by modeling the rhetorical moves that can spark them. For instance, he illustrates his framework and method for interpreting scripture in an April 1650 text, *An Humble Request to the Ministers of Both Universities and to All Lawyers in Every Inns-a-Court* (Sabine 419–37). In this pamphlet's dedicatory letter, he challenges university-trained divines and lawyers to refute his interpretation of scripture. "If reason and righteousness which is the foundation of Scriptures, and just Lawes do give it us: let us have our freedom quietly; if neither reason nor righteousness give us this freedom, we will lie still, and never trouble you more" (qtd. in Sabine 420). By invoking scriptural authority and offering a broad interpretation of both Testaments, as well as exegeses of selected passages, Winstanley legitimates his argument. He uses the authorized discourse of scriptural interpretation to suggest revisions of his society's legal and economic practices. His opening clauses draw on the seventeenth-century understanding of "right reason" as the product of the divine will. As the quoted passage implies, divine will and right reason should ground earthly legal systems. Within the next century, natural law and right reason would become synonymous, and Winstanley positions them as the appropriate interpretive lens for reading scripture. He implies that when laws and government diverge from the scriptural interpretation produced through those lenses, such laws and governments have fallen away from divine intent. By using biblical exegesis to argue for particular social changes, Winstanley shows poor audiences how to use such methods to construct comparable arguments. Thus in Gestalt terms he invites them to undertake rhetorical moves that can reorganize their experience of the social world.

Winstanley makes this modeling explicit by naming it and aligning it with practices associated with the poor. Later in the text, he uses his scriptural interpretations both to delineate his method and buttress his position. "And hereby I conclude, that these fore-mentioned Scriptures being but a gleaning of the Bible, gives a full warrant to all poore men, to build them houses, and plant corne upon the Commons and unnurtured land, for their comfortable livelihood, as they are part of Man-kind, being the right of their creation" (qtd. in Sabine 428). Winstanley's use of the word *gleaning* here works on three levels. First, he bolsters his argument about the commons by implicitly invoking a biblical injunction on gleaning. This divine admonition orders the rich to allow the poor to glean the grain dropped when hired hands have harvested their fields. Second, he names his own reading method as gleaning—learning the truth by combing the Bible bit by bit. Finally, he affirms his often-repeated belief that poor laypeople have the right and ability to interpret scripture by and for themselves. He positions his own reading as gleaning, an activity performed by the poor. This positioning explicitly invites poor audiences to use the rhetorical practices Winstanley names and enacts in his text.

There, the reading and interpretation performed by the poor produce truth, in implicit contrast with the scholarly readings of established divines. Poverty denotes deprivation of both material and educational resources. Thus *An Humble Request* challenges the university-educated clergy's monopoly on scriptural interpretation. At the same time, this passage fosters poor audiences' intellectual agency and challenges arguments against mechanick preaching and lay readings. Winstanley's allegorical interpretations of scripture try to motivate poor people to use reading and writing as forms of social action and to tie those practices to other forms as well. He supports his argument by articulating both his interpretive framework (of divine and natural law as right reason) and his method (gleaning). Perhaps even more importantly, his articulation of this framework and method offers other laypeople a model for legitimating and performing their own scriptural interpretations. By developing such rhetorical moves, poor laypeople could begin to reorganize their experiences and revise their rhetorical habits. They could thus undertake the self-revisions Goodman argues stem from changing such habits.

The second method used in Digger texts enacts rhetorical moves designed to increase proprioception of spiritual experience and the individual's own interpretation of such experiences. This method telescopes biblical history with ancient English history and contemporary events. For instance, in *The True Levellers Standard*, Winstanley reads Genesis's creation story as an allegory that explains how common people lost their intrinsic interpretive authority (Sabine 251–53). His reading depicts the fall as a combination of material/economic and intellectual enslavement. The well-to-do pursue material gain by exploiting the poor, while the poor pursue material gain by allowing themselves to be exploited. Thus the well-to-do enslave the poor because self-will enslaves both. By telescoping biblical history with ancient English history and myth, as well as with contemporary events, Winstanley portrays his own era as a boy whose imminent manhood will fulfill biblical history. The pamphlet asks poor audiences to identify themselves with the Israelites of biblical history, a practice familiar to them from sermons. Through its historical telescoping, the text urges audience members to form a community to work for the promised millennium by refusing the slavery of wage labor. That move, Winstanley argues, will signal the boy's transition into manhood and thus the beginning of biblical history's fulfillment.

In fact, *The New Law* forthrightly declares that "these single hearted ones [the poor and despised] are made to look into themselves, wherein they can read the work of the whole Creation, and see that History seated within themselves" (qtd. in Sabine 213). Thus, like Winstanley's allegorical readings, his historical telescoping encourages greater proprioception by asking audiences to discern particular kinds of spiritual experiences. Winstanley describes three "Methods of Divine discovery [or revelation of history]" (qtd. in Sabine 160–61). Moses embodies the first method, which involves "outward testimony . . . a man that was mixed with flesh and spirit" (qtd. in Sabine 161); the Apostles' testimony embodies the second method, namely, the witnessing of Christ by those who saw him; and the power of God appearing in each person embodies the third method, which will emerge at the end of history, a time Winstanley believes is at hand:

> Even so that single body [Christ's] is a type: That the same Spirit that filled every member of that one body, should in these last dayes be sent into whole mankind, and every branch shall be a joint or member of the mysticall body, or severall spreadings forth of the vine, being all filled with the one Spirit, Christ the anointing, who fils all with himself, and so he becomes the alone King of Righteousnesse and peace that rules in man. And the powers of the flesh which is the Serpent or curse, shall be subdued under him, and man-kind shall be made onely subject to this one Spirit, which shall dwell bodily in every one, as he dwelt bodily in the man Christ Jesus, who was the Son of man. . . . Even so, the man Christ Jesus, the great Prophet, declared in general termes what should be in later times; leaving it to every son and daughter, to declare their particular experiences, when the Spirit doth rise up in them, and manifests himself to them. . . . Even so the Lamb Christ Jesus, or that single body, gives way to the holy Ghost, or spreading Spirit. . . . The Son of man declares, that both outward forms, customs and types of *Moses* worship under that ministration at *Jerusalem*, likewise all forms and customs, and types of this ministration of himself as the Lamb held forth at a distance to be our Mediatour, should all cease and give way to the spirituall worship of the

Father in the latter dayes; or to the spreading of the Divine power in men, the one law of Righteousnesse, being the teacher of all. . . . So that . . . the rising up of Christ in sons and daughters . . . is his second comming. (qtd. in Sabine 161–62)

Challenging the Puritans' belief in predestination and the salvation of only a few elect, Winstanley declares that all shall be saved. In the process, he validates each person's interpretation of his own experiences as part of the movement of history. By prompting poor audiences to pursue such rhetorical moves, he positions them to expand their proprioception of such experiences, as a necessary step in articulating and interpreting them. Throughout *The New Law*, Winstanley names the poor as the first group destined to experience God's presence within themselves. When he says that Christ will give way to the "spreading Spirit," Winstanley names the spiritual renewal of each person as the ultimate fulfillment of both biblical and contemporary history in his own time. And he depicts the poor as this fulfillment's vanguard.

By asking poor audiences to see poverty not as a sign of God's disfavor (as other Protestant sects often did) but as a mark of divine presence, Winstanley encourages them to reorganize the evidence of their experience. This divine presence provides the experience that generates inspired biblical interpretations with more validity than those offered by clergy who have not sought knowledge of God through internal experience. Again, Winstanley's urging to expand proprioceptive awareness of spiritual experience simultaneously repositions audiences' relations to the social system. Thus the above passage also opposes established churches by disavowing any particular rituals of worship. Instead, it espouses communion with God based in individual experience. Perhaps most radically, the passage concludes by equating individual and communal renewal with the Christian millennial vision. In other words, Winstanley positions such renewal and its revision of material and spiritual practices as the transformation that will inaugurate the reformed society of the new millennium. Like his related method of scriptural interpretation and exegesis, Winstanley's historical telescoping urges audiences to see themselves as agents who can remake their identities and their society. From a Gestalt perspective, it encourages them to make greater contact with their own agency.

The Digger texts' first two methods form the basis of their third, which involves critiquing contemporary sociopolitical and economic practices. With the fourth method, personal-experience accounts, the third models specific kinds of rhetorical moves for reconstructing the self. Like the rhetorical strategies enacted by the first two methods, these moves position audiences to

increase spiritual proprioception and revise systemic perception, to use interpretive practices authoritatively, and to develop a shared figure and energy for
pursuing it. To produce the third method's critique, Winstanley again telescopes biblical history with English history in *The True Levellers Standard*. He
equates contemporary England's governors with both the Bible's "*Babylonish*
power" and ancient England's "*Norman* yoke" (qtd. in Sabine 259). He concludes, "Take notice, that *England* is not a Free People, till the Poor that have
no Land, have a free allowance to dig and labour the Commons, and so live
as Comfortably as the landlords that live in their Inclosures" (qtd. in Sabine
260). Similarly, *The New Law* builds on Winstanley's interpretation of heaven
and hell as states of mind and heart within individuals. The text uses this
interpretation to critique the established clergy's alternate reading of heaven
and hell as both actual places and eternal afterlives. "But, poor Creatures," he
says to the lower sorts, "you are deceived; this expectation of glory without
you, will vanish, you shall never see it; this outward heaven is not the durable
Heaven; this is a fancy which your false Teachers put into your heads to please
you with, while they pick your purses, and betray your Christ into the hands
of flesh, and hold *Jacob* [the poor] under to be a servant still to Lord *Esau* [the
wealthy]" (qtd. in Sabine 226–27). Through his scriptural interpretation and
historical telescoping, Winstanley criticizes the ideology that urges poor people to accept material deprivation in hopes of an eternal reward. This ideology requires the poor to pay the tithes that provide salaries for clergymen of the
established churches. Winstanley's critique shows that these clergy benefit
materially by propagating such teachings and discursively by monopolizing
the intellectual authority that produces scriptural interpretations.

In fact, he argues that this attempt to monopolize interpretive authority
supports efforts to subjugate the poor materially, intellectually, and spiritually. Winstanley undermines the monopoly by mobilizing common people to
take up their intellectual authority to work against this subjugation. *The New
Law* criticizes the clergy by equating them with the biblical villain-magician
Simon Magus (Sabine 214). Such passages challenge the clergy's status as stan-
dard-bearers of the upper middling sort in their attack on the poor and lower
sorts. In this role, clerics condemned commoners' culture as sinful and
immoral, thus supporting the upper middling sorts' efforts to regulate their
behavior and to make them into a submissive class of wage laborers. The clerical attack justified the era's intensifying, spreading poverty; the deepening
economic gulf between the better sorts and common people; and the aban-
donment of an older ethic of charity that used to help alleviate poverty. By
damning lay preaching and insisting that only university-trained divines could

legitimately interpret scripture, the clergy countered common people's efforts to mobilize their own intellectual authority through mechanick preaching.

Winstanley positions laypeople to reorganize their experience of clerical-lay relationships by increasing their awareness of the clergy's rhetorical strategies. Like Struggle's planners, he uses critique not for its own sake but to mobilize people toward a shared figure. Specifically, he enables poor laypeople to see themselves as authorized to undertake biblical interpretation to construct new socioeconomic and political practices. For instance, *The New Law*'s concluding passages critique clerical ideologies and habits to spur commoners to craft scriptural interpretations that initiate new social relations:

> People should all look up to him [Christ] for teaching, and acknowledge no other teacher and ruler but Christ, the Law of Right-eousnesse dwelling in every mans heart; the schollars would have the people to look up to them for teaching; and truly let me speak what I find, the more that you look upon them, or any men for teaching, the more you shall be wrapped up in confusion and bondage. . . . [The clergy and scholars] are branches of the Thornbush, that are full of sharp pricks, in regard they endeavour to uphold a forced maintenance from the people, whether they will or no; and force the people to be silent, to hear them preach hear-say: and not to gainsay or question what they say under pain of punishment, or being counted factious, or sowers of sedition. (qtd. in Sabine 240–41)

Winstanley's critique of scholars and clergy braces his argument for the primacy of common laypeople's interpretations. *The New Law* is a sustained effort not only to legitimate their readings but to resituate the locus of authority in the sanctioned discourse of biblical exegesis. That is, Winstanley seeks to shift this locus from academic readings to interpretations grounded in common laypeople's experiences. By contrasting the habit of looking to others for ideas with the process of looking to one's internal experience, Winstanley implicitly opposes abstraction to language uses that encourage contact. By urging the development of the individual's own ideas through proprioception, he encourages poor laypeople to reorganize their experiences by grounding their worldviews in a richer awareness of their own capacities and their perceptions' significance. *The New Law* validates laypeople's practices of intellectual discussion and textual analysis through Winstanley's use of critique, which proposes—and models—specific, concrete action. As Struggle's prompts enact the rhetorical moves the program asks participants to undertake, Winstanley's texts demonstrate the rhetorical moves he encourages. Common people used these practices to craft new spiritual and social ideals and to reconstruct themselves as agents struggling to produce a new worldview and a new political and socioeconomic order. Winstanley's writerly methods legitimate this process through an authorized discourse and further it by mobilizing poor audience members. In Gestalt terms, they encourage poor audiences to pursue creative adjustment to material newly available to them, namely the practice of biblical interpretation.

In their fourth method, Digger texts knit accounts of personal experience into textual analyses to amplify their themes and arguments. Like their use of critique, the texts' use of personal experience models rhetorical moves for audiences to undertake. When authors and audiences pursue such moves, they extend their experiments with creative adjustments to new material circumstances. They use personal experiences not only to develop their ideas but to construct plans for action and spiritual authority to support those plans. Thus they expand the newly available practice of scriptural interpretation to incorporate spiritually grounded interpretation of personal experience. This use of personal experience characterizes a broadside written by a group of Wellingborough Diggers, *A Declaration of the Grounds and Reasons why we the Poor Inhabitants of the Town of Wellinborrow, in the Country of Northampton, have begun and give consent to Dig up, Manure and Sow Corn upon the Common, and Waste Ground, called Bareshanke, Belonging to the Inhabitants of Wellinborrow, by those that have Subscribed, and Hundreds more that give Consent.* The manifesto opens by citing scripture to argue "that God made the Earth for the use and comfort of all Mankind." It follows by citing recent acts of Parliament "to make England a Free Common-wealth" (qtd. in Sabine 649, 650). Next, the broadside describes signers' efforts to seek work through their local justices, those efforts' futility, and their economically desperate situation. "We are necessitated from our present necessity to do this," they declare, "And now we consider that the Earth is our Mother, and that God hath given it to the children of men, and that the common and waste Grounds belong to the poor, and that we have a right to the common ground both from the law of the Land, Reason and Scriptures; and therefore we have begun to bestow our righteous labor upon it" (qtd. in Sabine 650). Like Winstanley's texts, this broadside weaves scriptural interpretation (and reason) into social critique and accounts of personal experience to draw conclusions that also announce the writers' present and planned actions. This demonstrates the group's clear mobilization to act in pursuit of a shared figure, jointly farming the common land.

Two of Winstanley's texts show how Digger writers used personal experience to construct such plans and the spiritual authority to justify them. Both *The True Levellers Standard* and *The New Law* also share this combination of methods and culminate by announcing action. Winstanley describes his material and spiritual experiences at various points throughout *The New Law*, and in one case he depicts a trance as a divinely inspired experience:

> As I was in a trance not long since. . . . I heard these words, *Worke together. Eat bread together*, declare all this abroad. Likewise I heard these words. *Whosoever it is that labours in the earth, for any person or persons, that lifts up themselves as Lord & Rulers over others, and that doth not look upon themselves equal to others in the Creation, The hand of the Lord shall be upon that labourer: I the Lord have spoke it and I will do it*; Declare all this abroad.
>
> After I was raised up, I was made to remember very fresh what I had seen and heard, & did declare al things to them that were with me, and I was filled with abundance of quiet peace and secret joy. And since that time those words have been like very fruitfull seed, that have brought forth increase in my heart, which I am much prest in spirit to declare all abroad. (qtd. in Sabine 190)

The trance fulfills two rhetorical purposes. First, it provides the sanction of divine revelation for Winstanley's position. At the same time, it validates common laypeople's practices of drawing conclusions and plans of action based on their spiritual experiences. To legitimate his own use of that practice in this passage, Winstanley follows his depiction of the trance by describing how he publicized his experience and then felt peace and joy. The "fruitfull seed" passage demonstrates the validity of individual spiritual experience as a basis for action. Winstanley's approach shows a common layman using his own interpretive framework to replace that of the established clergy. As the passage demonstrates, this use enables Winstanley to interpret his experience and to infer right ethical action from his interpretation. Through this method, he demonstrates the efficacy of lay interpretations rather than merely arguing for it. Winstanley offers an identity for poor audience members to take up. In it, they use their interpretations and inferences not only to advocate a new vision of community but to put that vision into practice. Thus he invites poor laypeople to weave their spiritual experiences with knowledge of their day-to-day lives and with social critiques to make and pursue plans for a revised society. Like Struggle's training materials and prompts, Winstanley's texts ask audiences to experiment with new rhetorical moves designed to reorganize their experience. By encouraging revised proprioception of their spiritual experiences, these moves enable people to interpret such experiences to construct spiritually grounded plans for action and rationales for those plans. Developing the rhetorical habits of such interpretation positions poor audiences to revise their relationships with their social environments by seeking ethical guidance from internal experience and interpretive practices rather than from others' interpretations.

Again, Winstanley models the moves for such work. By constructing interpretations through the lens of his own spiritual experience, he highlights how the poor can intervene in the existing economic and political system by refusing to sell their labor for wages. He shows how they can use this approach to initiate transformations of contemporary economic practices. Instead of sanctioning their role in a system that subjugates, impoverishes, and exploits them, Winstanley urges common people to revise their identities, to consider themselves equal to others. In turn, that revision opens the way to a renewed community that lives collectively. Thus Digger texts' methods urge common laypeople to reconstruct their identities and communities. They channel this audience's energies into transforming themselves and their society. Read through Gestalt lenses, the actions of groups like the Wellingborough Diggers suggest that such texts and the discussions they generated sparked some poor people to develop and pursue shared figures of social change.

Levellers' Blossoming

Pamphlets, discussions, and other literate practices also played a key role in mobilizing the Leveller movement. While preaching still spread new ideas most quickly and effectively during the Civil War, pamphlets were rapidly overtaking its monopoly. The popular Leveller leader John Lilburne wrote "in his short lifetime several score of pamphlets" (Brailsford 73). Many prompted audiences to protest England's arbitrary legal system and mandatory state religion. After a year in prison for smuggling a Puritan minister's manuscript into England for publication, Lilburne spirited a written appeal for help to his fellow London apprentices. Many were sectarians familiar with religious oppression, and they rioted to support Lilburne's demand for a public trial.

Still, the Leveller was not freed until 1640, two and a half years after he had gone to prison, when a new Parliament with a Presbyterian majority freed those imprisoned for religious nonconformity to Anglican strictures. But the Presbyterian Parliament imposed its own religious dictatorship. In May 1648, it passed the Blasphemy Ordinance, which made it a felony, punishable by death, to admit non-Presbyterian beliefs about the trinity or incarnation, even in private conversation. One who argued that Christ's crucifixion would save everyone, not only the elect, could face life imprisonment. Blasphemers were branded on the cheek with the letter "B" for the first offense and executed for the second. Many other beliefs were punishable by lifetime imprisonment unless the offender renounced them publicly. Under the new ordinance, sectarians were subject to life imprisonment or worse by virtue of their beliefs.

Facing such sanctions, they extended biblical interpretations to English law, equating God's law with natural law or right reason and religious freedom with political freedom. They translated religious interpretive authority into political interpretive authority and demanded political equality. Material privations sharpened these political aims. Poor harvests in the 1640s led to dearth. Grain prices doubled; the pease meal poor people ate was expensive and scarce. Some Londoners starved to death, while others seized corn from its owners. In the winter of 1647–1648, the combination of want and religious and political repression led the Levellers to organize what one historian describes as the first democratically organized political party (Brailsford 309). Members contributed weekly dues according to income to help publish and distribute pamphlets. They demanded freedom of worship, religious assembly, discussion, and publishing and equality of rich and poor before the law (Brailsford 461–62).

In addition to publishing pamphlets regularly, the Levellers produced a weekly party newspaper and petitioned. Their petitions helped sway Cromwell to try and execute Charles I, though he had formerly opposed doing so. They contributed to a December 1648 purge in which Parliament shifted from Presbyterian to Independent control, though even then the government continued to repress sectarian religious practices. The petitions united civilian and army Levellers, who used them to spark public debates and activism. New Model soldiers, defying martial law that curtailed their right to petition, visited a Hertfordshire town, fixed Lilburne's petitions to marketplace posts, then read the petitions aloud and urged citizens to support Leveller proposals for governmental reform. They encouraged resistance to the unpopular excise tax and refusal to provide the free room and board Parliament demanded citizens offer soldiers. They risked the firing squad to make their petitions the center of commoners' heated public discussions. Not long after the Hertfordshire incident, Lilburne and other Leveller leaders were arrested. Within days, eighty men presented to Parliament a petition signed by ten thousand supporters demanding the prisoners' release or court trial (rather than military or

Parliamentary trial). Leveller women followed with two appeals of their own, and Parliament promised Lilburne and his allies a fair trial before a jury. Like pamphlets, petitions not only energized public debates but also mobilized activism that often generated governmental response.

Diggers' Blossoming

As sectarian craftsmen and small tradesmen organized themselves into the Leveller party, Gerrard Winstanley's spiritual journey continued while he worked as a cowherd in Surrey. In 1648 he walked a path linking mysticism with social and self-revision, beginning his fruitful writing career by producing five pamphlets within a year. The last of these five, *The New Law*, worked to mobilize the poor people excluded even by the Levellers. The poorest people—beggars, servants, and those dispossessed of farms or trades—had been abandoned by the Levellers in the revised versions of their *Agreement of the People*. Those agreements excluded these types of people from the vote because the well heeled feared that servants and other employees might vote according to their employers' instructions. Similarly, they feared that beggars' and vagrants' votes could be bought or blackmailed. Further, the urban Levellers had little to offer the rural poor, those expelled from their lands by enclosing landlords. Despite such peasants' protests against the appropriation of their smallholdings, the Levellers as a whole never took a strong stand against enclosure. In the third and last draft of their proposed *Agreement*, they "ignore the agrarian question altogether" (Brailsford 449). Excluded from the Levellers' *Agreements*, many of these people made a trek like Winstanley's: through religious discussion, they moved into communal efforts to revise society more drastically than even the Levellers intended.

During the Civil Wars, these people's hopes for millennial reform had crumbled. Hayes describes the pattern of disappointment: "One by one the Presbyterians, the Independents, and, in [1648], even the Levellers seemed to renege on their promise to carry out full-scale reform of society based on a widening of the franchise" (7). After seeing the Civil War's sufferings and the defeats of those seeking wider reforms, Winstanley and his fellows concluded that it was futile and unethical to try to impose social renewal by force. They also believed that God worked through people's minds and hearts, that only individuals' personal transformations could bring about a transformed society. Winstanley describes reason, or God's guidance, as "that living power of light that is in all things" (qtd. in Brailsford 663). At the same time, the True Levellers believed their group project would promote the spread of that light and thus the personal transformations that would spark social change.

The New Law, published in January 1649, apparently motivated a small group to pursue its plan to reshape English society. On Sunday April 1, several joined at St. George's Hill in the county of Surrey to undertake this project. There, they began to sow carrots, parsnips, and beans in the commonly owned land, considered by most to be waste ground where little or nothing would grow. More people joined them within a day, and by April 23 they numbered fifty. During the year in which they sustained their project, the group invited all of England's poor people to join them. They hoped thousands would do so.

As Hayes explains, they chose their location carefully to attract fellow reformers and to promote their enterprise. He notes that the Diggers could have selected any remote, fertile patch of land if they had just wanted to live and farm communally. Instead, they chose a spot known for its barrenness and located not far outside London, within easy reach of the press. This meant they would attract publicity, and indeed the April 1649 newsbooks buzzed with often-contemptuous reports of the little group. It also meant that they would be able to use the London presses themselves. Further, their proximity to the city would allow the London poor to join the group easily if they chose. Finally, their choice of infertile land suggests the Diggers believed their endeavor was so strong it would flourish even if they farmed waste ground. As Hayes concludes, "They did everything they could to play up the symbolic aspect of the experiment. Winstanley knew the increasingly oppressive and intolerable conditions surrounding the Civil Wars called for a reinterpretation of history—for a 'new' mythology" (148). This new mythology was the True Levellers' vision of the millennium, the society of peace, justice, and equity they believed they were helping to initiate.

Because they saw God's law, natural law, and reason as synonymous, the Diggers used scripture to move those laws from a primarily religious realm into the social world. Ernest Lee Tuveson shows how this transition shaped Western thought more broadly in his study of the idea of progress. Tuveson describes how the idea evolved over several hundred years and explains that by the end of that period, "Providence [or God's plan for the world] could assume a disguise as 'natural law,' and St. Augustine's City of God [the transformed millennial society] become the human race progressing culturally and materially" (7). The Diggers helped to spark this evolution by identifying God with divine law, reason, and natural law. Cultural and material progress anchored their vision of a millennial society. They did not intend to disguise the religious foundations of their philosophical framework, though. Rather, they struggled to materialize their interpretations of scripture into a concrete New

Jerusalem by founding a community that would share equally in work and worldly goods. Hayes describes Winstanley's project as "an attempt to put into practice what others had preached, to transform words into deed, to make the abstract concrete. . . . He self-consciously and deliberately sets out to change biblical figures of speech into specific acts because he actually wants to bring about the heavenly kingdom on earth" (26).

Thus interpreting scripture to envision a renewed society led these people to take other action to try to realize their ideal. They lived, worked, and ate together on St. George's Hill. They planted vegetables and beans on the commons. They published explanations of their plan and invitations to join in it. These actions all contributed to their effort to use shared resources and labor to forge a new kind of community—one that would provide equal material, intellectual, and spiritual support to all of its members. The Levellers sought to alleviate the poor's sufferings; the True Levellers sought to eliminate poverty.

Near the end of April, they published a little manifesto to spread the news of their endeavor and their invitation. They titled their piece *The True Levellers Standard Advanced: Or, The State of community opened, and Presented to the Sons of Men* (Sabine 251–66). The pamphlet directly addresses England's poor, urging them to refuse to work for others and instead to unite and work together to produce food for themselves. It explains the venture at St. George's Hill and, rather than asking the well-to-do to give to the poor, it speaks to the poor themselves. Specifically, it exhorts them to change their situation by forming their own community, arguing that if individuals work to revise their day-to-day habits and attitudes, larger transformations will follow. Winstanley himself provides a quiet but forceful example. His pilgrimage from privileged London tradesman with conventional religious attitudes to penniless sectarian seeker led him to connect with the rural poor and other impoverished people. His own self-revision both sparked and participated in the communal St. George's Hill project, a collective transformation.

Within six months, a group of Buckinghamshire radicals joined the effort by writing three short pamphlets passionately advocating the same approach to social change. The first two, *Light Shining in Buckinghamshire* and *More Light Shining in Buckinghamshire*, draw on the radical religious tradition of the Anabaptists, sectarians who had fled persecution in Continental Europe and settled in Buckinghamshire (Sabine 611–23, 627–40). Both pieces advocate the Levellers' plan for political equality, legal reform, and religious freedom. But they extend this plan to include economic equality as well, arguing, as Brailsford puts it, that God's law shows that "commonwealth means equality. It must ensure to each man a just portion wherewith to live" (Brailsford 445). To make this argument, *More Light* uses almost the exact words of an Anabaptist sermon written nearly a hundred years before and passed down among the sect's refugee descendants. Like Winstanley and his colleagues, this pamphlet argues that common land and land previously owned by the ousted king and church should go not to wealthy enclosers but to the poor. Like the St. George's Hill band, the Buckinghamshire group wove the threads of England's radical traditions with the new Protestant activities of lay interpretation and the Anabaptists' belief in common ownership to ground new practices.

The third Buckinghamshire pamphlet shows that some better-off people shared this dream of social renewal as well. *A Declaration of the Wel-Affected in the County of Buckinghamshire* both declares its support for the poor people tilling the commons and promises to aid them in their efforts (Sabine 643–47). As Linebaugh and Rediker show, such efforts were a frequent response by the dispossessed all around the Atlantic as they faced destitution and pressure to accept back-breaking wage labor. In addition to similar efforts in the Americas, these historians describe a July 1647 revolt in Naples, in which a fisherman named Masaniello led the city's poor in a rebellion against oppressive taxes on food and other staple goods. Sailors brought word of the revolt to England, and just after the Putney Debates, one London speaker compared it with the Leveller drive for democracy (112–13, 116). Thus the St. George's Hill and Buckinghamshire projects paralleled other commoners' intermittent efforts in lands trading across the Atlantic.

Yet at St. George's Hill, as often happened at the sites of other such endeavors, the local well-to-do felt threatened. Unlike the middling sorts in Buckinghamshire, they did not offer support. Local gentry perceived the undertaking as a potential threat to their property, and during the first few weeks of April, they took the little group by force, first to the little town of Walton and next to larger Kingston. But each time authorities released the group. Frustrated, the better sorts complained to the Council of State appointed to govern England after Charles's execution, and the council asked General Fairfax to drive Winstanley and his colleagues from St. George's Hill.

One of Fairfax's captains visited the site and reported that the True Levellers were no threat, saying they had agreed to explain their project to the general. On April 20, Winstanley and another of his party, William Everard, did so. The news sheets reported that they presented themselves respectfully and civilly. But both insisted on wearing their hats before Fairfax, though convention dictated they doff their caps to a social superior. When asked why, they declared that the general "was but their fellow-creature" (qtd. in Berens 38). Thus they quietly defied seventeenth-century England's customs upholding hierarchy and privilege. They explained their faith, their commitment to renounce violence and attacks on private property, and their group's project. Their speech balanced them across the tightrope: it proclaimed their beliefs and plans—gaining them further publicity in the news sheets—without posing a serious threat in the general's eyes. He took no military action against the budding community.

Connection

Digger texts' rhetorical strategies also position different audiences to shift their perceptions of their own and others' identities, as a Gestalt analysis shows. By prompting audiences to expand awareness and experiment with rhetorical moves that produce revised contact styles, the texts poise audiences to construct a nonhierarchical authority grounded in acceptance of competing groups as spiritual and social equals. To do so, they move back and forth among various addressees and use a structure suited to both oral and silent reading.

By rotating among direct addresses to various audiences, Winstanley's texts play a reverse musical chairs that offers seating even to readers not yet ready to accept the Digger project. But Winstanley first uses this movable address to prompt different audiences toward contact with revised self-perceptions. For instance, in *An Humble Request*, dedicated in its opening letter to ministers and lawyers, Winstanley directly addresses these powerful groups to reposition discursive authority by subjecting them to God's judgment as articulated through right reason. "*Ministers and Lawyers,*" he demands, "will you all stand looking on, and see the *Lords* of *Mannors* exercise *Kingly* Power over the poor men that claime their creation-right in the earth, and be silent?" He continues, "You would be called dispensers of Justice: here is a point of justice for you to decide: this is the point upon which you shall either stand or fall, be saved or damned; for you are put upon the tryal" (qtd. in Sabine 433). By simultaneously appealing to and interrogating lawyers and clergy, Winstanley positions them as both judging his case and being judged by the light of reason's authority. Because he grounds this authority largely in the lower sorts' interpretations, this passage subjects lawyers and clergy to the judgment of poor audiences.

Winstanley exercises this judgment by depicting landlords who oppress the Diggers as hypocritical, violent, untrustworthy, and unreasonable. He describes how a local landowner used both litigation and violence to try to remove the Diggers from the commons they occupied. *An Humble Request* describes the interaction between Winstanley and the True Levellers on one side and Parson Platt, the landowner, on the other. The pamphlet reports that after conversation with Winstanley, Platt "was very moderate," promised to read the Diggers' explanation of their reasoning, and assured them that if they refrained from cutting wood on the commons he would not disturb their houses (qtd. in Sabine 433). But less than a week later Platt returned without discussion, bringing fifty men who joined him in burning the group's houses and belongings. The same night, Platt sent men to intimidate the band, who had stayed on the commons despite the destruction of their goods. Platt's men threatened to kill those who did not depart. Winstanley describes the True Levellers' conversation with their harassers:

> And some of the Diggers asked them, why they would do thus cruelly by them, they answered, because you do not know God, nor will not come to Church.
>
> Surely if the God of these men, by their going to Church, teach both their preacher [Platt] and they, to do such cruel deedes; we will neither come to Church, nor serve their God. Mr. *Plat* in his Sermons can say, *live in peace with all men, and love your Enemies*: Therefore if the Diggers were enemies, he ought to love them in action; but it is a true badge of an hypocrite, to say, and not to do.
>
> Let every Mans action be tried, and see who serves God, They or the Diggers. Mr. *Plat* and the Gentlemen (so would be called) that were with him, were full of rage, and gnashed their tongues with vexation; but the Diggers are patient, chearfull, quiet in spirit, loving to those that have burned their houses. (qtd. in Sabine 434)

Here Winstanley responds to the legal and social arguments being made against the True Levellers, arguments that position the group as violent, unreasonable, immoral, and atheistic. *An Humble Request* not only claims the group's godliness, morality, civility, and reason, but also enacts them. It positions Platt and his cohorts as violent and unreasonable, while depicting the Diggers as nonviolent seekers of justice who use discussion, writing, and appeals to authorized discourses. Winstanley's direct address to clergy and lawyers embodies reasoned argument—discussion based in the shared discourses of scriptural authority, civil law, and natural law. This approach contrasts sharply with Platt's use of force and intimidation against the Diggers. By juxtaposing the two approaches, Winstanley urges readers to revise their perceptions of both upper and lower sorts. He depicts the former as violent, uncivil, and unreasonable, in contrast with the typical representation of these groups as the seat of civil order. Similarly, he flips the usual depiction of the poor as lawless and uncivil by presenting the Diggers as peaceful, Godly, and reasonable. Thus Winstanley performs reasoned interaction textually by using direct address to structure the pamphlet as one side of a discussion that makes its case through the day's authorized discourses. In Gestalt terms, he models rhetorical moves poor audiences can use to construct themselves as equal rather than subservient and as reasonable and civil rather than disorderly. Thus he shifts discursive legitimacy from the university-educated lawyers and ministers to the supposedly ignorant people at St. George's Hill, encouraging revised perceptions of each group's identity and social role.

Winstanley develops these alternative perceptions by equating oppressive landlords with the prototype of fallen humanity. Yet he builds complexity into that depiction by showing all audiences how such fallen oppressors can win redemption. Again, he uses direct address. For instance, *The True Levellers Standard* instructs those in power on how to understand and treat the St. George's Hill project:

> O you *A-dams* of the Earth, you have rich Clothing, full Bellies, have your Honors and Ease . . . do the worst thou canst . . . the poor people whom thou oppresses, shall be the Saviours of the land; For the blessing is rising up in them, and thou shalt be ashamed.
>
> And thus you Powers of England, and of the whole World, we have declared our Reasons, why we have begun to dig upon *George* hill in Surrey. One thing I must tell you more. . . . if thou wilt find Mercy, *Let Israel go Free;* break in pieces quickly the Band of particular Propriety [individual property ownership], dis-own this oppressing Murder, Oppression and Thievery of buying and Selling of Land, owning of landlords, and paying of Rents, and give thy Free Consent to make the Earth a common Treasury without grumbling. . . . If thou wilt not *let Israel go Free* . . . Then know, that whereas I brought *Ten* Plagues upon him [pharaoh], I will *Multiply* my Plagues upon thee, till I make thee weary, and miserably ashamed: And *I will bring out my People with a strong hand, and stretched out arme.*
>
> Thus we have discharged our Souls in declaring the Cause of our Digging upon *George-Hill* in *Surrey*, that the Great Councel and Army of the land may take notice of it, That there is no intent of Tumult or Fighting, but only to get Bread to eat, with the sweat of our brows; working together in righteousness, and eating the blessings of the

earth in peace. (qtd. in Sabine 264–66)

This excerpt begins by directly addressing the better sorts to locate them explicitly within the history the pamphlet has already presented. The piece asks such readers to reimagine their position in both seventeenth-century English society and history. By calling them Adams of the earth, the text aligns them with the Bible's allegorical figure for the fallen state. Thus it prompts all audiences toward a revised perception of their identity and the effects of their desires. This move contextualizes the pamphlet's description of the St. George's Hill group's current actions, plans, reasoned justifications, and renunciation of violence. In this context, the St. George's Hill endeavor redeems civil society from the sin of encouraging individual ownership of resources divinely intended for common use.

Through this revised view of social reality and the relations among social groups, Winstanley's text positions receptive well-to-do audiences to reorganize their experience by showing them how they can partake of the coming redemption. Thus by locating well-to-do readers within its historical schema, the text tries to make them more receptive to the Diggers' project. The passage explains how such readers can support the coming changes and soften their lot in the process. In contrast, it next describes the painful consequences of obstructing history. Yet even these consequences appear as a tempered punishment that rhetorically enacts and models gentleness. In the context of the promise of mercy for those who support the process of making wealth common, the threatened punishment appears as a temporary condition leading to penance and ultimate redemption. By juxtaposing these two possibilities for the better sorts, Winstanley shows them how they can help and urges them to at least tolerate the Digger movement on ethical and self-interested grounds. Through direct address, Winstanley tries to shift this audience from distanced judgment into involvement by directly implicating them in his history and worldview. Thus direct address prepares the ground for Winstanley's instructions to the better sorts on how to respond to the True Levellers' project. In Gestalt terms, it prompts them to shift their experience by offering them a revised vision of redemption.

At the same time, Winstanley's texts prompt poor audiences to recognize how they exercise agency in the existing historical circumstances. Using direct address, he positions them to expand awareness of their own choices and those choices' effects. For example, *The New Law* addresses poor readers to mobilize them toward specific actions:

Therefore you dust of the earth, that are trod under foot, you poor

people that makes both schollars and rich men your oppressours by
your labours, Take notice of your priviledge, the Law of Righteousnesse is now declared.

If you labour the earth, and work for others that lives at ease, and
follows the waies of the flesh by your labours, eating the bread which
you get by the sweat of your brows, not their own: Know this, that the
hand of the Lord shal break out upon every such hireling labourer, and
you shal perish with the covetous rich men, that have held, and yet
doth hold the Creation under the bondage of the curse. . . . when the
Lord doth shew unto me the place and manner, how he wil have us
that are called common people, to manure and work upon the common Lands, I will then go forth and declare it in my action, to eat my
bread with the sweat of my brows, without either giving or taking hire,
looking upon the Land as freely mine as anothers; I have now peace in
the Spirit, and I have an inward perswasion that the spirit of the poor,
shal be drawn forth ere long, to act materially this Law of Righteousnesse. (qtd. in Sabine 194–95)

The shifting pronouns in this excerpt mark Winstanley's effort to change
his audience's self-conceptions. Specifically, he urges poor audiences to initiate
social reform by practicing communal subsistence farming. His direct address
and its biblical terms urge readers toward two actions: to see themselves as
privileged agents of history and to refuse wage labor in an effort to transform
economic relations. To make contact with their own agency, poor audiences
must recognize how they create the conditions of their oppression. They need
experiential recognition of their agency in the situation to perceive alternate
possibilities and to mobilize their energies toward the figure of common ownership. The threat of divine retribution against those who "take hire" evokes
the inevitable outcome of the history Winstanley posits. By putting poor audiences' choices in the context of this history, he illustrates the large-scale consequences of those choices and positions poor audiences to expand awareness
of their own agency.

But perhaps even more crucial is the move from addressing his audience
as "you" to "us that are called common people." This is especially so because
the shift occurs in the context of Winstanley's declaration of his personal
intention to take up the project. This shift from second- to first-person address
asks poor audiences to move from self-images of disempowerment to self-
images of agency, both local and historical. It includes these audiences in the

"us" to whom God will assign a local project that initiates global change. That is, the shift asks audiences to join the Lord's vanguard by working to transform the earth according to divine law. In Gestalt terms, Winstanley's rhetorical strategies position audiences to make greater contact with their own agency and range of possible choices.

Similarly, these strategies encourage broader awareness of potential affiliations. In these writings, Winstanley's shifts in direct address tend to consolidate audiences into opposing groups of poorer and better sorts. Yet ultimately such shifts urge upper and lower sorts to accept one another, to make peace, and to pursue a shared figure of common ownership. Thus Winstanley's texts both establish and dissolve us/them dichotomies. *The True Levellers Standard* moves back and forth between these efforts. First it emphasizes the St. George's Hill group's cohesiveness and dedication to their cause, but later it proclaims their inclusiveness, declaring, "We find the streaming out of Love in our hearts towards all; to enemies as well as friends; we would have none live in Beggery, Poverty, or Sorrow, but that every one might enjoy the benefits of his creation" (qtd. in Sabine 256–58, 262). Similarly, *The New Law* moves quickly and repeatedly back and forth between addressing the poorer and better sorts. It urges the first to create a community and the second to reform. But it follows these moves by asking both groups to consolidate themselves into a unified body of English people:

> There are yet three doors of hope for *England* to escape destroying and plagues [of the apocalypse]:
> First, let every one leave off running after others for knowledge and comfort, and wait upon the spirit of Reason, til he break forth out of the Clouds of your heart, and manifest himself within you. This is . . . to make choyce of the Lord, the true Teacher of every one in their own inward experience. . . . Secondly, Let every one open his bags and barns, that al may feed upon the crops of the earth, that the burden of povertie may be removed: Leave of this buying and selling of Land, or of the fruits of the earth; and as it was in the light of Reason first made, so let it be in action, amongst all a common Treasurie. . . . And let this word of the Lord be acted amongst all, work together, eat bread together. . . .
> Thirdly. Leave off dominion and Lordship one over another. . . . If every one would speedily set about the doing of these three particulars I have mentioned, the Creation would thereby be lift up out of

bondage, and our Maker would have the glory of the works of his own hands. (qtd. in Sabine 200–1)

Here Winstanley addresses "every one." He does not differentiate between common and better sorts in explaining how to avoid disaster and usher in the new millennium. Rather, he urges all groups to take up the same set of intellectual and material actions. In his shift from addressing disparate audiences individually to addressing all audiences simultaneously, Winstanley integrates the separate groups into a unified community that shares a worldview and a plan for social transformation. He addresses specific groups throughout his texts to prompt them to revise their particular self-conceptions, attitudes, and actions. But by subsequently addressing all groups at once, Winstanley builds on his earlier efforts to consolidate poor audiences into a community. As often, his rhetorical moves model habits that construct an inclusive identity that promotes concord. They do not abolish the community's boundaries but rather reposition the well-to-do to include them in it. Thus Winstanley's texts use an ethic of exclusion to consolidate a sense of group identity but then eliminate that exclusion by redefining and repositioning excluded groups as lost kin. In Gestalt terms, they encourage audiences to increase awareness of the humanity of other groups with divergent interests.

The Diggers' fate suggests this strategy brought mixed success. I know of no instances in which upper sorts actively supported the Diggers' efforts, other than the letter from the Buckinghamshire middling sorts. This circumstance suggests that while their texts helped define a figure shared by some (perhaps many) lower sorts, they did not make common ownership figural for most of the upper sorts. Still, the fact that both civil and military authorities repeatedly allowed the True Levellers to continue their project implies the texts succeeded in positioning the group as peaceful, godly, and reasonable to upper sorts as well as lower. Thus the texts' strategy of urging mutual acceptance, peacemaking, and pursuit of a shared figure apparently succeeded in two of its three goals with some key audiences.

Finally, Winstanley's texts invite functionally illiterate audiences to take up interpretive authority. They model rhetorical moves that foster inclusiveness by encouraging flexibility at the contact boundary. These moves use a structure that suits them to both oral and silent reading.[2] Several features of *The New Law* support this view of the texts. First, its chapters often unfold through a set of several steps. For instance, Winstanley sometimes opens a chapter by invoking his own experience of God's revelation, then follows quickly with a citation and reading of a scriptural passage. Next, the chapter provides a historical explanation of contemporary conditions and depicts seventeenth-century England as sitting on the brink of history's fulfillment. *The New Law* renders these steps in differing orders as variations on a theme. For example, it builds its biblical case by citing different parts of the Old and New Testaments in different chapters, it uses a historical lens to interpret various contemporary practices, and it describes different facets of Winstanley's spiritual and material experiences to ground its larger claims about God's workings within individuals. This use of variations on a theme facilitates oral reading by providing listeners with expectations for the text's structure and yet allowing the writer to make new points and build his argument within the frame of the text's established pattern.

Another structural feature that suggests *The New Law*'s chapters were written to be read aloud as well as silently is their size. While the text runs roughly one hundred pages in Sabine's edition, its chapters average four to six pages, with a few extending to ten or twelve pages. Sect members could easily read chapters of this size aloud during meetings. Thus members who could not read but wished to hear and discuss the text could do so. Further, Winstanley often concludes the chapters with pithy biblical quotations or other lines calculated to spark audiences' investment in *The New Law*'s project of personal and social change. Take, for instance, the concluding lines of chapters six, seven, nine, and ten: "*And so to lead captivity captive, and let the prisoners of hope go free. Rev. 6.11*"; "For now the Father is raissing up a people to himself out of the dust, and of the stones, that is, poor despised people, that are trod upon like dust and stones, shal now be raised up, and be made the blessing of the earth, *and the high mountaines shall be laid low, the lofty looks of men shal be pulled down, and the Lord alone shall be exalted in this day of his power*"; "For *Jacob* now must have the blessing, he is blessed, yea and shal be blessed, and *Esau* shal become his servant; *The poor shal inherit the earth*"; "The light and life of Christ within the heart, discovers all darknesse, and delivers mankind from bondage; *And besides him there is no Saviour*" (qtd. in Sabine 183, 190, 208–9, 214).

Such scriptural citations appear throughout Winstanley's prose. By interlacing them throughout the text, he again echoes sermons' composition. This structure particularly suits his audience, who not only recognized it from their extensive experience with sermons but knew scripture so intimately that they could quickly grasp biblical references with complex, multilayered implications and associations. Further, key images, also often scriptural, appear again and again throughout *The New Law*. For instance, Winstanley repeatedly uses Jacob as a symbol of the poor and downtrodden, Esau as an emblem of rich oppressors, and Israel as an image of both the poor collected into community and the coming millennial society. This pattern produces another set of variations on a theme. Like the pattern created by Winstanley's use of a set of repeated textual moves, this one reinforces his themes, provides audiences with a structure, and yet allows the writer to build and complicate his argument. Thus while this use of aesthetic language differs somewhat from Goodman's definition, it still accomplishes the end he attributes to aesthetic language: greater contact with some aspect of experience, here the possible relation of self and society presented in Winstanley's argument.

Finally, *The New Law* uses a question-and-answer format regularly, sometimes by posing a question and providing Winstanley's response, sometimes by positioning the implied questioner as a scoffer or Doubting Thomas. Through this format, Winstanley positions skeptics as cynics who lack faith. Of course, he also uses it to anticipate and reply to challenges to his interpretations of scripture and history and his vision of social change. Further, this format allows Winstanley to textually reproduce the structure of sectarians' meetings by imitating their process of discussion and debate. Because many audience members were familiar with that structure, Winstanley's imitation of it better equips his texts to engage this audience. Composing pieces designed to be read aloud as well as silently complements sects' practices of public reading, discussion, and interpretation. Most importantly, this composition works against the exclusion of people who could not read for themselves, an exclusion that strongly concerned Winstanley. Given that he targets especially the poorer sorts who tended to read and interpret communally, composing texts for both oral and silent reading provides him a practical and ethical approach. This form enables his texts to reach and work for that audience in ways texts written primarily for silent reading could not. Further, this structure enacts Winstanley's argument for universal interpretive authority and models another rhetorical strategy that fosters inclusiveness by encouraging multiple, flexible approaches to contact with others. It prompts audiences to take up such strategies, positioning them to practice habits of inclusion. Thus Winstanley uses shifts among various addressees to try to transform audiences' self-conceptions and actions. By using textual moves that connect with a primary audience's intellectual and interpretive practices, thus drawing on their structured ground, Winstanley increases his chances of motivating that audience to undertake personal and social revisions. From a Gestalt perspective, his rhetorical strategies construct and model a nonhierarchical authority that positions all people as spiritual and social equals.

Levellers' Fruition

The challenges of negotiating audiences with conflicting interests ultimately split the Diggers from their most probable allies, the Levellers. When the Independents gained control of Parliament in late 1648, the Levellers strove to craft a third version of their *Agreement of the People* to win approval from both their constituents and the new government. But by spring the negotiations had stalled and on March 26, not a week before the Diggers began tilling St. George's Hill, Lilburne and several other Leveller leaders were imprisoned in the Tower of London. Meanwhile, their opponents exploited the similarity between the Leveller and True Leveller names to accuse the former of desiring to abolish private property (Frank 234 n. 88). Desperate, Lilburne and his fellows repudiated their rural cousins and withdrew their prior support for land reform, favoring the interests of craftspeople over those of the wage laborers and displacing the rural poor represented by the True Levellers (Manning 313).

The army Levellers tried to force the issue by brewing a rebellion in the ranks of the New Model. Several hundred mutinied in Oxfordshire County, following Corporal William Thompson, who had published *England's Standard Advanced*, demanding that Parliament and the army implement the Levellers' third *Agreement*. Soldiers from two regiments to the south and another two from the east rebelled as well and contacted sympathetic troops in western England, planning a rendezvous at Bristol. Cromwell, fearing a nationwide revolt, marched with carefully chosen men to prevent the eastern troops from making contact (Petegorsky 158–59). Pursued by emissaries offering assurances that the generals wanted to negotiate and would not attack, the rebels gladly agreed and quartered at the town of Burford, barely posting a guard. At midnight, Cromwell attacked from both sides, capturing 340 Levellers while another 500 escaped. Its negotiating power gone, the movement melted. Yet its ideas lived on to shape England's future social and political reforms, not least progress toward universal suffrage (Petegorsky 116; Frank 245; Brailsford xii).

Diggers' Fruition

The St. George's Hill group pursued their project for nearly a year after Cromwell crushed the army Levellers at Burford. But although they had gained Fairfax's tolerance (if not his blessing), their trials at the hands of surrounding landowners intensified. The threatened local gentry attacked the community both physically and legally. Winstanley documents these attacks in a pamphlet publicizing the group's hardships. The piece describes how, over and over, the gentry took or destroyed the band's tools, pulled down houses they had built, beat and severely wounded them, and uprooted their crops. But, Winstanley declares, "those Diggers that remain . . . are cheerful; taking the spoyling [spoiling] of their Goods patiently, and rejoycing that they are counted worthy to suffer persecution for Righteousnesse sake: and they follow their work close[ly]. . . . Poverty is their greatest burthen [burden]; and if any thing do break them from the Work, it will be that" (qtd. in Sabine 304–5).

The group had forsworn violence, and they tried to wage peace through Winstanley's pen. For instance, after describing the gentry's abuses, Winstanley takes care to mention that although the landowners brought soldiers, the New Model men refused to take part in the attacks and regretted the abuses they watched. After other soldiers stationed nearby beat a man and a boy, stole their clothing, and burnt a Digger house in early June of 1649, Winstanley wrote a thirteen-page letter to General Fairfax asking not for the troopers' punishment but that the soldiers leave the Diggers in peace (Hayes 151–52).

Still, Winstanley did not hesitate to denounce actions he saw as evil. Two days after the soldiers' attack, locals bludgeoned four Diggers into unconsciousness, nearly killing one. Winstanley documented the assault the same day by writing the pamphlet *A Declaration of the Bloudie and Unchristian Acting of William Starr and John Taylor of Walton* (Hayes 153). He carried his denunciations into the national arena as well by writing in early July 1649 *An Appeal to the House of Commons, Desiring their Answer; Whether the Common-People shall have the quiet enjoyment of the* Commons *and* Waste Lands; *Or whether they shall be under the will of* Lords *of* Mannors *still*. He demands that Parliament make good its promises to establish a government based in Christian principles and freedom for common people (Hayes 153–55). Yet while condemning such actions, Winstanley never rejects the people who committed them, insisting they are redeemable. Hayes explains, "By seeing the hostile tenant farmers as vulnerable and manipulatable Winstanley shows understanding for the very people who have injured him most and tries to build a coalition between the poor and the lower-middle-class strong enough to withstand the increasing pressure from the gentry who control Parliament" (207).

The St. George's Hill group sent more letters to Fairfax and published more pamphlets in response to many of the persecutions they faced. They used writing to show the justice of their case, the virtue of their project, and the tenacity of their effort. And always they wrote to invite all readers, even those who had wronged them, to revise their worldviews and join the budding project.

Despite the hardships of poverty, assaults, hostile neighbors, and lawsuits, the True Levellers' project bloomed, if only briefly. Facing legal harassment and destroyed crops, they moved from St. George's Hill to a nearby heath. There they tilled the land, built four houses, and planted winter grain. But they again suffered repeated legal actions, destruction of their houses and tools, and physical violence. The Surrey ministers preached against them, urging local people to refuse the band food or lodging. Still, by April 1650 the group had raised eleven acres of grain and built six or seven houses (Sabine 18–20; Petegorsky 173). In the process, their writings, emissaries, and example inspired others to take up the project in separate locales.

In the early spring of 1650, facing privation and hunger but continuing to work, the group sent out messengers who traveled to more than thirty towns and villages in Surrey and four or five surrounding counties. The travelers carried a letter signed by twenty-five of the St. George's Hill group. The letter describes the group's poverty and requests financial assistance, promises the band will continue working to free the land for the poor, and urges other poor people to band together and begin cultivating their local commons. In some places, poorer residents did so. For instance, the letter seems to have motivated the Wellingborough group of Northamptonshire County, some sixty miles north of St. George's Hill, to write the broadside declaring their intention to farm a local commons. As Petegorsky explains, their manifesto declares "In March the 'poor inhabitants' of the town announced that they had begun to dig upon the 'common and waste-ground called Bareshank,' that several freeholders had agreed to surrender their claim to the commons and that some farmers had already offered them seed" (174). The broadsheet published their belief in everyone's right to use and enjoy the land (Brailsford 658). Similarly, poor people from the town of Coxhall, one county east of Surrey, began to till the common land. In Gloucestershire, several counties west, the poorer sorts tried to level enclosures and restore formerly common land to the people in June 1650. Thus the St. George's Hill group's determined fight to sustain their community and to use writing and discussion to prompt other poor people to join their endeavor energized some of those people to undertake the project for themselves.

Although all of these attempts succumbed to their richer neighbors' physical violence and legal attacks, the True Levellers' work inspired many. The St. George's Hill group persisted until the odds overwhelmed them. Petegorsky describes the project's annihilation:

A week before Easter [of 1650], Parson Platt, one of the Diggers' most persistent persecutors, together with a Mr. Sutton, pulled down a house and struck a man and woman working on the heath. Despite

Platt's promise that if the Diggers cut no wood from the heath he would no longer molest them, he returned a week later with several men, set fire to the Diggers' houses, burned their furniture and scattered their belongings. The Diggers were threatened with death if they attempted to resume their activities. To prevent their return, Platt and Sutton hired several men to maintain a twenty-four-hour vigil on the heath. With that [the Diggers' project] . . . seems to have come to an end. (175)

Like the Levellers' attempts to gain political representation for the middling sorts, the True Levellers' efforts to build an inclusive, equitable community dissolved under assaults from stronger contemporary forces. But also like the Levellers' beliefs, the Diggers' ideas inspired others in later years and far-flung places to attempt to construct a socioeconomic system based on the equitable distribution of resources.

Linebaugh and Rediker show how these ideas crossed the Atlantic, carried by sailors, slaves, and indentured servants to the Americas and Caribbean (248–326). Many escaped or rebelled, seeking to form alternative democratic communities that shared resources in common. Such groups included democratically governed pirate convoys, cross-race rebel coalitions in the colonial Americas, and maroon communities of escaped slaves, indigenous people, and European poor in the Caribbean and Roanoke. Digger beliefs inspired religious movements in 1730s America and writers such as Samuel Adams Jr., who in 1748 started the weekly *Independent Advertiser* to echo Digger ideas on redistributing land, commoners' need to recognize their own power, and the equality of men who are all "by Nature on a Level" (qtd. in Linebaugh and Rediker 217).

Some British colonial authorities returned leveling ideas to England, as when Colonel Edward Marcus Despard, former governor of Honduras, formed the antislavery, pro-redistribution London Corresponding Society in 1792. Robert Wedderburn, son of an Afro-Caribbean slave woman and her white owner, addressed Jamaican and English audiences in journals and pamphlets that circulated on both sides of the Atlantic. Echoing Winstanley's language, he holds that the encloser who had "turned his brother from his right [to land] was a tyrant, a robber, and a murderer" and that God had given the earth to "the children of men" (qtd. in Linebaugh and Rediker 314). While these activists did not manage to redistribute resources across class lines, they successfully fought slavery, which was abolished in the British Caribbean on August 1, 1838. The Diggers' ideas also invigorated working-class thinking in nineteenth-century Britain. Carolyn Steedman points to memoirs by John Pearman, who soldiered in India, then worked in England as a policeman. She argues that Pearman developed his position on race and class equality partly from his reading of Winstanley's texts (Steedman 5, 270–71 n. 10). While many of these radicals renounced Winstanley's commitment to nonviolence and lost his emphasis on self-revision, they nonetheless brought some True Leveller ideals into their centuries' social movements.

Transformation

Revising self-conceptions is central to Winstanley's approach, and his texts prompt such work by experimenting with dialectical rhetorical strategies. They enact the risk and loss Wheeler says is inherent in personal change, and they experiment with rhetorical strategies for reintegrating the self. This risk and loss result from the destructuring of self prompted by the texts' joining-and-analyzing, which examines poorer audiences' choices in relating to the better sorts and the social order. By highlighting lower sorts' unaware choices, this joining-and-analyzing destructures a self-portrait that presumes poor audiences' powerlessness. Digger texts encourage a revised self-conception by exploring specific tensions between individual agency and larger social and historical forces. They reintegrate the self as personal and social agent by synthesizing these opposing forces and modeling this synthesis for audiences.

Thematically and formally, their syntheses generate a dialectic between theory and other kinds of action. This dialectic moves the texts back and forth from individual to community focus, from material to spiritual experiences, and from urging specific local action to predicting sweeping social change. It produces a spiral that honors each side in these oppositions. Rather than establishing a compromised middle ground, it synthesizes these poles to revise dynamics and relationships, both individual and social. By using language that promotes contact, these syntheses position audiences to recompose the relationships between the experiences and abstractions linked to each pole. Thus they reconfigure agency in several specific ways.

The first focuses on the relation between self and spiritual authority. *The True Levellers Standard Advanced* examines this kind of agency by demonstrating the links between material and spiritual experiences. It highlights how individual identities intersect with community structures:

> And so selfish imagination . . . did set up one man to teach and
> rule over another; and thereby the Spirit was killed, and man was

brought into bondage, and became a greater Slave to such of his own kind, then the Beasts of the field were to him.

And hereupon, The Earth (which was made to be a Common Treasury of relief for all, both Beasts and Men) was hedged in to Inclosures by the teachers and rulers, and the others were made Servants and Slaves. . . . But this coming in of Bondage . . . this ruling and teaching power without, doth *dam* up the Spirit of Peace and Liberty; First within the heart, by filling it with slavish fears of others. Secondly without, by giving the bodies of one to be imprisoned, punished and oppressed by the outward power of another. . . . And Israels rejecting of outward teachers and rulers to embrace the Lord, and to be all taught and ruled by that righteous King, that *Jeremiah* Prophesied shall rule in the new Heavens and new earth in the latter dayes, will be their Restauration from bondage. (qtd. in Sabine 252)

Here Winstanley explicitly links material oppression on one hand with spiritual and intellectual coercion on the other. While spiritual and intellectual coercion occur first in Winstanley's history, the two kinds of oppression seem to intensify one another. This passage encourages poorer audiences to make contact with their active (but perhaps unaware) choices in constructing the coercive relationship. It suggests they can change it by collectively rejecting the intellectual and spiritual authority of England's clergy and universities. In place of that authority, Winstanley advises laypeople to rely on their own practices of experientially based reading, interpretation, and discussion. Because God provides the guiding light of reason within each person, people can replace enslaving spiritual and intellectual authority with right reason by turning within. Thus Winstanley argues that people can change material conditions of exploitation and oppression only by reconfiguring their relationship to spiritual authority, shifting its locus from the established clergy to their own spiritual experiences. This shift transforms people's spiritual and intellectual habits. It destructures a view of the poor as powerless, risking such self-conceptions in the reach for new self-understandings. Through it, poorer audiences can remake collective practices and dynamics if they work in the context of a community actively committed to reforming itself. Thus individual change grounds communal change. For Winstanley, individual and social practices shape each other, and the generative tension between them produces society's dynamics and material conditions. By defining individual agency through this dialectic, he highlights the role of social forces yet models a personal agency that works in a mutually constructive relationship with them.

Winstanley's second reconfiguration of agency focuses on the relation between self and material resources. *The New Law* builds on the revised relation between self and spiritual authority to establish a similar, mutually formative relationship between material conditions and individuals' attitudes and habits:

> While the man of unrighteousnesse raigns in and over man-kinde, truly every body wee see is filled with sorrow and complainings, and it is not without cause.
>
> As the powers and wisdome of the flesh hath filled the earth with injustice, oppression and complainings, by mowing [moving] the earth into the hands of a few covetous, unrighteous men, who assumes a lordship over others, declaring themselves thereby to be men of the basest spirits.
>
> Even so, when the spreading power of wisdome and truth, fils the earth man-kinde, hee wil take off that bondage, and give a universall liberty, and there shal be no more complainings against oppression, poverty, or injustice.
>
> When every son and daughter shall be made more comfortable to that one body of Jesus the anointed, and the same power rules in them, as in him, every one according to their measure, the oppression shall cease, and the rising up of this universal power, shal destroy and subdue the selfish power. (qtd. in Sabine 180–81)

Here material conditions shape people's attitudes and habits, but such attitudes and habits also initiate material privations. Further, Winstanley argues, revising behaviors and beliefs will help transform social, economic, and political relationships. His portrait of change reintegrates the initial depiction of self as victim of injustice and oppression into a self grounded in personal spiritual experience and so empowered to "take off that bondage and give a universall liberty." Perceiving one's internal sources of spiritual authority produces one's capacity to exercise agency in the material world. By synthesizing the individual with the communal and the material with the spiritual/intellectual, Winstanley links social construction to individual agency. In the resulting creative tension, personal and social change can extend one another.

These syntheses ground another dialectic, this one between urging specific local action and predicting sweeping social transformation. Through that synthesis, Winstanley achieves his third reconfiguration of agency, which focuses on the relations between self and historical forces. Like many writers before him who describe the coming Christian millennium and many writers after who reconstruct that millennium into a vision of perfected society, Winstanley tells a story of history. This story describes history's path and coming end. In comparable accounts by writers as divergent as Hegel, Marx, Dewey, and Hitler, history operates through humans rather than because of them.[3] Winstanley's history works similarly: it is powered by a supernatural force. But unlike many of the ideologically diverse writers who follow him, Winstanley deals gently with people in forecasting the path to his predicted utopia. That is, he alternates between stressing its inevitability and insisting that it cannot be imposed on some by others. Like Wayne's argument in planning Struggle, Winstanley's approach promotes revised experiences that encourage people to come to ideological change on their own rather than attempting to impose such change. Similarly, his texts move from describing holistic social transformation to advocating specific local action for particular groups in their existing conditions. An example appears in *The True Levellers Standard*:

> For the People have . . . laid out their Monies, and shed their Bloud [in the Civil Wars] . . . that the Oppressed might be set Free, Prison doors opened, and the Poor peoples hearts comforted by an universal Consent of making the Earth a Common Treasury, that they may live together as one House of Israel, united in brotherly love into one Spirit; and having a comfortable livelihood in the Community of one Earth their Mother. . . . And this is one Reason of our digging and labouring the Earth one with another, That we might work in righteousness, and lift up the Creation from bondage; For so long as we own landlords in this Corrupt Settlement, we cannot work in righteousness; for we should still lift up the Curse, and tread down the Creation, dishonour the Spirit of universal Liberty, and hinder the work of Restauration.
>
> Secondly, In that we begin to Digge upon *George-Hill*, to eate our Bread together by righteous labour, and sweat of our browes. . . . And that not only this Common, or Heath should be taken in and Manured by the People, but all the Commons and waste Ground in *England*, and in the whole World, shall be taken in by the People in righteousness, not owning any propriety; but taking the Earth to be a Common Treasury, as it was first made for all. (qtd. in Sabine 260)

Here Winstanley moves back and forth from telling world history to explaining and advocating the St. George's Hill group's very local project. The pamphlet's form as a manifesto encourages this kind of back and forth, producing a text that theorizes sociopolitical and economic change on the one hand and promotes a specific local project on the other. In fact, each move justifies and explains the other. The dialectic between them grounds the group's practices outside their texts. Specifically, these practices involve moving back and forth between intellectual discussion and material action such as communal subsistence farming. By linking the abstractions of his historical vision with such concrete local practices, Winstanley encourages audiences to make contact with the larger social potential of their choices. Thus he situates local, personal agency within such grand narratives, reintegrating the relation between self and larger historical forces. In these dialectics, each pole (theoretical/material and local/systemic) develops its opposite. The theory articulated in *The New Law* no doubt helped make the St. George's Hill project more meaningful to potential allies. Yet the work of the project itself prompted the Diggers to publish *The True Levellers Standard* to intervene in the larger social order and to protect themselves from military and civil authorities' potential repression.

The quoted passage from *The True Levellers Standard* thus shows the group working to accept the larger systems they cannot change and yet to change what they can, namely their personal and collective participation in the existing economic and sociopolitical systems. In Gestalt terms, it illustrates how they have seized environmentally available resources to pursue their goals, a crucial step in defining a practice of local agency that can work successfully with and in larger historical forces. Thus they move back and forth between acknowledging systems' power and maximizing their own agency, between depicting world history and working in their present.

Through these shifts, they move in and out of their predicted social future. This motion grounds Winstanley's fourth reconfiguration of agency, which focuses on the relation between self and others and so redefines the relation between self and civil authority. The Diggers use their vision of history's promised end to motivate audiences to revise their self-conceptions and habits. This use instantiates the kind of move Wayne argued Struggle needed to make to inspire participants with hope and purpose. But at the same time, Digger texts' shifts to contemporary circumstances repeatedly renounce any effort to impose their desired ends—the ideal society—on others. *The New Law* offers good examples of such back-and-forth moves:

> But this [the world's transformation] is not done by the hands of a few,
> or by unrighteous men, that would put the tyrannical government out

of other mens hands, and keep it in their own heart [or hands],[4] as we feel this to be a burden of our age. But it is done by the universall spreading of the divine power, which is Christ in mankind making them all to act in one spirit, and in and after one law of reason and equity. (qtd. in Sabine 180)

I do not speak that any particular men shall go and take their neighbours goods by violence, or robbery (I abhor it) as the condition of the men of the Nations are ready to do in this fleshly setled government of the world, but every one is to wait, till the Lord Christ do spread himself in multiplicities of bodies, making them all of one heart and one mind, acting in the righteousnesse one to another. It must be one power in all, making all to give their consent to confirm this law of righteousnesse and reason. (qtd. in Sabine 182–83)

The Civil Wars' violence had shown the True Levellers the destructive, dehumanizing aspects of revolution and its succession of coups. *The New Law* responds to these circumstances by promising a transformed society and striving to guide readers' energies toward such transformation. Yet at the same time it dissuades them from pursuing it through armed struggle. It declares such efforts yet another instance of the era's tyranny, and it urges readers instead to change their own self-conceptions and relationships with society's groups and practices. Like some of Winstanley's other textual moves, the insistence on nonviolence emphasizes that everyone is redeemable. Despite the spiritual and psychological pain in store for the recalcitrant well-to-do, they too will ultimately be saved and join the transformed millennial society. These rhetorical moves enact respect not only for Digger allies' individual agency but for opponents' agency as well. They construct a communal, consensual ground for civil authority and prioritize voluntary self-government that rejects coercive methods as well as voicelessness, armed rebellion as well as absolute authority. They support others' right to hold and act on different worldviews and define a limited set of acceptable means for pursuing social change. Thus Winstanley envisions an ideal society that will exclude no one and yet will obtain no one's inclusion by force. His texts establish ever-expanding boundaries around his future utopia. His efforts to forestall violent attempts to instantiate this utopia crucially reposition his history and its predicted ideal society. His texts put this goal into a dialectical relationship with Winstanley's present rather than attempting to annul that present. In short, *The New Law* carefully alternates between inspiring audiences toward its goals and directing their pursuit of those goals.

Thus the Digger texts reintegrate the self as an agent in dialectical relation to larger social, historical, and ideological forces. They use productive tensions between their dialectics' poles to synthesize sweeping world histories with local project descriptions, individual with communal focuses, and material with spiritual/intellectual experiences. They reconfigure aspects of individual agency to work with and in such larger forces. At the same time, these syntheses emphasize the role of social systems and seek to change those systems. The St. George's Hill group used their texts' dialectics to synthesize their community's intellectual and material practices, accomplishing two related goals. First, they constructed a history that reached backward and forward to culminate in their millennial vision by including all yet respecting others' agency. Second, they worked toward their vision by accepting and working within their present. By experimenting with rhetorical moves that achieve these syntheses, Winstanley's texts model language practices for fostering an individual agency that acts in dialectic with systemic forces.

5

Where We're At

LIKE THE Diggers, Struggle's participants used literate practices to shift their contact styles. As with the Diggers, this shift changed their relationships with others and with the larger systems they inhabited. Five of the eight summer 1996 Struggle participants took part in the individual, semistructured interviews, which used open-ended, focused questions. My analysis concentrates on Diane's interview because it most clearly illustrates a participant's use of Struggle's rhetorical strategies. I summarize moments in other participants' interviews when they relate directly to the analysis. Because Diane's interview focuses on her relationship with her son Ian, who participated with her in Struggle, I include brief excerpts from Ian's interview.

• • •

The pocket-sized tape recorder sat on the Umoja Room table's African-print cloth, obtrusive despite its microcassette size, especially when I double-checked the tape while Diane and I arranged ourselves near one end of the table. Her voice slightly gravelly and deeper from a head cold, Diane asked about my research, and I explained my interest in linking college-level education with communities such as those Struggle served. She affirmed the value of such work, and said, emphasizing grammar instruction, that school alone does not teach students "exactly the techniques they need when they go to college." I mentioned our conversation the preceding summer on how Ian's middle school teacher had encouraged him to write about his favorite topic, animals. I said I thought that would encourage his interest in writing and in learning the grammar and mechanics that concerned Diane.

The conversation shifted to Diane's efforts to focus Ian's attention on school. "I want to stay focused with him this year because of the fact that I feel that he'll have a tendency to get caught up with his classmates and goof off a little bit," she commented, explaining that he sometimes shifted his concentration from school to social life. "Well, he had a tendency to go that way, but I stayed on him about it, you know. I don't think he did as well as he could have done, you know? But there were times that he did apply himself; there were times that I made him apply himself, OK?" she continued. "But during those times, he was influenced a little by his classmates about what was going on in the street. But I stayed on him to say, 'This is not the way it's going to be. No matter what.'"

Listening to Diane, I remembered the steely note in her tone the previous year when her final-session Struggle conversation with Ian had emphasized her efforts to support him in school even when he resisted the work. During the preceding school year, she said, she had taken Ian to school because he had developed a habit of tardiness. She had arranged with her employer to arrive and leave later, Diane explained, so she could drive Ian to school to ensure that he arrived on time.

Describing Ian's changes in the current school year, which had begun several weeks before the interview, she said, "This year he took the initiative to get up, get dressed, and leave in a timely fashion." After I expressed approval, she commented, "He's matured a little bit." Noting that he had just entered ninth grade, she said, "I've seen a tremendous change in him, especially since he worked this summer." I told her that during his interview Ian had mentioned his summer job with a Community House program, and Diane replied that since he had held the position, Ian had shown much more respect for his parents' jobs. "He understands now what it means to get up and go to work, no matter whether you want to be there or not, you know?"

"Right," I answered quietly, recalling Ian's repeated expression of concern about finding a path that would lead him into an adult profession that met his needs for both material security and satisfaction in his work. He aired the concern both during his Struggle participation and during his interview. This concern figured centrally in at least three of the five interviews and pulsed strongly through a fourth. One adult participant had stressed the importance of holding a job she enjoyed and that offered her some autonomy in her work. Another, Joanne, had described facing a pay cut that probably totaled 20 to 30 percent of her income. She emphasized the stress of deciding how to handle the situation because she loved her job but did not know whether she could manage on the smaller paycheck. When I asked about her practical plans, she said she was taking things day by day to keep herself from worrying excessively.

As Diane continued describing Ian's response to his first job, she implicitly addressed these issues. "He liked the point about having his own money and not having to ask Mom or Dad," she commented. "And I think he loved the fact that he could say, '*Mom, I–I'll* take care of that,' you know?" She continued, quoting Ian, "'I have a little bit of money, I will take care of that.' To me that was a little sense of responsibility." Noting that he had opened his own bank account and kept it open even after the summer job had ended, she continued, "He was influential in buying his school clothes. I did not have to buy his school clothes this year. And he was very selective about where. . . . Last year, he just gave me a hard time about everything because, I believe, it was my money, and he didn't know the value of it. This year, he knows the value of it. And he was very selective."

"So he learned to shop," I commented.

"Yes, he did. He learned the value. Of money." Extending the point, Diane remarked, "He learned the value of time. Definitely, you know? Because, as I was trying to get to show him last year, being on time, when you have responsibilities like that, you must be able to compensate for that responsibility, and it means that if you're running late, you need to call and let them know you're running late. You can't assume that people know what's going on with you or [that] they can read your mind. You must speak your mind. If you're running late, it's your responsibility to call your job and say you're running late and why. OK? If you cannot attend, you need to call and let them know you cannot attend, instead of not showing up at all. No show, no call, you know?" Reiterating that Ian had learned more responsibility, she concluded, "I see a tremendous improvement."

Describing Ian's changes, Diane said she had perceived him as experiencing an "identity crisis," which had begun before the Struggle project and continued during the following year. Mentioning that the two of them had often blown up at each other prior to Ian's changes, she commented, "I have a feeling that since the Struggle program, since the work program [which supplied Ian's summer job], we don't do blowups like that anymore. We can talk them out. Definitely. *Ev-very* once in a while it has to go a little further than that, that it's . . . a demand. 'I'm demanding that you . . . as your parent, that you have to do something,' OK? But normally," she continued softly, "if we get mad at each other, then one of us is able to come back and apologize. I have seen him do that. At one time, it was beneath him to apologize. You know, 'I don't do that,'" she mimicked. "You know? But now he'll come back and say, 'Well, Mom, it was my fault,' and 'I'm sorry,' and we'll take it from that level. Or vice versa, I will go to him, and I'll say, 'I apologize for hollering or screaming at you, but these are the things that bring this out. And this is why I went to that level with you, because I should not have to go to the third or fourth request of asking you to do something.

"But after I go to the third time of saying, 'I need you to do something' or not do something, and it doesn't work, I've gotten to the point now, that I don't get upset at him. I just do it myself because I feel that he'll come back. And he'll want something from me, OK? And my motto has always been to give someone a dose of their own medicine. So when he comes back to me to say, 'Ma, I want something' or 'Mom, I need you to do something,' then, I try to do what he did to me. I either don't hear him; I don't answer him. Or," she said, extending the word, "I say 'OK' and don't do it, you know? And then when he comes back to say, 'Well, Mom, why didn't you do this?' or 'Mom, I asked you to do this,' then I can come back and say, 'Well, you know the shoe is on the other foot. Earlier today, you and I went through [a] similar situation, where I said, 'Ian, I needed you to do this, and you ignored me or you just didn't do it, or you took your good old time,'" she continued, elongating the phrase, "'about doing that.' I say, 'Now you see how it feels,'" she concluded, emphasizing each word. "'Because you need your mother to do the same thing.' You know?"

"So you do bring it to that explicit level of saying [why you did what you did]?" I asked.

"Oh yes. I do," Diane replied decisively. "Yes, exactly. I want you to see why. I want you not only to see it but to feel it and experience it. Definitely. So maybe next time, it'll be a little better." Diane described some specific examples, then commented, "I'm telling him, 'That's mutual respect. You want me to have respect for you. I'm the mother and you're the son. It has to be an equal thing.' . . . At this point, because he's so much older, and he's maturing, you have to equalize things . . . mutual respect. So, this is where I'm at with Gerald," she concluded, referring to Ian by his given name rather than the family nickname he typically used at the Community House.

Noting that strengthening relationships, especially parent-teen relationships, was at the heart of Struggle, I suggested we discuss Diane's work with Jody, her teenage Struggle partner. I asked what she had gained from that work, what was important to her about working with an unrelated partner. Later, I explained, I would ask her to link her answer to her relationship with Ian.

"What I got, or what was important," she began meditatively. "Listening. To listen to what Jody was saying, actually listening to what he was saying." She paused, exhaling. "Respecting, basically." She continued, "And maybe then advising. As to say, 'Well, Jody, I believe if I were in that particular situation, this is how I would handle it,' instead of telling Jody, 'This is how you should handle it.' I don't believe you should ever tell anybody how to go about maintaining or dealing with his business. I believe that you have to use yourself always as an example. I wanted Jody to identify by using myself as an example." She continued, "One of the things that Jody and I talked a lot about was [that] when I was younger, believe me, we did similar things, OK? And I would explain to Jody, 'Oh, Jody, when I was younger, I did something very similar to that,' you know? And maybe how I handled that situation. Or how I did not handle that situation and what the outcomes were."

Diane's account echoed with the notes of Ian's description of a changing relationship between himself and Diane. I interviewed him just before talking with her, and as she spoke, their descriptions harmonized.[1] When I asked him how family members reacted lately to disagreements, he emphasized the changed dynamics. "Sometimes we don't even argue, we just [pause]. We say one thing, another, and it goes. [We] go our separate ways on it."

"Do you ever just talk things out?" I asked.

Noting that Diane now sent him to his room only rarely, he added, "We talk, too. After we settle down first. So that we go back and talk about it." Sketching a recurring dispute about his desire to venture out of his neighborhood and downtown, he explained that sometimes after a talk he would get permission to go later.

Continuing the description of her Struggle work with Jody, Diane noted that she often prompted him to consider "both sides of the situation" he was describing. When I requested an example, she mentioned Jody's love of sports. Reiterating that every situation had its good and bad sides, she applied the formula to Jody's interest. Diane demonstrated, repeating her words to Jody, "'The good side is the fact that you're interested in sports. And what it may be able to do for you [and] your goals.' OK, his goal was to . . . be able to have a home for his mother. He talked a lot about wanting to have a home for his mother."

Diane went on to explain that her conversation with Jody had focused on asking him "What is it you need to do?" to pursue his goal. "I didn't know if he considered it a bad side," she explained, "that you have to stay focused, OK?" She clarified, "You have to do well in school, and I believe nowadays young kids think that's something bad. 'Oh, I have to do well in school. I can't deal with certain friends'—you know, is being [a] bad [side of the situation]." Tying Jody's situation to her own prior experiences, she said, "I know, when I was younger, Jody's age or older, when my parents told me there were certain friends that I was not allowed to associate with, I considered that to be bad. But . . . in the other sense, I'm telling Jody that you may have heard that to be bad, but look at your goal, look at your dream. Look what it is that your friends may be into that may hinder [pause for emphasis] you from obtaining this goal that you one day may want to have for your mother. And yourself." Concluding her example, Diane said she emphasized "what you may have to let go of in order to achieve. And whether or not you're willing. If you're willing or you're strong enough to be able to do something like that."

"To do that letting go so that you can stay focused?" I asked.

"Mmhmn. Mmhmn. And if not, then," she paused, "what is it that I can do, or what is it that the Struggle program can do to help you?" Diane's next comments seemed to call implicitly for such negotiation. After asking what she or Struggle could do to help Jody pursue his goals, she continued, "Maybe it might not be me, maybe it might be you," she said, gesturing toward me. "Or maybe it might be Miss Joyce. Or Pastor Wayne. You know. Somebody within the program that you [Jody] may be able to relate to, who may be able to help you understand and guide you in letting go of some of the rougher parts of your life, OK?"

Expanding her focus, she continued, "I really look at the streets, for young kids, as being rough. Definitely. I really do. Especially nowadays because there's so much happening out there in the streets, you know, and I don't believe that you should totally give up the street because the street does educate. But I do believe that they need to be able to [pause] know the difference, OK?"

"And when you say 'know the difference,' you mean between . . . ?" I asked.

"What's good and what's bad out there."

"OK. Like . . . how far is too far?"

"How far is too far," Diane affirmed. "When you're being approached, OK?"

Emphasizing that she believed Struggle educated children on that issue through exchanges with adults, she explained, "To say, if you're ever approached, if you ever come into situations like that while you're out there in the street, mostly my thing is to think. Think about it before you just jump into it, you know?"

Diane's emphasis uncannily echoed Ian's earlier description of what had been important to him about his work with his adult Struggle partner, Maureen. Near the beginning of my interview with Ian, I asked him, "What makes you say it was a good project? What would you say you got out of it?" He replied, Maybe 'cause you worked with other people that you don't know, know about or [pause] I dunno, mostly just talkin'. Git me off the street. Now that was good, too. 'Cause I usually be hangin' up the street sometime."

When I asked what he had liked about talking with his adult partner or about working with people he did not know, Ian replied after a moment's silence, "I dunno; she really talked about what's goin' on in her family. An' I talked about what's goin' on in my family, so we had some type of a similar problem." I asked which problems he had in mind, and Ian answered without hesitation, "Like the areas we live in." He added, "Or, growin' up now, there's a lot of crime out there that ev'rybody . . . You still gotta keep your head straight so you don't get caught up in that mess. 'Cause where I live at, the Hill, they've got a whole lotta stuff up there, 'specially Robinson Court. They got a whole lotta stuff. I don't really hang up there. Prob'ly get up there an' play football once in a while but nuttin' much. . . . Since we [he and Maureen] talked about that kinda stuff . . ." he continued. "'Cause we have similar things to worry about."

When I asked whether the conversations with Maureen had helped him to deal with those things, Ian paused, then answered, "It helped a little bit. 'Cause when we started talkin' about that, I really realized that [pause] there's a lotta stuff goin' down out there today. You can't be caught up in that mess."

"OK," I answered quietly. "What made you realize it more from talking to her?"

"The way she just talked about all that . . . the killing, and the drug stuff out there. 'Cause I know a couple that sell drugs up there, an' . . . She just got me straight on stuff like that." He continued, "I wasn't really payin' that much attention before she started talking 'cause I usually just go up there ev'ry day, but [pause] I don't really go up there no more. . . ." Here I could hear the cadences of his mother's speech. Explaining, he said, "I go to the parks or go to my friends' houses or some'n' or stay on the street. I don't really do all that stuff no more."

"Instead of bein' up at Robinson Court?" I asked.

"Yeah. Or Upper Webster, . . . I don't really go up there no more. Pay no attention to them."

"Well," I replied, "that sounds like a big change."

"It is," Ian breathed, his pitch rising, then falling markedly, despite his quiet speech. "Mostly, I don't know . . . I just don't do that anymore."

His intonation seemed to preclude hearing his description as glib, evoking instead emotional dimensions beyond my knowledge. Ian's words echoed in my ears as I listened to Diane. She continued, "Because sometimes if you just take one minute and think about what it is that you are ready to get yourself into, you may not do that. Or you still may do it, but you may do it with a conscience, OK? To say, 'Well, I was told if I do this, then this may be the outcome of this,'" she said. "And sometimes just thinking about that will stop you from doing what it is you're doing. Even after you have already started doing that." She concluded, "And as I explained it to Jody, and as I explain it to my son, it's just common sense."

I mentioned that this could be difficult for teens because they sometimes felt so caught up in the moment, and she replied, "Right. But I'm saying common sense will let you just think about it. One moment. One moment. If you just think about it for a moment, there may be . . . a level of hesitation there. Definitely. You may have the strength—or the courage—to say, 'No. No, this is not me.' And another thing that I think was important for me to try to express to Jody—and I use Jody in the same sense as I use my son, because they're both the same age—that you have to be an individual. I express to them to be an individual and not a follower, you know?" She explained that in conversations with Ian, "I tell him, 'One day—you may not know—you may be a leader. Because you were an individual first, and not a follower.' So a lot of times when my son is confused about certain things," she continued, "I stress to him to be an individual. When you're in situations where you just don't know what to do, think about being an individual first. Definitely."

At that point, I asked Diane if we could return to what she said she had gained from working with Jody, her teen Struggle partner, namely, listening and conveying mutual respect. When she agreed, I asked, "Would you say that doing that work with Jody helped you to change your relationship with Ian in ways that you wanted to? Or that it made a difference, a positive difference, in your relationship with Ian?"

"Yes, it did," she replied, her tone rising, then falling, in decisive emphasis. "I do think so because I looked at the fact that I advised, OK? Because he was not my son, so therefore I couldn't demand that he do things." Later, hearing the echo of Struggle's instructional materials in Diane's response, I concluded that if she had taken up this language, she had probably done so because it intersected with her deep commitment to parenting Ian well. "Because I learned how to advise Jody," she continued, "I believe I was able to carry that over into the relationship that I had with Ian. And now I don't . . . demand so much that he do things, OK? Or get angry to the point that it's a physical anger, OK? I try to advise my son as if [pause] this is the way that it should be done." She went on, "I listen more to what he says, and I learned that if I want to strike up a conversation with my son, I have to actually go for the things that interest him first," she concluded.

After referring to the preceding summer's conversations about Ian's love for animals, Diane commented, "Since then, my son has become a great lover of cars." After the interview, I wondered whether Diane had taken up this emphasis on Ian's interests as a result of our conversations on the link between interest and learning. I mentioned that Ian had raised the topic during his interview and attributed his new interest to Diane's gift of a magazine subscription.

"I don't know if you know that," I said, explaining why I had mentioned it.

"No," she replied. "No. In fact, he mentioned that not too long ago, was I going to renew my subscription to *Motor Trend*. And at that point in time, I would tell him that I didn't take it out in the first place, somebody else did it for me. And I just passed it on to him because I was not interested in *Motor Trend*. Well, that's great. I didn't know, but I'm glad to hear it. Definitely. That may make me take it out again. Definitely."

• • •

A Gestalt analysis of Diane's and Ian's interviews illustrates how their Struggle work prompted them to reorganize the evidence of their experiences and thus to experiment with alternative rhetorical strategies. In doing so, they began changing their contact styles. My examination of Diane's rhetorical strategies implies a revision of Goodman's distinction between aesthetic (or contact-producing) and verbalizing (or alienating) language practices by redefining aesthetics in terms of function and form, rather than primarily in terms of form.

Both Diane and Ian found key conditions of their experience changed during their Struggle work, and those changes prompted shifts in their organization, or interpretation, of these experiences. Struggle offered such changed conditions because its structure produced adult-teen relationships that paralleled parent-child relationships but also incorporated significant differences. This structure prompted adult and teen Struggle partners to experiment with new rhetorical strategies and allowed them to experience an alternative relational style.

For instance, Diane's description of her work with Jody, her teen Struggle partner, emphasized how the program's structure changed the conditions of her experience, in Goodman's terms. As a result, the evidence provided by those conditions shifted for her, and her experience of them changed. She pointed out one key difference in these conditions when she stressed that she could not demand that Jody do things because he was not her son. As a result, she adopted the rhetorical strategies of advising and listening. In explaining how her work with Jody transferred to her relationship with her son, Diane noted that she found herself demanding things from Ian less frequently and responding less often with visceral anger. This shift in her emotional and physiological experience illustrates the impact of her revised perception and subsequently changed rhetorical habits. Those habits developed from her work with Jody, in which she described using herself as an example and encouraging him to consider both sides of a situation. Her characterization of the interactive approach she used with Jody, "respecting basically," describes the contact style she initiated with Ian by bringing new rhetorical moves into their exchanges.

In his interview, Ian explained how his work with his adult Struggle partner, Maureen, similarly led him to interpret his experience differently. When I asked him why he had said Struggle was a good project, Ian emphasized the benefit of talking with a formerly unknown adult about the dangers of living in poor, crime-ridden neighborhoods. Because Maureen had risked involvement with the drug trade and suffered serious consequences as a result, Ian's perception of these dangers shifted. He had heard descriptions of them from his mother before joining Struggle, but the changed conditions of his interaction with Maureen positioned him differently and encouraged greater contact. Ian's description of his revised perception of those dangers and practices for dealing with them (such as changing his regular haunts) suggests he had reinterpreted the conditions of his experience on the basis of his interactions with Maureen. Further, his speech's echo of his mother's cadences implies he may have begun to take up some of her concerns about street life after his conversations with Maureen. Thus he revised his interpretations of both his neighborhood's conditions and his mother's position on them.

Both Ian and Diane described using new rhetorical moves in their post-Struggle interactions with one another. Such moves suggest that their reorganizations of experience led mother and son to experiment with changing their rhetorical habits and thus their contact styles. For instance, in explaining how she sometimes gave Ian a dose of his own medicine by failing to keep a promise to him when he had done the same with her, Diane indicated she had linked an established rhetorical move with a new one. She said she had long believed in prompting people to experience the effects generated by their own behavior, so in using that strategy, she drew on an established habit. But Diane also emphasized that in her interactions with Ian she had stopped repeating requests and getting upset, instead paralleling his treatment of her. She wanted Ian to experience the emotions she had. Her formulation evokes Goodman's emphasis on experience as the decisive factor in changing communication patterns. It demonstrates how Diane married rhetorical strategies learned in Struggle with carefully chosen existing strategies to shift her contact style with Ian. Her work exemplifies the reintegration Goodman associates with growth.

Similarly, she described her own and Ian's new uses of apology to defuse conflicts, emphasizing that before they participated in Struggle, he would not apologize. Both she and Ian pointed out that the two experienced fewer blowups, and he commented that some arguments were even avoided entirely, because mother and son were able to calm down and then talk through their differences. The parallels between their descriptions, particularly given that neither heard the other's interview, suggest not only that they had begun developing new rhetorical habits but that those rhetorical habits were changing their contact styles and their relationship. (In their interviews, Janine and her adult partner each described similar changes in family rhetorical patterns and attributed those changes to the rhetorical strategies they learned in their Struggle interactions.) Finally, Diane's stress on her post-Struggle efforts to engage Ian in conversation by appealing to his interests indicates another rhetorical move she used to establish a contact style based on respect.

Some of the rhetorical habits Diane described have implications for Goodman's theory of aesthetic language. They emerge in her explanation of how she used common sayings to prompt Jody and Ian to develop greater awareness of their range of available choices and the implications of those choices. Goodman opposes aesthetic language uses to clichés, arguing that the former encourage contact while the latter consist of verbalizing, or abstracted talk that promotes alienation. But Diane's explanation illustrates a complex, rather than oversimplified, approach to situations, an approach carefully crafted to encourage greater contact and expanded awareness.

For instance, Diane's admonition to consider both sides of the situation initially sounds likely to foster black-and-white thinking. Because such thinking cannot address the complex dynamics of desire and resistance, it is, in Goodman's terms, likely to increase alienation and decrease contact with a person's own experience. Yet Diane's description of how she used the admonition with Jody reveals a multifaceted approach. By repeatedly using the term *friends* to describe associates Jody might need to avoid, she highlighted the situation's complexity. While she depicted these people as bad influences who might hinder Jody in his goals, her semantics also emphasized their personhood and emotional connections to her teen partner.

Diane's use of the truism "think before you just jump into it" similarly incorporates multiple possibilities. She glossed her use by explaining that thinking beforehand might lead a teen to not do something, or at least to do it "with a conscience." Calling the habit of thinking associated with this saying common sense, Diane said it could prompt a moment of hesitation that might give a teen the ability to reject a temptation. Both of her alternative possibilities, doing something with a conscience or hesitating long enough to recognize personal discomfort, involve augmenting proprioception and perception. In each scenario, the adolescent contacts conflicted feelings about a potential choice and as a result perceives the choice differently. The scenarios illustrate how Diane was using common wisdom to encourage Jody and Ian to increase their contact with their own internal experiences and thus to shift their perceptions of external circumstances.

Her formulation of the scenarios acknowledges the possibility of internal conflict and of delay between changed perception and changed action. In Gestalt terms, it allows space for teens to make contact with their desires and resistances and thus to generate creative responses as a result of their expanded contact. Like Struggle's prompts and Winstanley's uses of biblical verses, Diane's version of common sense encourages teens to shift their perceptions of external circumstances by positioning them to extend their proprioception. Ian's account of how his perception of his neighborhood and its dangers changed after his conversations with Maureen suggests he engaged in just the kind of hesitation, increased proprioception, and shifted perception his mother advocated when she invoked common sense.

Complex uses of clichés appeared in other interviewees' descriptions as well. Joanne explained how she had applied the idea that "when times are hard, you don't have to just keep yourself down. You can get up." Saying that she had needed to learn stress management to control newly diagnosed diabetes, she noted that she had used those techniques to deal with an impending pay cut. Janine described how she had insisted a peer refrain from judging a deaf adult. The other teen, she explained, had mistaken sign language for gang signs until pressed to listen before judging. Like Diane's uses of common wisdom, Joanne's draws on a truism to expand proprioception and so to shift perception. Janine's positioned her peer to extend her contact with a situation before moving into action.

In each case, the use, rather than the form, of clichéd language determined its role in diminishing or expanding contact. These cases suggest revisions to Goodman's definition of aesthetic language. Such revisions would make his distinction between aesthetic and verbalizing language more useful. They suggest that to define a language practice as aesthetic, we must examine its effects for users (both speaker or writer and audience). That is, we must try to understand, insofar as possible, the phenomenological experiences of writer and audience. Only then can we establish which forms foster contact for which audiences and under what circumstances. Rather than strictly a matter of form, aesthetics in this view becomes a function we can understand only by combining formal analysis with empirical study of specific language uses and their conditions. Such combined examinations provide a richer, more nuanced understanding of what effects various language forms produce with diverse speakers and audiences in different circumstances. Thus revising Goodman's theory of aesthetic language encourages us to study patterns in the ways various groups use different rhetorical forms to promote or diminish contact.

• • •

As Diane spoke, I remembered Ian's efforts during his interview to make connections between his interests and possible future careers. Twice he mourned his high school's loss of its football program due to lack of funding. Mentioning the possibility of football and biology scholarships to college, Ian reemphasized his interest in veterinary school during the interview and mentioned reading books on the subject. "Animal books. Or car mechanic. I know a lot about cars and stuff. Some'n' to get a job that I can live the rest of life for, but [pause] those are the three subjects I wanna do, then [football, veterinary work, and auto repair]."

"When did you think of car mechanics?" I asked. "Because I don't remember you talking about that."

"I didn't really get into cars until my mom started orderin' these car magazines. To keep me doin' some'n'. I just would take 'em to school an' after we do work I read 'em an' just got interested in 'em," he continued, accenting each syllable of "interested." "'Cause they talk on stuff about the cars, like the valves, the horsepower, the fuel chambers." As he concluded, Ian's speech grew quiet but emphatic, as if to underscore his interest.

"You're really getting into the nuts and bolts of the engine, then?" I asked, struck by his description, which accented not the cars' prowess but the knowledge of their workings.

"Yeah. I don't know how, but they just kinda took me by storm. I just got interested in 'em." Later, though, Ian returned to his interests in football and veterinary school, naming those as his main options. Only after the interview did I recall that he had already said, "I'm still thinkin' 'bout the vet'inarian an' football, but mechanics, that's just a third idea. Just in case."

He described the mechanic option as a job to "live the rest of life for," just before referring to his three career ideas. Initially, I heard only an interest in financial security in his words. But later I concluded that in the context of his emphasis on his interests, the word *for* suggested Ian's quest for a sense of fulfillment in his future work.

I described to Diane Ian's thoughtfulness about potential future paths. She replied that she often used herself as an example with Ian, especially regarding education. "One of the things I always tell Ian is that, well, he's going to graduate. I tell him that 'you're going to graduate from school.' There's no excuse, there's no reason, no nothing in this world that can justify why you did not graduate from school unless you are not on the face of this earth. And that is beyond my decision." Diane explained how she used her own life as an example, citing her father's insistence that his five daughters graduate from high school. His demands had pushed them to do so, she explained, but he had provided no support, leaving that entirely to her mother. Diane speculated that she might have performed better academically and in sports if he had taken a more active role and described how she explained to Ian her own commitment to actively support him.

She noted, "I told him [Ian], 'I'm not going to be like that. You're going to graduate from school. I'm going to tell you in the same means my father told me. You're going to graduate from school. But the only thing that I'm going to do that my father didn't do for us, is that I'm going to be there to help you. I'm going to help you in school." Listening, I admired Diane's sophisticated, self-conscious efforts to simultaneously draw from and revise her family's practices and discourses. This approach suggested that Diane's use of Struggle's moves and her interaction with her teen partner, Jody, were intellectual tools she had taken up to pursue that ongoing project. I commented that her approach differed significantly from her father's.

Agreeing, she said she supported Ian by helping him organize his assignments, keeping in touch with his teachers, and providing help and encouragement to complete his homework. "School's very important because [pause] if I would've applied myself back then, then a lot of the things that I'm doing now, I would not have to do." When I asked for clarification, she explained, "Basically, I had to go back and reeducate myself. And I'm trying to help them [her children] not to have to do that. In order for me to be where I am and doing the things that I'm doing, I had to go back and reeducate myself."

Linking her adolescent experience with her children's, Diane concluded, "Not only am I making it [graduation] a demand for Gerald and Shamila [her daughter], but I'm showing them the means of how to go about doing that. The alternatives, you know? There are alternatives here. There are choices here. [They] may not always be choices you want to make. But they are choices," she finished articulating her words distinctly and slowly. "So therefore, if you make that choice, then nine chances out of ten you've got to stick to it, you know? But you do have a choice." She reiterated this position, then repeated, "It may not be the choice you want to make, but . . . you have a choice. You're not a victim. 'You're not a victim,' that's what I tell them.

Believe it or not, I saw that on TV, and it just came to light: yes, that definitely makes sense. 'You're not a victim because you do have choices. It may not be the choice you want to make, but it is a choice. There are people who don't have choices in this world, who are victims. But you're not one of them,'" Diane concluded, articulating the last five words with soft intensity.

She reiterated her emphasis on agency in discussions with Ian, her efforts to point out his limited but available range of choices. "I just always get him to open up his eyes and see that his situation is not as bad as he thinks it is. Definitely. Hopefully he'll capitalize on it. And make the right choices." Explaining that she encouraged Ian to get involved in activities that would prompt thinking, she commented, "If we get back to the Struggle program, the Struggle program makes you think. Definitely. It makes you think."

I said Diane seemed to be helping Ian find the tools he needed to pursue his dreams. "I'm hoping so," she replied. "I leave it open. My eyes, basically, open, because what you see is not always the way it is. I try to be very open-minded, but I also try to [pause] weigh out—how do I want to say it?—justice. You know? Both sides of the scale." Reiterating her emphasis on pausing to think, Diane noted that she encouraged Ian to ask people if he could get back to them if he needed time to think about a decision. She said she also urged him to explain his decisions. "I think people are more understanding . . . or more likely to understand." I commented that this approach could encourage listeners to respect the decision being explained.

"Definitely," Diane replied. "Yes, so that's where we're at."

• • •

In addition to revealing Struggle participants' accomplishments, constructing a Gestalt reading of their interviews changed my perceptions, rhetorical habits, and contact style. I came to see and use critical theory differently. That change revised my goals as an ethnographer, and prompted me to rethink my understanding of the relations between individual and systemic change. The interviews expanded my contact to shift my perceptions, interactive habits, and contact style.

Developing this interpretation of the interviews shifted my view of critical theory, prompting me to reground it in Struggle participants' uses of cultural products, rhetorical strategies, and literate practices. For instance, before joining Struggle, I valued work on the violence inherent in schooling by such researchers as Erickson, Graff, Ogbu, and Willis. Years after my Struggle participation, I still value this work, but I use it differently. In my earlier readings, I understood it primarily as an argument for systemic change; a demonstration that schooling socializes working-class students into materially exploitative, psychologically eviscerating roles; and a warning about how false consciousness hobbles efforts toward systemic change by siphoning people's energies from collective movements into individual advancement. Working with Struggle's participants brought me greater awareness of their experiences of the issues facing many working-class and African American families. Through it, I heard alternate accounts of the sociocultural conditions faced by the groups such educational researchers study. This contact shifted my perception.

For example, hearing Diane's account of how Ian learned to handle his first job and new pocket money, I recalled Ian's growing recognition that his neighborhood offered dangerous opportunities. These characterizations repositioned Ian's Struggle emphasis on schooling and its socialization. They suggested people in Ian's and Diane's circumstances might knowingly choose this socialization, despite its costs. They emphasized its power to help Ian avoid the quicksand of street life by going to college and establishing a career rather than joining the one in ten African American men between twenty-five and twenty-nine in prison (see "Crime").

Similarly, Diane's admonitions to Jody about choosing his associates carefully heightened my awareness of the potential uses of ideology. I had respected critical theory's point that calls for sacrifice in the name of education can produce self-serving, bourgeois efforts to socialize people from outside white middle-class culture into its worldview. But that call sounded quite different to me when Diane articulated it because I had seen her concern for Ian and Jody and her commitment to helping Ian avoid the devastating circumstances his partner Maureen had faced. While I did not feel authorized to make such a call, my contact with the Struggle participants' concerns and goals led me to support marginalized groups when they made that choice.

Thus my use of critical theory shifted. I concluded that if I read schooling's socialization strictly as co-optation or false consciousness that undermines social-justice movements, I would need to ignore Struggle participants' concerns. I would take the position that Ian and Diane should sacrifice his individual chances to instead invest their energies in pursuing systemic change. I decided I could not ethically take that position for anyone else. My Struggle contact increased my awareness that I had chosen to professionalize in a way I hoped would promote such change but that did not entail the kind of systemic challenge Winstanley's group undertook. That contact strengthened my sense of obligation to support others' efforts to negotiate their own compromises with the existing socioeconomic order.

I did not see that order as any less exploitative or problematic. But the Struggle interviews prompted me to revise my approach to addressing it. Issues such as interviewees' recurring concern about balancing job satisfaction with income led me away from an idealist position toward a more negotiated approach. For instance, that concern changed how I use Spivak's interpretations of Marx. She reads his work as both deploying and erasing humanist social values when he envisions fair relations of production and exchange (see esp. "Limits and Openings" 97–98, 108–9). I had found her reading persuasive but stopped with its conclusion that institutions, even revolutionary efforts, inevitably reify ideals and push people into more or less ill-fitting roles. I had focused on Spivak's warnings against imposing an agenda on others, the impossibility of representing others, and the dangers of accepting uncritically the repressive ideologies often espoused by exploited groups.

The Struggle interviews persuaded me that individuals within such groups exercise agency, however limited, in choosing whether and how to negotiate proffered agendas; that they often use ideology in complex, strategic ways; and that investigating people's felt experiences can give at least partial voice to erased values rather than trying to evade them. For instance, when Diane took up my emphasis on honoring learners' interests, her commitment to supporting Ian's academic and personal development suggests she did so to further her own long-established agenda. Thus investigating others' phenomenological experiences supports explicit negotiations between ideals and felt experience. In this case the interviews moved me away from privileging abstract theories of revolutionary social change that impose their visions on others without respect for those others' concrete objections. They suggest that privileging such theories undermines the possibilities for me, as an academic, to build coalitions with community members and groups. Instead, they led me to study community members' perceptions of their experiences and to negotiate my own goals, such as systemic change, with the goals of those most exploited by the existing system. They imply that to work toward social change without imposing ideals on others, I need to include support for people most systemically exploited. In taking this approach, I seek, like Winstanley, to synthesize ideals with existing conditions, to reconcile my values with others' to promote an equitable, inclusive community that invites rather than coerces membership.

This changed use of critical theory prompted me to revise my goals in doing ethnography. I had been strongly influenced by critical ethnography's emphasis on seeking creative writing strategies to address the problems of representation. For instance, critical ethnography's arguments on the dangers of (mis)representing one's subjects led me to try to craft more dialogic depictions in which I included subjects' self-representations.[2] Its arguments on incorporating social change as part of ethnography's agenda led me to try to make my text accessible to my subjects as well as to academic readers. The new use of critical theory prompted by my Struggle work did not erase these goals but made them secondary to another set.

These newer goals emphasize understanding existing conditions and my subjects' phenomenological experiences of them to reconcile my ideals with both. To negotiate with others, I need to understand their perceptions and experiences insofar as I can. To do so, I must increase my awareness of how I participate in the existing exploitative system. As Lu and Horner argue, I can best address ideology and the gaps between representation and experience by examining the gaps between my own representations and experiences. Through that work, I develop greater awareness of my role in perpetuating existing inequities and stronger potential for changing my participation. That awareness heightens my sensitivity to the nuances of others' experiences. Critical theory showed me the all-pervasiveness of ideologies, discourses, and power relations. The Struggle interviews highlighted participants' strategic work with them. Hearing that work and its efficacy and complexity, I, like Winstanley, decided that the best way I can encourage social change is to revise my own role within such systems. I concluded that as one person changes her role in an interactive system, its dynamics shift, inviting other participants to change their roles and so revising the system itself.[3]

Thus my goals as an ethnographer moved toward increasing my holistic contact with subjects' perceptions and with my role in the systems we inhabit. The new approach to critical theory persuaded me that empirical work, particularly qualitative research, provides a crucial tool in expanding such contact. This contact reshapes the intersection of the abstract with the concrete and of ideals with existing circumstances. It highlights the need—and the viable possibilities—for changing all four. As Goodman shows, it fosters spontaneous reorganizations of awareness and so encourages new contact styles. Thus it provides a concrete way for academics to develop coalitions with the people who figure centrally in critical theory.

As Goodman explains, such growth takes root in the experience of risk, loss, and change inherent in genuine contact. The Struggle interviews pushed me to undertake this process. For instance, they revised my initial response to Diane's declaration at the end of the Struggle project that one of her goals for Ian was for him to buy a house for her. Traditional psychological theory reads such a parent-child relationship as an unhealthy reverse dependency in which the parent seeks inappropriate support from a child. Influenced by this view, I felt uncomfortable when Diane mentioned her hope. But during the post-Struggle interview, when she mentioned encouraging Jody toward a similar goal, I realized it might embody a more communal, interdependent ethic than the individualist, independent persona (or myth) privileged by mainstream psychology. To see this alternative possibility, I needed to risk my adherence to the model I had initially held.

Such shifts both resulted from and encouraged a developing contact process in which ethnography unearths my presuppositions and puts them into dialogue with those of my subjects. This contact process demands that I respect those self-representations rather than simply filing them within the categories provided by my preexisting conceptual systems (though of course it inevitably involves integrating them with those conceptual systems as well). This contact style better positions me not only to listen to subjects but, in Spivak's terms, to speak to them.

This new contact reorganized my understanding of systemic change. Rather than perceiving individual agency as myth, co-opted action, or impossibility, I came to hear its dialectic with systemic and historical forces. Despite the power of ideology, discourse, and institutional structure, I heard in the Struggle interviews the echoes of an agency with personal and systemic implications. Diane's use of truisms about common sense, individualism, and choices recognized that however desirable systemic change might be, teens such as Ian and Jody have to live in their existing circumstances. Her strategies respected those circumstances' constraints while offering rhetorical habits designed to help such adolescents flourish. That approach could move young, urban black men from the stereotypical roles assigned them by mainstream discourses into other scripts.

Such possibilities emerge in several interviewees' emphasis on linking desires for job satisfaction with the goal of financial security. This emphasis challenges an institutionalized education that teaches working-class and lower-middle-class people to tolerate boredom and define themselves either as rebels or compliant employees (see Erickson, Graff, Ogbu, and Willis). Like the Diggers' challenge to their assigned social role as wage laborers, it has the potential to revise a system that demands an underclass of unemployed, underemployed, and poor people. Like Winstanley's project, it strives to shift people's experiences and expectations of work. For instance, in her interview, Janine described "working toward [her] talent," an approach advocated by a teacher she seated at her metaphoric Struggle table of advisers. Through that approach, she developed her initial plan to pursue a health care career, which she saw as a realistic goal, by defining it more specifically. She first planned to become a nurse but later decided to pursue pediatric nursing for deaf children because it better fit her interest in helping people with disabilities. Janine reshaped her approach to the work, positioning her desired job not only as a means of subsistence but also as a source of personal satisfaction. Further, she integrated her teacher's rhetorical strategy (and suggestion of a career teaching sight- and hearing-impaired children) with her prior interest in health care work. Her shift illustrates the power of Wayne's approach to work as destiny. It highlights the power of limited individual agency that works dialectically with systemic forces.

Similarly, in her interview Joanne explained she had not often thought about her goals before participating in Struggle but that doing so had shifted her concerns. She moved from her focus on wanting children to "goals that I can do," namely, asking her employer to finance the courses she needed to become certified as a nurse's aide. These cases suggest that Diane's use of truisms to emphasize agency can support the goals of people most affected by exploitative systems, rather than reinforcing self-destructive behaviors or solidifying class boundaries. While middle-class whites might believe the myth of absolute agency, in Struggle I heard participants' often sharply felt lack of agency. Further, I heard how they used Struggle's rhetorical practices to support a limited agency that both advanced their individual interests and carried implications for systemic change. With that recognition and in a current context in which I did not see a strong coalition for social change emerging, I shifted my own work toward this change, from seeking collective efforts to supporting such individual revisions.

6

To Feel That You Are a Citizen

COLLECTIVE MOVEMENTS toward social change emerged in the unionizing effort that swept U.S. industries in the 1930s and 1940s. The movement that unionized the steel industry in the greater Pittsburgh region and a local segment of this group, in Aliquippa, Pa., both used literate practices to promote personal and social change.

A geographically isolated company town whose civil and financial institutions were virtually all owned by the resident steel firm, Aliquippa (like many company towns) curtailed the circulation of information and ideas through civic repression, economic blackmail, and outright violence. Local unionizers started their own newspaper, the *Union Press*, not only to circulate information but also to model for readers a complex, scaffolded set of rhetorical strategies designed to reconstruct readers' contact styles and so promote a collective agenda. Excerpts of *Press* pieces, analyzed in the context of the histories of both movements, show how these activists' texts respond to their community's particular sociopolitical and economic circumstances. They use the changed conditions of experience provided by such factors as the new National Recovery Administration to address those circumstances.

In contrast with the Digger and Leveller efforts, the unionizing movements illustrate not the risk of annihilation by the larger society but the risk of co-optation. Like the seventeenth-century groups, the unionizers' platform posed a threat to their society's established habits of behavior and perception. But unlike its English counterpart, the U.S. political-economic system dealt with this threat by co-opting the activist movement rather than trying to destroy it. This approach almost surely resulted from fears of communist revolution generated by the unrest of the Great Depression and the specter of Russian Bolshevism. Local activists' strong political agenda and grassroots control were subsumed by a hierarchical, centrally run national union with close ties to the political establishment. To gain this establishment's tolerance, the union movement eschewed its initial goals of grassroots governance and far-reaching revisions of the socioeconomic and political orders.

Steeltown Simmers

The Bessemer furnaces' thick, dark smoke hung over the valleys, permanently obscuring the sun. Flame spurted intermittently from the blast furnaces to illuminate the clouds of smoke and surrounding hills with a volcanic light that bathed cavernous, often unpaved streets. Residents coughed, choked, and spat, laboring to breathe in a locale dominated by the mills' smokestacks. James Parton (later quoted by Lincoln Steffens) called Pittsburgh at the beginning of the twentieth century "hell with the lid off" (Bell 25; Powers xii, 2).[1]

By this period the surreal landscape created by the mills spanned the Pittsburgh region's rivers in the towns of Clairton, Glassport, McKeesport, Duquesne, Braddock, Rankin, Munhall, and Homestead to the southeast (Davin 5; Powers 2); Saltsburg, Apollo, Vandergrift, Leechburg, Natrona, Brackenridge, and New Kensington to the northeast (Meyehuber 42–43); and, gripping the steep hills, Aliquippa and Ambridge to the northwest. The mills' fumes permeated work and civic life in Steeltown, as the *Bulletin Index*, Pittsburgh's weekly magazine, christened the region (Davin 5). John A. Fitch, after a year's sociological research, describes plants in 1910 Steeltown operating continuously, most men working six 12-hour shifts one week and eight the next. Companies squeezed eight shifts into a seven-day workweek through the "long turn," which required men to work twenty-four hours every other Sunday to get twenty-four hours off the next. By 1910, steelworkers' holidays had been reduced to Christmas and July Fourth, while blast furnace crewmen could not take even these (Fitch 175–77).

"It is commonly understood that the United States Steel Corporation is the dominant force in politics in the mill towns," Fitch notes (229). George Powers, a 1930s union activist, explains that the company ran the local government, police force, and Republican Party, having established a one-party system: "On the day before elections, the steel company pay office placed sample ballots in the men's pay envelopes" (19). Steel firms had purged unions from their plants after the 1892 Homestead strike (Brooks 28). Yet Fitch depicts the steelworkers as seething, ripe for a "socialistic" political movement (235, 243). When the American Federation of Labor's (AFL's) 1919 effort to organize the steel industry crumpled under corporate red baiting, the firms suppressed civil rights, forbidding gatherings of four or more strikers, invading and searching houses, and beating occupants (Brooks 39).

Aliquippa Simmers

In Aliquippa, Steeltown's second largest community, no mill hand left the two Jones & Laughlin Steel Company (J & L) plants in response to the 1919 strike call. No AFL organizer could even enter town (Brooks 29; Casebeer 614). In the early 1900s, the two most important towns in the Beaver Valley, the Ohio River region west of Pittsburgh, were Ambridge and its sister Aliquippa, then known as Woodlawn (Brooks 111). In 1906, J & L broke ground for the first of its two largest steel plants on a seven-and-a-half-mile tract along the Ohio and, through its subsidiary, the Woodlawn Land Company, founded Woodlawn, its company town (Casebeer 629; Brooks 112).

J & L planned the town to maximize its control of Woodlawn citizens. One main road surrounded by ridges traverses Aliquippa, and on these hills the corporation built one housing plan per ridge, populating each plan with a particular ethnic group or mix of groups. Thus residents of one plan could not enter another without first descending the hill into town (Casebeer 619). Isolation of ethnic groups was deliberate and effective, and as in the rest of Steeltown, the Republican Party was the company's instrument. Steelworker Mike Zahorsky explains, in an interview with historian Eric Davin, "You couldn't get a job if you were a Democrat. It was like living in Russia, Siberia. . . . The company had their stooges out and you didn't know who you were talking to. . . . You couldn't trust a fellow you knew for 25 or 30 years" (qtd. in Davin 20–21). During the 1920s, J & L transported workers from mills to polls without regard to age or citizenship and pressured them to vote Republican (Casebeer 634).

J & L's viceroy from the teens through the thirties was J. A. C. Ruffner, school district and borough tax collector, chairman of the local Republican Party, director of both the Woodlawn Building and Loan and the Woodlawn Trust Company, and director and vice president of the First National Bank of Aliquippa. Ruffner also published the town's only newspaper, the *Aliquippa Gazette*, which printed, according to an out-of-town reporter, only "anti-union shrieking" and frequently ran boxed front-page stories warning residents against specific union agitators from outside the area (Davin 24; Casebeer 631). Ruffner's lieutenants were J & L police chief Harry G. Mauk and Aliquippa police chief and squire (or magistrate) Mike Kane, who also served as state chairman of the union-busting Constitutional Defense League (Davin 21, 22–23). Pete Muselin, a Croatian-immigrant steel worker who opposed J & L domination, describes Kane riding a motorcycle into boardinghouse kitchens, shouting, "Break it up, you Hunkies!" to disperse small groups of men playing cards and singing (Muselin 70). According to Muselin, the town's official and company police forces, the steel firm, and the town council were closely knit:

> The J&L police carried their guns openly wherever they went. Their purpose was to intimidate people. . . . The [J & L] coal and iron police were domiciled right next to the J&L main office there in Aliquippa. . . . They had all their machine guns, all their paraphernalia and tear gas and what have you, in there. And they had a shooting range right next door. Every day we could see them off of mom's dining room window, practicing with pistols, rifles, and so on. . . .
>
> If there was a vacancy on the police force in town, it was always filled with a Jones and Laughlin coal and iron policeman. . . . The borough council was composed of strictly Jones and Laughlin people and the town's professionals. . . . The council made the ordinances to suit J&L. . . . I would defy [the ordinances] on the grounds that they were unconstitutional. They would tell me . . . "We make the rules. This is not the United States. This is Woodlawn, and we're going to do what we please because J&L gives bread and butter to all these people. (69–70)

Lots along Franklin Avenue, the town's main thoroughfare, were available to merchants only through the Woodlawn Land Company. J & L owned the water company, the railroad, the bus company, and the trolleys. The only supplier of clothes and sundries was the Pittsburgh Mercantile Company, J & L's company store, which sold on credit and deducted payments from workers' paychecks (Casebeer 630–31). By the early 1930s, the corporation was the United States' fourth-largest steel company, and the Aliquippa Works alone, without J & L's other plants, would have ranked sixth nationally in both employment and gross tonnage (Casebeer 628). The corporation had achieved its success by controlling its Aliquippa workforce through civic domination.

In his 1933 book, *Labor and Steel*, historian Horace B. Davis notes steel firms' deliberate choice of isolated locations. He then explains the process of civic control:

> In [a company] town the steel company commonly exercises in fact, if not in law, all the functions of government. The company dominates education and organized religion. It is the state.
>
> The forces that police the steel communities exercise governmen-

tal authority but typically are paid by the companies and [are] responsible directly to them. In time of industrial peace, the mills and company towns are policed by special deputy sheriffs, usually in uniforms.
. . . In Pennsylvania these guards were formerly . . . known as the "coal
and iron police." . . . All [coal and iron police] commissions were
revoked in 1931, but the legal basis of the system remains unchanged.
The United States is the only important industrial country which per-
mits private payment of officers of the law. (qtd. in Casebeer 626–27)

These company-dominated police forces stifled unionizing efforts in
Aliquippa, charging anyone recruiting new union members with suspicious
activity, then arresting, questioning, and searching potential union activists.
They fined and beat anyone found carrying union cards (Casebeer 633). An
Erie school inspector reported that in the mid-twenties J & L officials had
revamped the Aliquippa schools, claiming they should prepare students not to
enter college and professions but to become "good workmen in the mill"
(Casebeer 632; "Inept School System"). Casebeer explains that workers were
fired not only for joining the Democratic Party but also for reading anarchist
literature. Muselin describes how the Aliquippa police periodically raided his
house, taking all books, periodicals, and bulletins, Marxist or not, and never
returning them (70).

On one occasion Muselin began to read the Declaration of Independence
aloud in public, and a policeman promptly accused him of sedition, declaring,
"That's communistic stuff you're reading!" As Muselin pronounced the phrase,
"all men are created equal," the officer arrested him (Muselin 70). Although
he was released on that occasion, by 1932, Muselin had spent three years in the
Allegheny County workhouse, often deprived of nearly all food and water, on
charges of violating Pennsylvania's sedition law by holding a union meeting.
That year, he and three of his four colleagues were released on the order of the
state pardon board. The fifth prisoner had died from mistreatment and medical neglect a few months earlier (Muselin 71–73).

Reading Instructions

A Gestalt analysis reveals one crucial dimension of Aliquippans' developing strategy for gaining civic power: producing a pedagogy by generating the
kind of subversive reading material local police had tried to eradicate. An
analysis of Aliquippa's working-class newspaper, the *Union Press*, illustrates

how this instruction works. Journal issues published from August through October of 1937, the strategically crucial months between the newspaper's first edition and the November 1937 elections, include examples of the first prong of the *Press*'s pedagogical strategy: reading instructions. The paper prompts readers to stake out a new relationship to knowledge, to pursue and use it for their own purposes, by promoting their experience of three phenomena: collective identity, the potential of learning as a tool, and related perceptual habits.

• • •

One of Aliquippans' key moves in the battle against J & L's civic control was to challenge the firm's media monopoly in the form of Ruffner's *Aliquippa Gazette* by founding their own journal, the *Union Press*. The paper calls itself the "Official Organ of Lodge 1211, SWOC [Steel Workers' Organizing Committee], CIO [Committee for Industrial Organization], A.A. of I.S. and T.W. of N.A. [Amalgamated Association of Iron, Steel, and Tin Workers of North America]," and its August 11, 1937, opening issue requests, in a boxed, front-page notice, that "all those who wish to work for the UNION PRESS either as reporters, columnists or business agents, please meet me [Ralph Rudd, editor] at the Union Office . . . next Monday, between 2 P.M. and 9 P.M" ("Will All Those Who Wish to Work"). Not only does the journal address local issues, it invites—and gets—community participation in its production.[2] Its pages lay out the connections among union, political, and social issues, running stories such as "State Law Now Prohibits Employment of Company Thugs as Deputy Sheriffs" alongside "Union Conducts Mass Meetings on [Political] Registration" and "How to Settle Your Grievance Under Contract." The *Union Press* served Aliquippa activists as a crucial weapon in their battle with J & L's network of community control. It subverted the company's information machine not only by printing stories on workers' legal and political rights but also by undertaking a pedagogical project to instruct working-class Aliquippans in particular ways of reading, in means to manufacture their experience into knowledge, and in steps for reshaping their individual and collective identities. These efforts expanded readers' contact in several areas. The first involves awareness of collective identity; the second, awareness of learning and knowledge as potential tools in the struggle for working-class power; and the last, experiments with a set of rhetorical forms that model new perceptual habits.

The *Press*'s masthead launches its effort to prompt workers to see themselves, and their relation to knowledge, through new lenses. To reposition the relationship between labor and capital, the masthead includes this excerpt from Abraham Lincoln's 1861 message to Congress:

> There is one point . . . to which I ask a brief attention. It is the effort to place capital on an equal footing with, if not above, labor, in the structure of government. It is assumed that labor is available only in connection with capital; that nobody labors unless somebody else, owning capital, somehow, by the use of it, induces him to labor. . . . Now, there is no such relation between capital and labor as assumed. . . . Labor is prior to and independent of capital. Capital is only the fruit of labor, and could never have existed if labor had not first existed. Labor is the superior of capital, and deserves much the higher consideration.

By quoting one of America's most famous and respected (and, notably, Republican) presidents, the masthead repositions the status, priority, and social significance of labor. It thus authorizes not only the unionization movement but also the *Press*'s own mission and lenses for viewing the world. The Lincoln epigraph sanctions the *Press*'s effort to transform the social, political, and economic relations between labor and capital, a project the paper undertakes by revising journalistic modes of authorizing knowledge and readers' expected relation to that knowledge. Its defining introductory move encourages readers' awareness of a culturally revered figure's support of labor, an awareness designed to foster readers' perception of their collective identity and its significance and potential power.

The *Press* builds on this opener by presenting self- and community education as a tool for pursuing material goals. "We Learn Union," which appears in the October 6 issue, excerpts part of the discussion held in a class on parliamentary law sponsored by the Aliquippa union local's Educational Committee. The class, it explains, is to train members in how to run meetings. "We are learning how to do business in our meetings quickly and efficiently. More important still, we are learning to do business fairly, democratically, for we are learning the rights of minorities, the rights of an individual on the floor of a democratic meeting. And most important of all we are learning to respect the will of the majority, and to be ruled by it." This description works to expand readers' awareness of the need to learn new rhetorical strategies designed to generate democratic contact styles. By linking the procedural rules to a list of the benefits they provide, the description transforms the knowledge of parliamentary law from abstract, de-contextualized information into a potential tool readers can use. It links the abstract rules to aspects of readers' structured ground, namely, the shared goal of initiating effective, equitable union meetings that can enable the Aliquippa activists to develop collective strategies for reclaiming their civil rights.

"We Learn" is also careful to distinguish between learning how to do and learning what to do; union members themselves must define their policies, it insists. And the Educational Committee hopes to use the method of parliamentary law to discuss precisely those issues:

> Parliamentary procedure is only the first step. It only teaches us how to do in meetings what we want to do there. It does not teach us what we want to do, what policies we should follow to build a strong union and make it accomplish what it should. . . . We hope to discuss the changes we want when our next contract is drawn up. We hope to study and discuss the problem of high prices and low wages to see what more the union can do than it is doing now. We may go into the problem of high rents and slum clearance, and the problem of public health. And perhaps we will make a study of labor's entrance into politics, both here and abroad, to try to develop a better understanding of the possibilities of the future.
>
> There is no limit to the subjects we can study nor to the opinions we can express. Labor must educate itself to understand what it is doing and why, so that it can advance unhampered by its own ignorance to a higher standard of living and a wider freedom.

Again, the paper links the process of learning new practices of language use to shared goals already existing in readers' structured ground, here by listing long-standing problems the union plans to address through education. In Gestalt terms, by heightening readers' awareness of education's potential as a tool to solve such problems, the journal broadens their perception of their possible field of action. In promoting such uses of education, it fosters an activist, agency-oriented contact style.

The article draws on readers' structured ground in other ways as well. Just before the quoted paragraphs, it contrasts depictions of the parliamentary procedures with a nondemocratic union meeting and acknowledges that the parliamentary-law classes may sound "stuck up." This double move first validates readers' potential resistance to the emphasis on formal learning by acknowledging suspicions about such instruction in readers' own idiom, that is, by using familiar rhetorical moves. In Gestalt terms, such validation of resistance is a crucial step needed to engage people in working with blocks to awareness and new behavioral options. This move also depicts education as essential to pursuing freedom. In the quoted paragraphs, which conclude the article, training in parliamentary law unlocks activists' access to political action—both study and strategizing—on the problems confronting them in daily life, from financial stresses to housing to health conditions. Entering the political arena emerges as one powerful way to address these problems. But the piece presents education, both in parliamentary procedure and in the issues mentioned, as the practice needed to cultivate such political work. The article uses the parliamentary-law course as its springboard to define education in a broad range of subjects as key to activists' hopes for transforming their community.

The *Union Press* thus works to shift readers' perceptions of education by expanding their contact with its potential as a tool to pursue their figural goals. It prompts readers to look at knowledge and learning not as tools of the elite (or something stuck up) but as weapons they themselves can take up in their quest to transform their living conditions. One of the ways the *Press* does this work is by revising objectivist modes of journalism and journalistic knowledge production in its own newspaper writing strategies.[3] Its first issue spearheads this retooling in its lead article, positioned top right, above the fold, and highlighted with extra white space and a wider typeface. "Union Wins First 15 Discharge Cases" reads the banner stretched across the top of the first issue, while the lead article's title trumpets, "Discharged Union Men All Put Back To Work." Just below, a boldface subheading proclaims, "12 Men From Open Hearth Department, 1 Each From Cold Rolls, Restaurant And By-Products Plant, Win Jobs Back." The interplay among these titles voices not only the union's challenge to J & L but, as the introduction to the *Union Press*'s first issue's lead story, the journal's as well. The headlines work in concert with the story's opening paragraph to torque objectivist journalism by frankly declaring the paper's allegiance. "Every one of the 15 union men who have been discharged from the mill here in Aliquippa since the strike and plant election last May has been put back to work, through the efforts of the union's officers and grievance committee," emphasizes the article's opener. By using the lead article of its first issue not merely to report on civic events but instead to mark that article, and in fact, that issue, as the explicit public relations and public education arm of the Aliquippa activist movement, the journal in effect renounces mainstream journalism's quasi-objectivity in favor of a more forthright acknowledgment of its sociopolitical investments.

In fact, the *Press* works to revamp mainstream journalism's portrayals of working-class Aliquippans, and this twist supports the paper's efforts to teach readers to redefine their relations to knowledge. As part of an extended controversy over J & L's de facto administration of local schools, the October 6 *Press* reprints an *Erie Daily Times* article written a year and a half earlier by Erie's school director, Bertha Winter Mahoney. In the piece, Mahoney derides J & L's political control of the school board, its policy of firing any school employee whose politics challenged the company, its decrepit buildings and furnishings, and its unplanned, unmonitored instructional system.[4] But she explains Aliquippans' tolerance of this criminally inadequate educational system by characterizing them as "unprotesting mill hands," noting that 70 percent were "of foreign birth or parentage" and more than three-quarters were "dependent upon the mill for their sustenance and very existence" (4, 1). Thus Mahoney paints Aliquippans not only as powerless in the face of J & L's regime but as unable to comprehend the crippling effects of the company's school system on their children.

In another reprint, "Ruffner Led Vigilante Committee," this time from the *New Masses*, Margerite Young depicts J & L's reign of terror in part by portraying workers and their families as brave but ignorant. Notably, in an article that spans many columns both on page 1 and in its continuation on page 2, her only quotation from the union activists she describes relays two sentences in broken English by "a motherly woman whose Slavic face was luminous as she said, 'Boss tell husband better keep out of union. We not scared, not scared by company, not scared of vigilante, not scared of nothing only God.'" She thus presents the Aliquippa activists as unable to speak for themselves, inarticulate, and charmingly childlike. While Mahoney and Young both sympathize with Aliquippans and lay bare J & L's rule of terror, they picture those Aliquippans as passive, uneducated, and, ultimately, incapable of helping themselves.

Although the *Press* capitalizes on outside writers' cachet and legitimacy and uses their pieces to expose J & L tactics, the union paper's pedagogical project works explicitly and extensively against such depictions. For instance, Mahoney's piece appears on the front page, but below the fold and in fact positioned—strikingly—directly below the two lead pieces, both of which fall under the banner headline, "Democrats Challenge School Policies." The first piece under this banner is "Ask Questions," an article explaining that the two Democratic candidates for school director are challenging the Republican school administration's policies by means of the second piece. This open letter is titled "Text of Questionnaire" and addresses the candidates' series of questions on local school conditions and policies to "Dear Mr. Voter." Similarly,

Young's article takes second place in terms of headline and white space, as well as type size, to Democratic candidates' charges against Republican justices of the peace. Thus the *Press* editions that reprint Mahoney's and Young's articles use them in support of Aliquippan activists' causes but subordinate the reprints to local pieces that enact and foster—rather than argue for—working-class Aliquippa residents' political clout. The local pieces stage for readers the activists' challenge to J & L. They implicitly respond to Mahoney- and Young-style characterizations of Aliquippans as passive, weak, and ignorant by demonstrating the strength of Aliquippa's grassroots movement. They position readers to experience themselves not as the uneducated, inarticulate subjects of others' writing—of official, mainstream journalistic knowledge—but rather as the actors and writers of their collective self-depictions and sociopolitical project.

The placement of local and outsider articles accomplishes this move by putting readers into contact first with the pieces that represent them as intelligent, educable, and in the process of developing political sophistication and rhetorical expertise. Staging that contact first fundamentally changes readers' contact with Mahoney's and Young's infantilizing portrayals because it positions readers to experience themselves as developing political and rhetorical competence. It changes the conditions of readers' experiences of the latter articles and thus revises their perceptions of those articles' depictions. Just as Diane's contact with her adolescent Struggle partner changed the conditions of her experience of communicating with Ian and prompted her to develop new rhetorical practices, the *Union Press* layout encourages readers to undertake the rhetorical practices presented in the local articles. It not only presents the articles but also implicitly opposes their view of Aliquippans to the infantilizing pictures presented by Mahoney and Young. Through that opposition, the *Press* promotes readers' contact with the potential agency available to them by pursuing the kinds of analyses and rhetorical moves the local articles model.

Other articles build on this work by expanding readers' contact with rhetorical strategies used in political discussion and debate to promote a contact style of civic engagements. They highlight the conflicting ways of seeing the world embodied in the struggle for control of Aliquippa rather than attempting, like mainstream journalism, to suggest an ideal reader with a universal worldview. Like its twist on objectivist journalism, this *Union Press* writing strategy explicitly engages in political struggle by directly addressing different, conflicting readerships rather than imposing a fictional ideal reader.[5] The first of the *Press*'s September 29 editorials, "We Beg To Suggest—" enacts this shifting address to challenge union opponents after pointing out a recent successful agreement between union leaders and Aliquippa mill officials:

We call this fact to the attention of those workers in the mill who have said that the union was doing no good and would never be able to establish satisfactory relations with the company.

We call it to the attention of the United Iron and Steel Workers of Aliquippa, local and independent [members of J & L's company union], who, we have heard, are confident that on next February 28 they will end the relations between the company and the CIO [the recently formed sponsor of Aliquippa's new local branch of the AA of IS and TW of NA].

And particularly we call the relationship we have established to the attention of Messrs. Weir, Girdler and Grace, who will never sign contracts with the CIO because it is irresponsible and can lead only to strife and friction. . . . And finally, if we may be permitted a word of advice, we would suggest that these people ["those workers . . . who have said that the union was doing no good"] join the union and share in its benefits.

Instead of presuming a shared attitude and set of interests in its readers, the *Press* deliberately tweaks objectivist journalism (which speaks broadly to the general public) to address, directly and in succession, a series of audiences whose positions conflict with the effort to pry J & L's fingers from Aliquippa's civil life. The editorial uses a specific local event to challenge these audiences' interpretations of their circumstances, beginning with mill workers holding little faith in union efforts. The piece confronts each group's position, whether addressing antiunion workers, workers who remained in the company union, or the bitterly antiunion leaders of J & L's sister Little Steel firms (the major independents, those companies that had managed to avoid being swallowed by the industry's behemoth, U.S. Steel). Using its interpretation of a relevant local event, it challenges those positions in an effort to push each audience to revise its stance. In contrast to objectivist journalistic methods for addressing an audience, the *Press* seeks to sway readers not by addressing an ideal reader whose position real readers are implicitly urged to share but by modeling rhetorical strategies that foreground conflicting positions and use local events to grapple with those positions' interpretations. Like Winstanley's pamphlets and Struggle's training materials, it fosters people's experiments with such strategies by demonstrating them.

The *Press* also appeals specifically to local working-class readers by drawing extensively on familiar rhetorical practices—and thus on communal structured ground—in some of its columns. These regular features use a colloquial language and fragmented sentences and paragraphs that move rapidly back and forth among implicit addresses to various audiences, skipping quickly and without transition from one topic to another. Their references remain opaque to the reader without inside information and enable the columns to demonstrate knowledge, attitudes, and experiences shared by working-class readers while simultaneously working to consolidate readers' attitudes in support of the activist effort in Aliquippa and to direct readers' actions along particular courses. The October 13 edition's "The Spirits of 1843" column[6] demonstrates this style and its effects, first by addressing a particular abusive boss: "We hear that Ray Hale, the Committeeman from Soho is going to invite Supt. Riggs to sit on the next hot ingot that comes out of the pits . . . Riggs claims that those ingots are cold enough to sit on . . . And Hale doesn't believe him . . . Hale says that if he does sit on one he'll not sit down for a hell of a long time . . . Maybe he'll stand up and take notice that Union conditions are going to prevail in his sweat shop."

Later it calls for workers to take particular actions to strengthen the union's power to bargain with the company:

> We need shop stewards to keep us posted on some of the dirty things these Girdler bosses are trying to pull off . . . Give us the dope on them and we'll make them walk the chalk line . . . A certain big boss coerced a man at the coal handling department to revoke his case against the company . . . He dictated the revocation and made this man sign it . . . We warn him and other bosses here and now that if this practice is continued we shall enter cases with the N.L.R.B. [National Labor Relations Board] against them and the company . . . And you men that may have a case don't be afraid to bring them to your Grievance man . . . He'll fight your case for you . . .

In each of these excerpts, all ellipses appear in the original text. They function as part of its conversational style, which assumes readers would recognize the reference to Girdler. Readers were likely to know of Girdler's violently oppressive management, whose legacy remained among a corps of local supervisors although Girdler had left the Aliquippa plant many years previously, eventually becoming president of J & L and, later, Republic Steel (Casebeer 618). Similarly, the first excerpt suggests that Riggs pushes mill hands into working too closely with newly cast, still-hot ingots, but it essentially relies on readers' prior local knowledge of the practices and conditions prevailing under various supervisors. By using local knowledge and idiom, the *Press*'s columns provide a crucial element in building the paper's credibility with Aliquippa workers. They draw on working-class Aliquippans' structured ground by using their rhetorical habits and content knowledge, much as Winstanley uses sermonic rhetorical moves and Struggle's training materials use introductory moves based in community, rather than academic, discourse.

Such uses of this knowledge and idiom illustrate column writers' intellectual and experiential connection with working-class readers. Demonstrating this connection perhaps legitimates the articles written in the culturally sanctioned language of informative reporting. And it may smooth the way for pieces such as "We Learn Union" and its calls for workers to educate themselves even in procedures that may appear elitist. Further, it explicitly uses rhetorical habits from readers' structured ground to invite revised perceptions, thus supplementing the other articles' invitation to more formal rhetorical practices. Requests for readers to provide information on their bosses' behavior encourage an activist contact style. This style results from torquing established rhetorical habits, putting erstwhile gossip to official union use, thus reshaping perceptions of basic unfairness into union monitoring. Such invitations parallel Winstanley's exhortations to audiences to take up rhetorical authority and Struggle's positioning of Diane and Ian to experiment with rhetorical moves that ultimately helped them sidestep family conflicts.

The columns' use of fragmented style, local knowledge, and colloquial language also enables the second excerpt's aside, which explicitly addresses supervisors, warning them of union reprisals for their illegal, coercive actions, and, simultaneously, uses that warning to demonstrate union strength to unconvinced workers. In fact, the quoted passage positions the warning to supervisors as an example of the kind of abuses workers should report so that the union can act to redress them. The example is followed by another reminder to workers to report cases of company abuse to union grievance officers. The column uses this three part structure—urging reports, providing an example, and reinforcing the call to relate abuses—to prompt readers to undertake specific actions as part of the collective effort to wrest Aliquippa from J & L domination. By combining its call to action with an example of bosses' abuse, the piece not only demonstrates what kinds of infractions to report but also appeals directly to readers' local experience of such assaults to mobilize them to act individually as part of a collective effort. Specifically, it urges them to marshal their experience as official knowledge, as the kind of information that will bolster the activists' effort to bring J & L under community control and civil and constitutional law. Like Struggle's training materials and structure, it not only models such new rhetorical practices but also uses changed conditions of experience—here, the possibility of union action—to encourage experimentation with those practices. Thus the column builds on the newspaper's work to reposition readers' relations to knowledge by asking them to formulate their experience as a particular kind of legal and ethical knowledge—to take up a revised contact style.

The *Press*'s columns also advocate other kinds of action involving readers' uses of knowledge. Its October 20 "Ladies Only" column promotes a communal figure of political action and a revised sense of collective identity. It works to form readers into a "we" who analyze local social, political, and economic events and act politically in response. This work begins in its opening paragraph: "'On to victory and a new deal for Aliquippa' is a slogan aptly reaching the very core of Aliquippa's trouble. Too long have we been a subjected, dominated group of people, afraid to demand the rights given us by the Constitution of the United States. We need a new deal. . . . We have a right to live our own lives free from the present tie-up between politics and work."

This opening paragraph invokes the transformation of national politics and Aliquippa residents' constitutional rights and applies them to the town's particular situation to position readers as a "we" struggling for independence from J & L's grip on all of civic life. Once again, the journal heightens readers' awareness of changed conditions of their experience to urge them to experiment with the new rhetorical strategies it models. The column introduces these strategies through a step-by-step analysis of the Republican argument for the local school board president's innocence of all responsibility for the situation in Aliquippa's schools. In the culminating step in its analysis, the column insists on both the president's responsibility and readers' performance of their own analyses:

> It cannot be denied that Mrs. Wright has accomplished some good in her work. She has. But for her friends to tell us that she is responsible for all of the good done by the Board and could not help the wrong the Board did is to underestimate our intelligence. If she had enough influence to be elected the Board's President, [a]nd to make the members do certain things, she certainly had enough influence to prevent their doing other things.
>
> It is time for our opponents to know that we no longer swallow (wholesale) everything told us. We read about them, and think about them, and our decision[s] are based upon a composite of what we have read, seen, heard, and thought. Let them realize that we are an intelligent group of people and let them act accordingly.

This concluding paragraph constructs the "we" of readers as politically interested people who enact certain kinds of intellectual work that involve not only reading and evaluation of written information and sources but a synthesis of that information with their own experience and analyses. In short, it positions readers as practitioners of a complex interpretive system that integrates the pursuit and analysis of textual information with the analysis of other kinds of individual and community experience. By accusing opponents of presuming that working-class Aliquippans cannot and do not practice such intellectual work and thus of underestimating their intelligence, the column suggests that this work is both essential to Aliquippa's activist movement and the presumed practice of any working-class reader. Thus the piece works not only to marshal reader investments in sociopolitical action but also to foster the *Press*'s pedagogical project: prompting readers to shift their relation to knowledge from its passive objects to active users who seek and process various kinds of information, written and otherwise, and who analyze that information and integrate it into their own experience. This work, the paper insists, is the precursor to community transformation. In fostering it, the journal promotes new rhetorical habits and perceptions to initiate readers into an activist contact style.

Steeltown Seethes

The *Press* drew on energies generated by Roosevelt's 1933 National Recovery Administration (NRA). The NRA ameliorated Depression-era laborers' desperation by authorizing workers to organize themselves into unions. Labor reporter Harvey O'Connor describes the new policy's impact in Steeltown: "Along came the New Deal, and then came the NRA, and the effect was electric all up and down those valleys. . . . Steelworkers read in the newspapers about this NRA Section 7A that guaranteed you the right to organize. All over the steel country union locals sprang up spontaneously" (qtd. in Lynd 191).

Steelworkers watched the AFL's quickly successful drive to organize coal miners. In 1933, eager rank-and-file steel laborers moved to infiltrate the AA of IS and TW of NA (also known as the AA), a decrepit AFL craft union known for excluding blacks, immigrants, and unskilled workers. Rank-and-file leaders, white and black, established locals across Steeltown. AA membership grew from fewer than five thousand in 1933 to fifty thousand by February 1934 and involved 129 new lodges (Brody 15–16), as well as increased black membership (Dickerson 133; Brody 16; Powers 41–44). The rank-and-file movement was led largely by Clarence Irwin, who was committed to democratic unions and opposed AA president Mike Tighe's conservative policies (Powers 67). Irwin persuaded the 1933 AA convention delegates to demand that the steel firms recognize the new AA lodges or face a strike. When steel management refused, the rank-and-filers asked AA leadership for financial and other support (Brooks 56). Tighe denied support, and influential union allies advised against a strike at the behest of John L. Lewis, who headed the United Mine Workers (UMW) and hoped to organize steel (Lynd 198). Subsequent negotiations between union officials and the National Labor Board brought small results. Steelworkers in Braddock, Pa., bars heard the news of the failed negotiations over the radio and shredded their union cards (Lynd 198).

Aliquippa Seethes

In 1933, Aliquippa's Pete Muselin was helping to organize a strike against the Spang-Chalfant specialty steel plant in Ambridge, Aliquippa's sister city just across the Ohio River. Mobilized by the Depression, which left many Ambridge families without enough money for food, workers from its seven steel plants first formed an Unemployed Council to fight evictions and utility cutoffs, then allied themselves with the Communist-led Steel and Metal Workers Industrial Union (SMWIU). On October 3, workers at six of the Ambridge mills demanded recognition of their union. Five of the six closed peacefully when the companies requested time to consider. But at the Spang plant, company deputies threatened the union representatives with rifles, tear gas guns, and machine guns (Casebeer 637–38). The former head of J & L's Coal and Iron Police, Sheriff Charles O'Laughlin, was now Beaver County's chief law enforcement officer. O'Laughlin raised seventy-five men of his own and pressed Aliquippa's American Legion commander, William Shaffer, to raise another seventy-five. Led by Mike Kane and three other lieutenants, 248 newly appointed special deputies, including roughly fifty J & L employees, were organized into groups of four, each containing at least one ex-serviceman. Wielding submachine guns, tear gas bombs, shotguns, revolvers, and clubs, and wearing white handkerchief armbands for identification, the private army marched military-style on the Spang-Chalfant plant.

Many strikers and spectators ran at the onset of the Legionnaire force, but others stayed through the initial violence and O'Laughlin's order to disperse. Picketer Adam Pietrowsky, who had stood next to Pete Muselin's brother Tony, was killed. Deputies later admitted, during state-ordered hearings, that they had been gunning for Pete Muselin personally. He speculates that, mistaking

Tony for him, they had taken aim at the other Muselin and shot Pietrowsky instead (Muselin 74). The J & L militia injured roughly one hundred people, shooting most in the back. When the wounded sought treatment, local doctors interrogated and abused them, ripping bandages roughly and verbally battering the patients (Casebeer 640–41). In the aftermath, police traveled in bands to disperse groups of more than three at gun point, raided strikers' offices without warrants, confiscated records and cash, and arrested leaders, who spent days in jail before their release on habeas corpus. In all, J & L spent $24,811.40 to deputize and arm its militia and another $1,925.60 in May 1934 on riot guns, long-range tear gas projectiles, grenades, and ammunition (Casebeer 641).

But the firm's October 1933 effort to prevent "see[ing] the law thrown aside" failed. Many of the Aliquippans pressed to join O'Laughlin's militia refused. In an interview with historian Eric Davin, Aliquippa steel worker Frank Kromerich describes how he dissuaded his older brother from participating on the grounds that "it was not in the interest of our family or the people of Aliquippa" (10). Kromerich describes how the stirrings in Aliquippa during the 1932 elections had blossomed into full-fledged activism, despite continuing repression. That year, he says, "there was some trend that people wanted to vote for the first time, and were voting not as instructed by the people of the town which was the first indication that people were getting restless" (7). The older Croatians in Aliquippa remembered their ethnic group's deep involvement in the 1892 Homestead strike and in 1919 action, and they talked about the union (8). Kromerich himself joined the AA in late 1933. "I met a man who was an organizer, I asked to sign up in one of the taverns, I signed the card up and gave him the card, he told me that forget who he was, where he came from, and he says you're [sic] card will go to [A]mbridge, but I'm not going to take it over, it[']s going to go through a grapevine system" (10–11). Kromerich began signing others, black and white. Despite J & L's community control, between March and August of 1934, he explains, discussion of unionizing was increasing among the mill workers. "It was s[t]arting to become more open, more people started to talk about a union. . . . After '34, the discussion was getting stronger and stronger. People wouldn't run away from you when you talked about a union. Before soon as you mentioned the word 'union,' it would be just like a dynamite, they would scatter" (15).

Although they were followed by a J & L plainclothesman, two union activists drove to the AA's international office to obtain a charter for their new local, Beaver Valley Lodge #200. Mobilized by the new charter, two hundred more men joined (Casebeer 649). Both Casebeer and Davin describe a locally run organizing campaign not controlled by AA leadership or AFL operators (Casebeer 650–58; Davin 38). Casebeer explains that workers who had attended SMWIU meetings were angry with AA president Tighe's passive leadership. Aliquippa leaders such as AA lodge president Albert Atallah joined Clarence Irwin and others struggling to take control of the union, and Irwin often spoke at Aliquippa lodge meetings. Aliquippa unionizers undertook political activism as well. In 1934, the AA lodge established Aliquippa's Democratic Social Club, which local union organizer Dominic Del Turco described, according to Casebeer, as "the political arm of the union movement in Aliquippa" (Casebeer 657). Casebeer explains that people who feared walking publicly into union offices would take their union pledge cards into the Democratic Club (Casebeer 657). Even Philip Murray, who, with John L. Lewis, would organize the 1935 unionizing drive under the hierarchical SWOC, admitted that in 1934, "[Aliquippa] workers operating under their own motion, without any assistance from any international union, without any assistance from the American Federation of Labor, at that time organized 6,500 of the 8,000 workers at the Aliquippa plant into an independent union" (qtd. in Davin 38).

Although the 1934 effort crumbled with the move from strike to Washington negotiations, Muselin, Kromerich, Atallah, Irwin, and others continued fighting to control AA resources so they could effectively confront the steel firms.

Manufacturing Knowledge

Atallah and his colleagues' battle would eventually take local shape in the pages of the *Union Press*. The second prong of the journal's pedagogical strategy involves teaching readers to manufacture knowledge. The *Press* instructs readers in analyzing texts by examining those texts' rhetorical moves and underlying socioeconomic and political interests. It models for readers the rhetorical practices for extending an interpretation of local events into a position with further reach. The journal pursues this project by encouraging readers to juxtapose different kinds of awarenesses. Examining how it scaffolds directed experiments with multiple rhetorical strategies that support large-scale revisions of readers' intersecting rhetorical, perceptual, and evaluative habits provides a basis for extending Perls, Hefferline, and Goodman's model of change.

In its first issue, the *Press* launches a campaign to teach readers to analyze other texts with a page 1 top-center boxed piece titled "Remember . . ."A synthesis of editorial and exposé, "Remember" admonishes readers to evaluate the socioeconomic and political interests shaping texts to analyze those texts' content. Its first five paragraphs are a litany of clauses beginning with "If," for instance, "If you read that the Wagner Act is one-sided and should be amended to restrict the actions of labor unions." Each of these paragraphs is followed by a boldface, entirely capitalized injunction: "REMEMBER WHERE THE PROPAGANDA COMES FROM." This phrase leads into another series of paragraphs that begin with "Remember" and pithily detail some of the steel corporations' propaganda efforts.

> Remember that the National Citizens' Committee, organized in Johnstown and moved to New York City, paid for its first set of full-page newspaper advertisements approximately $65,000, which was supplied by Ernest T. Weir [owner of Weirton, West Virginia's National Steel Company].[7]
>
> Remember that those advertisements were written by Ketchum, MacLeod and Grove, Inc., a Pittsburgh advertising firm which is alleged to be tied in with Federal Laboratories, the strike-breakers' supply house for machine-guns and tear gas, and with National Railway Audit, a detective agency which hires out stool-pigeons and strike-breakers to employers afflicted with labor trouble.
>
> Remember that when the National Citizens' Committee, then supported by Weir, Grace and Girdler [Grace and Girdler were presidents of Bethlehem and Republic Steel, respectively], moved to New York it engaged the publicity firm of Thornby and Jones.
>
> Remember that Thornby of that firm is a friend of Edsel Ford and drew him in to back the Citizens' Committee.
>
> Remember that Weir, Girdler, Grace and Ford are the biggest and bitterest enemies of the workers' right to organize and that they are now using their money together to destroy that right by propaganda.
>
> Remember all this when y[o]u read the papers.

This set of cumulative paragraphs, in its reply to the introductory list of clauses, responds not by arguing against those clauses' positions but by exposing their socioeconomic roots. The paragraphs build on one another to demonstrate the steel corporations' attempt to choke the union movement through a public relations drive. By exposing the economic power behind this drive and the corporations' reach throughout the U.S. business community, the piece ties the steel barons' economic resources explicitly to media control.

By painting the firms' grip on local and national events, it builds to the punch of the last two sentences and powerfully positions the information provided by much mainstream media as propaganda. Thus it promotes new (or renewed) awareness of the links between political and economic issues, modeling the rhetorical and perceptual habits readers can use to interpret mainstream media themselves. Because heightened awareness expands an individual's potential field of actions, in this case it is likely to increase readers' sensitivity to such modeling. By tracing mainstream journalism's corporate roots, the article demonstrates a way of reading that evaluates and responds to texts' positions not primarily by examining their arguments but by tracking the socioeconomic interests that produced them. Given Goodman's definition of evaluation as largely a product of rhetorical strategies, this lesson in rhetorical practices lays the groundwork for revised habits of evaluation.

The *Press* extends this arm of its pedagogical strategy by using editorials not only to respond to and position its own reprinted articles but also to discuss local events to model for readers an analysis of the links among economic, political, and social systems. Following the paper's successful campaign to force school superintendent H. R. Vanderslice to resign, the October 20 edition's editorial column opens with the piece "Mr. Vanderslice Resigns." The editorial begins by sympathizing with Vanderslice and pointing out the impossibility of fulfilling the superintendent's position effectively given J & L's control of Aliquippa. But, it continues, "perhaps he made a mistake in coming to such a town in the first place. It should have been clear that a school administration couldn't be honest here." Building on this point, the editorial goes on to thoughtfully position both Vanderslice's work and progressive education in the context of Aliquippa's sociopolitical conditions.

> When he [Vanderslice] came he tried to establish a progressive plan of education, one which would teach the children to think for themselves and study for themselves, rather than drill them in the ideas of the governing politicians. He was allowed to carry out the form of progressive education, but the substance, progressive thought, was not permitted.
>
> With the rise of the union to bring new political freedom and new freedom of speech and thought, Aliquippa people were allowed to express their dissatisfaction with the school administration. Led by the Democratic Party, they attacked failure after failure and weakness after weakness, and have demanded a reconstruction of school policies to permit truly progressive education and progressive thought.

This analysis of Vanderslice's educational approach takes a more balanced, insightful approach than does the reprinted article by Bertha Winter Mahoney run by the *Press* two weeks earlier. In part, then, the editorial replies to and repositions that article not only by acknowledging the importance of Vanderslice's efforts to institute a progressive pedagogy in Aliquippa schools but also by demonstrating that a well-educated, well-connected professional was as vulnerable to J & L pressure as were the "unprotesting mill hands" of Mahoney's piece.

In fact, the article powerfully establishes the union and Aliquippa's newly viable Democratic Party as the agents that have finally made possible genuinely progressive thought—the substance of progressive education—in the community. By portraying the inability of educators and professionals to counter J & L's domination, the piece not only reminds readers of the firm's reach but illustrates the inefficacy of traditionally cited checks, like education and culture, on the corporate grasp. In the quoted passage, the editorial juxtaposes Vanderslice's failed attempt to instantiate progressive education with the union's successful introduction of new freedom in politics, speech, and thought, thus positioning the union as the essential prerequisite to intellectual and civic freedom, as the harbinger of truly progressive education. By prompting readers' awareness of the union's efficacy, the paper again encourages revised perceptions of workers' collective power.

Further, the editorial enacts the very progressive education it advocates. It extends the commentary on the events surrounding Vanderslice's resignation to an analysis of the current political situation in Aliquippa:

> The people's anger is more than the controlling politicians can face, so they have tried to escape their own responsibility by laying the blame on Messrs. Vanderslice and Leonard, Superintendent a[n]d Solicitor. Having some measure of pride, Mr. Vanderslice refuses to be made a whipping boy and resigns. Mr. Ruffner's newspaper, The Aliquippa Gazette, hails it as an admission of guilt which thereby excuses from all blame the Republican bosses themselves.
>
> When Mr. Ruffner cries against the policies of school administration, and when he condemns political coercion in the schools, voters only need ask, "Who has been tax-collector and Republican Chairman for the last twenty-four years?"

These paragraphs not only examine J & L's use of the local Republican Party to control the administration of Aliquippa's schools, they highlight the role of the town's Republican-controlled media in that process. By constructing an alternate reading of Vanderslice's resignation and using that reading to call into question the *Gazette*'s position, the editorial enacts for readers another means of reading corporate-controlled media. In addition to asking readers to analyze the socioeconomic interests behind such media, the *Press* asks them to confront its interpretations of events with alternative understandings. Like other articles, the editorial increases awareness of such rhetorical strategies by modeling them. Its concluding question pushes readers beyond adopting the union paper's interpretations and instead instructs them in the means to examine and challenge corporate mouthpieces' positions by analyzing the workings of local politics.

The journal thus torques the editorial as a written form that comments on local issues and extends it to educate readers in analyzing local events so they can interpret the information manufactured by mainstream media.

In fact, the editorial's instruction builds on a related front-page story in the same issue, "Vanderslice Resigns Position." This story, even more thoroughly than the editorial, carefully moves the issue of Aliquippa schools away from Vanderslice personally and links it directly with Republican domination of the school administration. Using an objectivist journalistic format, the article carefully establishes the *Aliquippa Gazette*'s status as Republican Party tool, describing it as "published by J.A.C. Ruffner, Republican candidate for Tax Collector and chairman of the Republican Party for more than twenty years." Having thus positioned Aliquippa's only other newspaper, the article goes on to juxtapose pieces of the local Republican Party platform for the upcoming election with pieces of Democratic candidates' "Text of Questionnaire" addressed to "Mr. Voter," printed by the *Press* two weeks previously. In effect, the story sets up the Republican position and then uses its own earlier printing of the questionnaire to undermine that position. It encourages readers to juxtapose awarenesses of both positions to shift their holistic perception of the election's issues.

Building on the interplay between those two texts, the article interprets the questionnaire to construct its own implicit response to the *Gazette*'s ingenuous use of Vanderslice as whipping boy: "The Democratic criticisms of the school system, however, are generally interpreted as aimed not alone at Mr. Vanderslice, but at the whole administration, which the Democrats charge is controlled by the Republicans." The story's moves model for readers a complex series of rhetorical practices in using texts. The article demonstrates that the *Gazette* uses Vanderslice in an attempt to deflect responsibility from the town's Republican administration and thus shows readers how to look for such diversionary devices. Its extended excerpts from both the Republican platform and the questionnaire illustrate for readers a method of recalling relevant texts and putting them into dialogue, via quotation, with one another. By using that dialogue to construct its concluding interpretation of the questionnaire— and thus its challenge to the *Gazette*'s position—this article models yet another method for interpreting and responding to the corporate-controlled media's texts. This method integrates a combination of rhetorical moves that model a shift in perceptual focus and evaluative frame.

The "Text of Questionnaire" addressed to "Mr. Voter" figures more extensively in this prong of the *Press*'s pedagogical strategy, for the journal teaches readers how to interpret not only rival newspapers' and political parties' texts but also its own. Once again, its instruction involves heightening and juxtaposing different kinds of awareness. The questionnaire's sister piece, "Ask Questions," appears with it under the same banner headline, "Democrats Challenge School Policies," the October 6 edition's lead story. "Ask Questions" in fact frames—literally and figuratively—the questionnaire, and its frame both positions the questionnaire in Aliquippa politics and provides a set of reading instructions.

The article provides a context for its companion piece in the history of local politics and thus instructs readers in how to approach the questionnaire. Before and after its listing of both Democratic and Republican candidates and the latter group's years in office, "Ask Questions" invokes and comments on the current political campaign's historical context:

> In a drive for victory that many are confident will succeed, the Democratic Party is making a bid for control of the government of Aliquippa, seeking to overthrow the Republican Party which has been in office here for a generation. . . . Aliquippa leaders of the Democratic Party, however, assert that the length of time their opponents have spent in office is to the advantage of the Democrats, for, they say, the Republicans have not satisfied the voters, but have done many things against the will of the public. The open letter which Luger and Kirkwood have issued today is an effort to point out those things and gain support for a change in the city government. It is expected that other charges by the other candidates will be made against the remaining Republican officials to bear out the Democrats' claim that the Republican administration has been inefficient and corrupt.

By positioning the questionnaire as, simultaneously, a listing of and response to Aliquippa's grievances against J & L's civil regime, this article asks readers to interact with the Democratic candidates' text by reading its questions not as discrete current issues but rather as specific links in the mesh of community control. Thus, inquiries such as the questionnaire's "Isn't it true, Mr. Voter . . . [t]hat we have portable schools that are an insult to an American community? That schools where your children freeze in one end of the room and roast in the other end are obsolete? That our most remote communities would not tolerate such conditions?" might be read not only as an indictment of Aliquippa schools but as an effort to cut through a section of J & L's civic control. "Ask Questions" asks readers to understand such critiques as pointing out instances in which J & L's Republican regime has defied public opinion. As the concluding lines quoted suggest, the article prompts readers to understand the companion piece's questions as examples of Republican—J & L—repression and as issues pertaining to a particular political race or candidacy. Thus it instructs readers in how to evaluate specific questions in local politics through the lens of the town's grassroots effort to redistribute political and economic power. The double meaning implied in its title, "[Luger and Kirkwood] Ask Questions" versus "[You, the Reader] Ask Questions," helps teach readers how to take up those lenses. By heightening and juxtaposing particular kinds of awareness, it prompts readers' revised perceptions not only of local politics but of the rhetorical tools available for assessing those politics.

Notably, the story accomplishes this instruction by shuttling between a quasi-objective journalistic format and more explicit declarations of position. In most of the excerpt quoted, the piece uses an objectivist approach to distance itself from the Democratic Party's drive to reshape Aliquippa. Those lines affect a descriptive intent, as if "Ask Questions" merely means to convey neutral information on the ongoing political campaign and its participants. That format lends authority to the piece's historical contextualization of the Democratic candidates' text. But such quasi-neutrality contrasts with the piece's introduction of the questionnaire, which declares, "In an open letter to the voters of Aliquippa, through the pages of The Union Press, Paul A. Luger and Harrison Kirkwood, Democratic candidates for School Director, challenged today the policies of the present Republican School Administration." This sentence's construction proclaims what the *Press* has already enacted by publishing the questionnaire in larger type surrounded by more white space than is used for any other front-page piece—the newspaper is acting as a weapon in the grassroots battle for control of Aliquippa. This twist on objectivist journalism affords another kind of legitimation, one that affirms for readers the importance of taking up the instruction offered in "Ask Questions" and putting its reading practices into play in their assessment of the questionnaire.

The front page of the *Press*'s September 29 issue pairs a similar set of articles under the common headline, "Five-Day Work Week In Slack Is Guaranteed to Senior Employees." Under it appear two pieces, the first of which is "Text of Agreement," which prints the new interpretation of a problematic section of J & L's contract with the Aliquippa union, a document recently hammered out by union and J & L officials. The second piece, "Timko and Carr Sign Agreement," not only explicates the agreement's context but, again, teaches readers how to work with the text of the agreement itself.

After explaining that the agreement institutes new policies for assigning the limited work available during slack periods (long a sore issue with J & L employees), the piece provides both explanation and example:

> Curtailment of forces will be made in each department in such a way that the newest men will be laid off and the older ones will be "bumped" back down the scale of promotion in the same order that they advanced to their present positions. "That means that new men brought into the mill and assigned to advanced positions over the heads of older men will be laid off directly, instead of being demoted to positions they've never held," Mr. [Joseph] Timko [sub-regional director of the SWOC, the CIO's organizing arm] explained. "For instance," he said, "a new man brought in from West Virginia and given a good job in the Hot Mill will be demoted just the way he came in—back to West Virginia."
>
> "The agreement, signed by Mr. Carr and myself, is just as much a part of the contract now, so far as we are concerned here in the Aliquippa Works, as the original Section 6, and it will be incorporated into the new contract next February," Mr. Timko said.

Aliquippa workers were particularly angry with J & L's long-standing habit of importing workers from West Virginia during busy periods and retaining those workers over local employees with greater seniority during slack times. The article's use of Timko's quotation invokes this key local grievance to illustrate the new agreement's impact on it. The piece prompts readers to interpret the agreement's abstract formulations specifically in terms of their own local experience. It teaches them how to read such texts—in effect, any policy doc-

ument—in terms of their local effects. Here the *Press* prompts readers to juxtapose awareness of local events and their implications with awareness of
abstract principles. Through this juxtaposition, it models application of such
principles by drawing on a figural local issue, using that issue to teach analysis and application.

As with the "Text of Questionnaire" addressed to "Mr. Voter" and its
framing "Ask Questions" piece, the journal uses its layout to reinforce the relation between these two pieces and the significance of the reading practices
they model. The larger typeface and better position accorded to "Text of
Agreement" positions "Timko and Carr" as decidedly secondary to it. In the
language of layout, context and reading instructions appear important—both
articles are above the fold on the front page—but readers' work with the agreement itself is primary. "Timko and Carr" models a way of reading rather than
providing any definitive interpretation of its companion text. The September
29 edition's showcasing of "Text of Agreement" makes readers' work with that
model—rather than the presentation of the model—the paper's pedagogical
focus. The interplay between the two pieces works to prompt readers to take
up the project of interpreting a policy document through the lenses of their
local experience to gauge that document's effects.

A third pair of articles acts as the lead stories in the *Press*'s October 29 pre-
election issue. Both appear under a single triple-decker headline that spans
two-thirds of the front page, proclaiming, "Old Council Condemned/Affi-
davits, Pictures Prove Brutality/Kiefer Blames Burgess Sohn." Here again, the
framing article, "Man Beaten and Injured by Policeman," explains and contextualizes the real lead piece, "Text of Democrats' Statements and Affidavits."
The framing story begins by positioning the documents reproduced in its
companion piece as evidence:

> Affidavits signed by Nick Yagielo [the man beaten], Edward Jones,
> and Joaquim Martinez[,] witnesses of the beating, and sworn to before
> a notary public, are offered as conclusive evidence supporting the
> charges of brutality against the local Police Force which candidate for
> Burgess George L. Kiefer prefers in an [*sic*] questionnaire addressed to
> [incumbent] Burgess Morgan Sohn in this issue of THE UNION
> PRESS.
>   Other affidavits . . . attest to further beatings, unjust imprison-
> ment, and intimidation of voters by the police department, and to
> inefficiency or malfeasance by Justice of the Peace Mike Kane. Pay
> envelopes in the possession of the Democratic Party and reproduced

in THE UNION PRESS show that Justice of the Peace C. R. Hayward has ordered his fines and fees stopped out of the pay of certain prisoners.

The framing story thus uses an exposé format to illustrate rhetorical strategies for evaluating the affidavit texts as authorized accounts of individuals' experience, accounts with the force of legal evidence. In effect, the story asks readers to take the role of a jury evaluating Burgess Sohn in light of textual evidence reproduced for them by the *Press*, whose front page supplements the affidavits with large photographs of Yagielo's injuries and copies of the pay envelopes described. This instructional move culminates in the editor's note immediately following the framing story:

> American freedom of the press has protected our exposure of viciousness and corruption throughout the political campaign which is ending now. But there is no freedom without responsibility. We have sought to maintain our integrity as a newspaper by printing only demonstrable facts.
>
> The affidavits and photographs which appear on this page are samples of the evidence which backs the charges we have printed.— The editor.

Through its explicit appeal to the freedom of the press, the editor's note reminds readers of the very new reality of that freedom in Aliquippa and of the *Union Press*'s status as both the evidence and enactment of it. That is, it promotes renewed awareness of readers' recently changed conditions of experience. Because, in Goodman's terms, such changed conditions promote reinterpretations of experience, the reminder may heighten readers' awareness of potential environmental resources such as new rhetorical tools. By fostering this awareness of resources and of the abusive conditions still ongoing in Aliquippa, the journal prompts readers to juxtapose the two kinds of recognition, further emphasizing the need for such tools.

Freedom of the press thus appears as both prerequisite and introduction to readers' freedom of interpretation—readers need access to such information to interpret it. While the note's claims for journalistic responsibility would, in mainstream journalism, typically lead into claims for objectivity, here they instead enable the *Press* to position its reprinted texts (and pay envelopes and photographs) as both facts and evidence. Rather than declaring its objectivity, the paper claims a kind of legal validity that enables it to build a particular case. Thus the framing story and its editor's note begin modeling for readers means to legitimate their experience, to represent it as evidence, a weapon in the drive for community control. As a result, they encourage readers to reinterpret experience within the new evaluative frame offered by the rhetorical practices they illustrate.

The language of the local Democratic Party frames the affidavits even more closely, appearing before, between, and after them. The introductory paragraphs of "Text of Democrats' Statements and Affidavits" interweave a chatty, conversational voice with a more formal style, sometimes referring to Yagielo by his surname, sometimes by "Nick." They compare the Aliquippa police with the Spanish Inquisition and describe Yagielo's encounter with them, yet conclude, "But read his [Yagielo's] affidavit. This statement was sworn to after he had been to his personal physician following his final discharge from the police station" (1). As with the other reprinted texts, this format works with the front page's layout to position reading the affidavits as the central activity expected of readers. The party's language between and following the affidavits urges readers toward particular interpretations of the texts.

> Is anybody in Aliquippa safe?
>
> Citizens are asked to read these affidavits, then make up their minds to vote the entire gang of politicians responsible for present conditions out of office in November. . . .
>
> Do the people of Aliquippa want such Dark Ages brutality as this to continue? It might happen to any citizen of Aliquippa, black, white, rich or poor.
>
> No one can predict what these imported [from outside the local area] policemen of the Aliquippa police force will do.
>
> They have done plenty in the past and the events sworn to by Mr. Yagielo give evidence that they are not a thing of the past. . . .
>
> Has council taken any action to investigate this case? Or for that matter any other case? No one has heard of it.
>
> The only conclusion to be drawn is that either Burgess Sohn and council approve of these beatings or they don't care what happens to the average citizen of Aliquippa. . . .
>
> How much longer are the people going to stand for these conditions?
>
> We think until Democrats elected on November 2nd take office, and stop them.—THE DEMOCRATIC PARTY (1–2)

In these paragraphs, reading and interpretation appear as key actions, for they are directly linked with decision and further action (e.g., voting). While the Democratic Party's language frames the articles and plugs a particular interpretation of the experiences represented by Yagielo's and others' affidavits, it refrains from constructing those experiences into a story or argument built on paraphrase or quotation. Instead, the framing language remains just that in relation to the highlighted texts. Thus the interpretations it promotes, while of course crucial to its point, function most prominently as interpretations of another text that holds the central position. The combination of framing language and reprinted affidavits enacts a textual practice that models a way of building knowledge around experience and developing a course of action out of that knowledge. As Winstanley's pamphlets supported the Diggers' St. George's Hill project and Diane's Struggle work extended her parenting efforts, the *Press*'s rhetorical instruction promotes related actions in a wider social context.

In effect, the interplay among the affidavit texts, the Democratic Party's language, and the framing story illustrate for readers how to transform experience into evidence. They do so by modeling, naming, and encouraging a complex set of rhetorical moves, urging readers to experiment with these multiple moves. This process of scaffolding and directly sponsoring experiments with multiple, linked rhetorical practices extends Goodman's conception of change. It incorporates the spontaneous component of that change, recognizing that it can be encouraged but not mandated. Yet it also suggests that large-scale revisions of perceptual, rhetorical, and evaluative habits result not from a single experience of heightened awareness but from a series of linked experiences tied closely to modeling and explicit explanation (comparable to Wheeler's destructuring) of new alternative strategies.

The textual practice that conveys this instruction contrasts sharply with those that base evidence in professional authority or quote bits of individuals' speech to construct a journalist's story. Here, individuals' statements take the position of authorized evidence on which the newspaper and Democratic Party comment. This textual practice builds shared community knowledge (for instance, of police brutality) into valid evidence rather than imposing an interpretive framework external to the experience, as, for instance, happens in the pieces by Margerite Young and Bertha Winter Mahoney. Those stories afford little space for Aliquippa's working-class readers to use their experience in a process of knowledge production. The affidavits and their surrounding language, in contrast, enact a different textual practice that correlates with a different practice of knowledge construction—one in which working-class readers' experiences are represented as legitimated knowledge. Thus the interplay among the affidavits and the Democratic Party's and the *Press*'s language enacts—and models—for readers methods of constructing their experiences in the form of authorized knowledge that can act as evidence in their struggle with J & L's domination. The newspaper, in other words, instructs readers in intellectual practices that they can fashion into tools.

The *Press* explicitly drives home these tools' power in an October 13 editorial titled "We Publish—." After noting its publication of various company-union agreements, the piece explains its reasons for printing them.

> We have published these arguments and we will publish others in future issues of THE UNION PRESS, because we believe that every union member should study and understand the contract under which he is working. The text of the contract, like most legal texts, is subject to different interpretations and to different applications under different circumstances. It is by actual trial and judgment that the full meaning is brought out. . . . Each of [the agreements] is now the precedent for future settlements, for each of them defines specifically and interprets certain rights which union men have under their contract.
>
> That is why we publish them. Every union member owes it to himself to find out what his rights are, so that he may know when they are being violated, and so that he won't exceed them in his demands upon the union or corporation.
>
> Unionism does not come easily. Its possibilities and implications are broad and numerous. It takes practice and study and experience to understand how to be a good union man, and far more to become a good leader. On education depends the future of the labor movement and the future of America.

Here, the practices of study and self-education are directly linked to understanding and acting on one's situation. They enable workers to evaluate their circumstances and act accordingly. Action with texts interlocks with, supports, and enables other kinds of action, e.g., the practice, study, and experience needed to be a successful union member or leader; textual work appears here as a crucial step in fashioning oneself as a union member and extending Aliquippa's grassroots movement. Interpretation emerges as a key move in such textual work. The editorial initially positions interpretation as the quasi-legalistic process of trial and judgment, through which the meaning of such crucial documents as union-management contracts gets established. But by insisting that union members must study such agreements to evaluate their specific situations—to construct the meanings of their experiences—"We Publish" marks interpretation as the tool that enables union members to represent those experiences as evidence. It mandates an intellectual work that focuses particularly on many of the *Press*'s reprinted texts—the political platforms, agreements, and affidavits. As the editorial's conclusion illustrates, interpretation drives the grassroots effort to transform the future of not only local communities but the nation. By fostering readers' awareness of such tools' power, the journal further scaffolds their experiments with its suggested rhetorical, perceptual, and evaluative processes. Like Struggle's training materials and prompts and Winstanley's pieces, it integrates modeling, explanation, and persuasion in repeated cycles to support people in revising their contact styles. Together, these examples suggest that such revision extends beyond the insight provided by a single awareness experience and so requires larger support structures.

The *Press* extends its interpretive strategies through editorials that teach readers to use interpretations of their local experience to move back and forth among analyses of local and national issues in defining positions and taking actions. In fact, the October 13 issue builds on the "We Publish" editorial in the one immediately following it, "One-Third Organized." The piece opens by invoking what it describes as "the old cry" of "Buy union made goods!" "Seasoned unionists," it continues, "follow this practice religiously, but many of us, being new in the labor movement, have much to learn about what are union-made goods, and how to identify them." Using *Press* editors' recent study of the printing trades' union labels, the editorial goes on to an in-depth analysis of a particular set of union labels and their significance. By showing readers how to recognize unorganized, partially organized, and completely organized printers, it teaches them not only how to read the paper's own union label but why learning how to interpret such labels is important. Again, the journal prompts readers to juxtapose awarenesses, this time of a practice's significance and its procedures. By linking this juxtaposition to its larger structure of support for revising perceptual habits, the *Press* again encourages readers' awareness of their potential collective power. Specifically, the piece as a whole makes an implicit but forceful argument for the CIO's industry-wide approach to unionizing, as opposed to the AFL's craft-centered method. Through this cross-industry solidarity with the printers' and typographical unions, the *Press* bolsters a labor movement that spans U.S. industries and urges readers to do likewise. Thus it teaches them to construct interpretations leading to action with national implications.

An October 6 editorial, "The Union in Politics," similarly models interpretive moves that connect national events with local experience. The piece opens with a brief recapitulation of common arguments for why unions should "stay out of politics," such as the notion that if involved in politics, "the union . . . is bound either to alienate or to coerce some of its members." The editorial follows these arguments first by invoking the AFL's "vague and nebulous policy" on political involvement and then by reminding readers of Ohio and Pennsylvania politicians who crushed labor movements. It goes on to draw conclusions based on those events and to connect its conclusions with Aliquippans' local experiences.

> The point is that the civil government has control of the use of the armed forces—the police and the militia—and if labor does not control the government the employers will. It is an absolute necessity for the union to get into politics and come out on top.
>
> Aliquippa people have learned these lessons well. We knew what to expect of the local police officials during our [May 1937] strike, and it is because we knew and united solidly to resist their aggression that there was as little trouble here as there was.
>
> There were minorities among us in the primary campaign this year, but the union men are to be congratulated that they did not allow a serious split. And the minorities themselves are to be congratulated that they had the good grace to mend the minor splits that did occur, as soon as it became apparent what the majority wanted. That is of the essence of democracy. It is not dictatorship or coercion.
>
> Our lodge has endorsed the candidates of the Democratic Party. We are in politics up to our ears now, and rightly so. It is up to us to demonstrate that we have the will and the wit to st[i]ck together and win. We have a big stake in the election—there's no use kidding ourselves—and we must win.

In these paragraphs, the editorial's analysis of national politics grounds its argument for union activism in local politics, but this analysis is validated through an interpretation of Aliquippa events. The piece ties analysis of national events directly to its interpretation of Aliquippa's situation. By reading the events of the local Democratic primary, the editorial builds on that connection to refute the arguments cited in its opening and to conclude that its policy in Aliquippa has produced democracy rather than dictatorship. The link between interpretations of national events and interpretations of local events supports the piece's final declaration of the local union's position and the stakes involved. Putting Aliquippa events into national context enables its insistence that political action is crucial to the local grassroots movement. Thus the editorial models for readers the rhetorical moves of an analysis that interprets national and local events in light of one another to form a position.

Two more interconnected editorials, "Lay-Offs" and "And Why," which appear in that order in the October 20 *Union Press*, situate the union's approach and company policy around an issue that figures in both Aliquippa and national economics and politics. Both pieces address the problem of how to deal with layoffs and, in particular, the union's demand for a seniority clause. "Lay-Offs" describes the clause and union's reasons for pursuing it:

> But the union agreed to this [policy] believing that it would be better than the heart-breaking share-the-work policy which prevailed before. Then no one was certain where he stood. No one made a decent living. Now at least the older and more experienced workers in each department are safe, and in most cases they are the local residents. Others who are laid off know where they stand, and can go ahead and look for another job.
>
> The union recognizes that this is not enough. We recognize that we have a very difficult problem to face. Until we have built up the purchasing power of the people so as to prevent depressions, there will be slack times and unemployment. While we are working for adequate national purchasing power, we must institute a system of social insurance to help take care of the unemployed and carry them over the hard times. We hope that employers and other public-spirited citizens will join us in working for such an insurance system to take the edge off depression.

The first paragraph in this excerpt emphasizes the union's reasons for acting as it did in response to Aliquippa's local circumstances, particularly in its mention of ensuring jobs for local residents. But the following paragraph, the editorial's conclusion, acknowledges the policy's shortcomings and opens the question of market forces beyond the control not only of individual employees but of the union as well. By contextualizing the local union policy in broader economic terms, the piece not only invokes the union's larger mission of creating permanent prosperity but again implicitly argues for the union's political involvement by calling for a system of social insurance. The text thus models for readers a set of contextualizing rhetorical moves that link local experience with (inter)national market forces to produce a frame for both evaluating local policy and locating such policies within larger strategies, e.g., increasing purchasing power and lobbying for unemployment compensation.

The following editorial, "And Why," builds on this work by responding to charges that the union in fact caused layoffs from J & L. The piece first cites an industry-wide slump and then explains that "the cause of business slumps is inadequate purchasing power in the pockets of the consumers." Like the preceding piece, this editorial situates the union's role within a broader economic picture to argue for the union's global strategy of increasing purchasing power. "The captains of industry," it concludes, "have it within their power to provide for themselves an enduring market which would prevent any general business slump. If they have failed to do this, it is their own short-sightedness which is to blame, not the CIO." Together, these two editorials enact for readers an intellectual practice that responds to arguments by weaving interpretations of local experience into a representation of broader economic and political context to construct local initiatives and, simultaneously, to position those initiatives within a global plan. Their interplay helps the newspaper teach readers the rhetorical moves to combine analyses of other texts with interpretations of their own experiences to manufacture knowledge. As the *Press* itself demonstrates, this knowledge serves readers as a tool in developing a newly activist contact style seeking local and national transformation. The journal fosters this new contact style through a support structure that integrates the varied elements needed to encourage such self-revision.

Steeltown Boils

But in the summer of 1934, unionizers found little support, as Clarence Irwin and his allies faced steelworkers' despair. They put rank-and-file candidates up for national offices in the AA's fall 1934 elections and approached SMWIU for the funds, lawyers, and publicity needed to build a national movement. Rank-and-filers resolved to rely on "the power of their own organization, exercised by the calling of strikes if and when necessary" (Lynd 200). In retaliation, AA president Tighe expelled them as dissidents, and SMWIU followed Communist Party policy and refused to break with Tighe. Lynd explains, "The [SMWIU] resources which might have financed an organizing drive were used instead to campaign for re-instatement in the A[A]" (Lynd 201). SMWIU backed successful lawsuits that forced Tighe to reinstate the expelled locals but did not support rank-and-file strike efforts. Meanwhile, UMW leader John L. Lewis blocked planned rank-and-file strikes uniting mine and steel workers. Disillusioned steel workers again renounced their AA memberships.

Some joined Employee Representation Plans (ERPs), company-sponsored unions formed by the steel corporations to try to counter the union drives authorized by the NRA and exclude "outside unions" (Brooks 75). While many mill workers labeled the ERPs stool pigeons, some sought to seize control of them from management (Powers 50–51). For instance, Clairton's John Mullen and Duquesne's Elmer Maloy tried to counter Carnegie Steel's fragmentation of ERP power by uniting to pressure the firm to negotiate with representatives from several plants (Brooks 82–85). Meantime, Lewis had lost patience with AFL roadblocks to his efforts to direct steel unionizing. After repeated confrontations with its leadership, Lewis led the miners', printers', typographers', smelters', and other unions in a fall 1935 break with the AFL. They formed the CIO (Brooks 71; Powers 55). At the same time, the AA rank-and-filers were regrouping for another effort to seize control of the AFL by sweeping the upcoming 1936 convention into an active organizing campaign. They asked ERP leaders to join them (Powers 55–60).

Men such as Mullen and Maloy did so, organizing local political campaigns to try to make unionizing more feasible. In fall 1935 Mullen ran for city council and "got licked by a hundred votes" despite company opposition and the fact that Mullen spent "forty-seven dollars and they spent thousands" and "hauled men to the voting booths on company time . . . intimat[ing] that their jobs would be safer if they went along with the Corporation" (Brooks 8–9). In spring 1936, Steeltown activists, hearing that Lewis would be in nearby Greensburg, sought the CIO leader and urged him to begin a CIO-supported organizing drive in steel (Powers 63–65). Lewis agreed, planning to offer the AFL five hundred thousand dollars to organize the industry. Knowing the reactionary AA would oppose the move because Tighe feared losing control of the steel union, CIO staffers asked Aliquippa's Albert Atallah how to persuade the AFL to accept Lewis's offer.

Atallah proposed infiltrating the upcoming AA and AFL conventions, both scheduled for the end of April. At the Uniontown, Pa., AFL convention, Powers and other rank-and-filers agitated successfully to send a delegation recommending acceptance of Lewis's offer to the nearby Canonsburg, Pa., AA convention. Despite Tighe's attempt to prevent the expelled locals from joining the convention, Atallah's spokesmanship succeeded, and the new representatives won their seats and the acceptance of Lewis's offer. On June 17, 1936, Lewis established SWOC. Many ERP representatives, such as Maloy, began

working with SWOC even before they became members, planning to infiltrate the company unions for the new organization. By early 1937, ERP members deserted to SWOC in droves, as company union remnants agitated for
independence and SMWIU threw its resources behind SWOC, though the
CIO later discarded SMWIU organizers when they became inconvenient
(Lynd 203; Brody 28; Casebeer 668–69). U.S. Steel, facing the prospect of a
company-wide strike, agreed on March 2, 1937, to recognize SWOC's bargaining power and negotiated a contract signed on March 17.

But Lewis's leadership imposed tight hierarchical controls on rank-and-filers, requiring SWOC authorization for all local strike actions (Casebeer 667).
To win SWOC's desperately needed financial resources, rank-and-filers sacri-
ficed grassroots control. SWOC focused on national strategies, overlooking
local politics in favor of presidential politicking and publishing a union journal with no local news (Davin 54–55). Philip Murray, Lewis's lieutenant and
appointed SWOC leader, eventually renounced SWOC's political role, insisting, "The SWOC is not a political instrument" (qtd. in Davin 57).

Yet SWOC's drive succeeded only because it capitalized on the energies of
steel's dedicated grassroots organizers. Brody indicates that activists such as
Irwin and Atallah provided the outlet into which Lewis plugged CIO
resources (16). By directing and funding this network, SWOC furthered local
drives that netted 125,000 members between June 1936 and early 1937 (Brody
21). But as Lynd points out, the June 1933–April 1934 rank-and-file drive, with
little outside support (financial or otherwise), had signed roughly the same
number (191).

Despite Murray's apolitical rhetoric, the rank-and-filers organized grassroots political campaigns to win control of their communities. Powers explains
that in the early 1930s the Democratic Party in Steeltown "had no precinct
workers, no funds, no leadership, and no spirit" (131). Union activists faced
civic repression. For instance, just after John Mullen made his first open
SWOC speech in July 1936, his wife called to say the Clairton sheriff was evict-
ing the family from the company-owned house they rented. Mullen found his
wife and three children (two of whom had rheumatic fever) and his furniture
in the pouring rain. He quickly learned that the company had ordered every
local real estate agent to refuse to rent to him and found an apartment only by
moving at night into a place rented for him by a friend. He then decided to
run for mayor (Davin 35). In Duquesne, Elmer Maloy could not rent a hall for
a union meeting because the company directed banks to threaten hall owners
with mortgage foreclosure if they rented to him, or they rented halls on condition that their owners refuse to rent to Maloy. Like Mullen, Maloy decided

to run for mayor, and Davin says other Steeltown activists explained their 1937 political campaigns with comparable stories (40–41).

Despite the official Democratic Party's opposition, Maloy overwhelmingly carried the primary. Davin notes that other Steeltown organizers also used their union infrastructure to bring the moribund Democratic Party to life (57). Drawing on new public condemnation of recently exposed company violence and duplicity, activists met, canvassed, printed newsletters and flyers, and held Labor Day parades. Although Duquesne's official Democratic Party worked for the Republican candidate, Maloy won the election by a secure margin (Davin 42, 44). Not only did Mullen also take the Clairton mayor's seat, in November 1937, seventeen Steeltown communities put local government into the hands of "labor-liberal coalitions" (Powers 140). Only McKeesport's Republican mayor George Lysle survived. The November 11 Pittsburgh *Bulletin Index* ran a cover photo of Elmer Maloy, proclaiming, "Up and down the river, revolution!" (Davin 2).

Aliquippa Boils

Brooks depicts veteran UMW activist Joe Timko single-handedly organizing fearful Aliquippa workers at SWOC's behest. Local activists Mary Cozzicolli, Frank Kromerich, Ormond Montini, and Pete Muselin emphasize Aliquippa's fear but also its long-standing organizing efforts. Cozzicolli, who worked with other women in the mill's sorting room, describes the mid-1930s founding of the local Democratic Club (6), while Montini sketches unionizers' infiltration of the Music and Political Italian Club, the company's Republican-controlled organization in Aliquippa's Italian section (5, 9).

Such efforts provided Timko a base. He used the Democratic Club to call the first organization meeting. Eighteen steelworkers attended. J & L fired fourteen within two weeks. But Timko's second call drew forty-five people and his third, two hundred. The fired fourteen named themselves the Honor Roll Committee, whose membership hit fifty-two by summer's end, as J & L continued firings (Brooks 115–17).[8] An Honor Roll manifesto invoked members' legal rights, condemning the firm's actions and announcing their plan to unionize for Aliquippa's betterment (Casebeer 665–66). At the request of Democratic Club president Mike Kellar, Mary Cozzicolli formed a ladies' auxiliary to raise money. Through social events, the auxiliary supported union causes, fed strikers, and helped organize the voter registration drive (Cozzicolli 13).

Meanwhile, J & L used its civic officials to arrest members and deduct fines from their paychecks, search organizers' rooms and belongings, confiscate union literature and membership cards, and have spies "ostentatiously [take] down names and license numbers" at union meetings (Brooks 118). Through its company union, J & L issued a flyer detailing the evils of strikes and unions, the benefits J & L provided Aliquippa, and its opposition to any "outside union." It warns, "The $30,000,000 plant now being erected in Pittsburgh was lost to Aliquippa through labor agitation[,] and the value of every dwelling dropped to 30 cents on the dollar" (qtd. in Casebeer 671). A July 2, 1936, *Aliquippa Gazette* editorial calls union leaders racketeers scheming to extract dues from gullible co-workers and decries labor's potential political influence (Casebeer 671–72). In reply, Timko distributed his own leaflet, and by August, SWOC had started its *Steel Labor* newspaper. Organizers distributed it at mill gates, union meetings, and workers' doorsteps (Brooks 117).

The company used operatives to sow racism and undermine unionizing, but blacks increasingly identified with the AA "because of its potential to advance their interests" (Dickerson 135). Robert Vann, the nationally prominent black publisher of the *Pittsburgh Courier*, "lent the weight of his editorial pen to the CIO," and other black Pittsburgh leaders backed the Aliquippa organizers (Dickerson 138–39). SWOC sent black organizers as well as white to Aliquippa, and resident black activists played important roles in the Aliquippa local (Dickerson 142, 147).

Despite J & L's efforts, membership grew, bolstered by the March 1937 SWOC–U.S. Steel agreement. On April 12, 1937, two years after J & L fired the original Honor Roll Committee members, the Supreme Court upheld an NLRB decision ordering the firm to rehire the discharged men with back pay (Casebeer 664–65, 672). The ruling electrified Aliquippa. On May 12, Aliquippa workers struck J & L when the company refused to sign an exclusive bargaining contract with SWOC. But "[i]n a sense a group of steelworkers didn't strike as much as an entire town struck" (Casebeer 672–73).

Cozzicolli describes how even elderly women stood on the picket lines to prevent supplies for scab workers from entering the mill (8–9). According to a young organizer, "the workers took over the functions of government" (Casebeer 674). Traffic clogged the streets, forcing the bus company to suspend runs, while picketers commandeered the train terminal to prevent the trains, all owned by J & L, from stopping. Others blocked the Aliquippa side of the bridge to Ambridge, effectively closing Aliquippa (Casebeer 675). Two days later, as Pennsylvania's Democratic governor, George Earle, approached the mill with Timko, their car was halted by company police with raised rifles (Brooks 126). Earle ordered the company and the union to settle the matter peacefully, and J & L capitulated. Thirty-six hours after the strike began, chairman H. E. Lewis signed an exclusive bargaining contract on condition that SWOC win an NLRB election in Aliquippa mills (Casebeer 675). In the May 20 election, workers voted 17,028 to 7,207 for SWOC, and the committee negotiated a contract establishing it as exclusive bargaining agent (Brooks 127). The first exclusive bargaining agreement in the nation, secured in the first real industrial election, it positioned SWOC for battle with Little Steel, independent firms that undertook a long, bloody fight against unions after U.S. Steel's agreement with SWOC.

In summer 1937, Little Steel was led by Bethlehem Steel's president Eugene Grace and Tom M. ("Tommy Gun") Girdler, who started as J & L's Aliquippa general manager and eventually became president of Republic Steel Corporation (Casebeer 618). After extended efforts to negotiate, SWOC struck the firms in May 1937, quickly mobilizing ninety thousand workers. The companies deployed firearms, tear gas, and other weapons, as well as bribery, propaganda, and civil repression. They terrorized steel towns, killing picketers and wounding strikers and their family members (Brooks 143–44; Powers 108–10). Eventually, SWOC exposed their tactics in Congress's LaFollette investigation, which led to the firms' 1941 agreement to bargain with SWOC (Abel 104–5).

But like other rank-and-filers, Aliquippans traded local control for SWOC's support. Timko derailed a series of 1937 wildcat strikes pressing for safer working conditions (such as protection from falling hot steel; Casebeer 679). And Aliquippans fought for democratic local government without SWOC support. By 1935, Democratic registrations had shot from virtually none to 20,960, challenging Republicans' 45,675 in Beaver County. The union's 1937 candidates for local political offices pledged to reform the police force through civic (rather than company) control and to introduce New Deal programs such as the Works Progress Administration and Public Works Administration, which Republican officials had rejected. They won the burgess's (mayor's) seat and three of the four city council seats up for election. They ousted Ruffner from the tax collector's office. In the next elections, union candidates won the remaining council seats. One steelworker commented that it was "worth twelve dollars a year to be able to walk down the main street of Aliquippa, talk to anyone you want about anything you like, and feel that you are a citizen" (qtd. in Casebeer 680).

While SWOC's support was essential, it also destroyed rank-and-file activism. Local activists could not call a strike, set dues and initiation fees, or choose national leadership (Brody 28; Nyden 30). In 1942, when SWOC reorganized as the United Steelworkers of America, it institutionalized a rigid hierarchical structure (Brody 28) and shrank from political activism. Blacks seeking integration and local organizers such as Clarence Irwin, who had backed "a real Labor Party with no connection with any of the existing parties" (Lynd 204), saw their hopes fade (Davin 32, 62–63). Their desired grassroots challenge to corporate control of American communities evaporated into "the political company unionism of the two-party system" (Lynd 204).

Manufacturing Identities

Still, in mid-1930s Aliquippa, the *Union Press* sought a political voice for labor and helped grassroots activists to win civic control of their town from J & L, using the final prong of its pedagogical strategy: teaching readers how to remake their identities. The journal instructs readers on developing an activist contact style by prompting them to reposition their identities in relation to various groups. Some pieces use shop and neighborhood micropolitics to teach rhetorical strategies for changing entrenched practices in mill culture, strategies that link action on individual incidents with broader union efforts, thus promoting a contact style that integrates individual and collective forms of activism.

To address Aliquippa's entrenched racism, encouraged by corporate efforts to enflame racial tensions, the *Press* prompts readers to reposition themselves in relation to various groups. "Negro Problems Discussed," a story reprinted from Universal News Service on the National Negro Congress's upcoming second convention to be held the following month in Philadelphia, is positioned prominently in the top-left block of the paper's September 29 issue. It undertakes this work through an opening paragraph that describes blacks as an important CIO constituency and then notes that the convention invited all CIO affiliates to send delegates. The story's location on the page and opening paragraph mark black issues and integration into the CIO as important to the union drive as a whole, emphasizing that the invitation is an explicit effort to foster an interracial approach. In its list of issues to be "proposed for discussion and action" at the convention, the article includes "[t]he organization of Negro workers with their white fellow workers into democratically controlled trade unions." This item links action on black advancement integrally with advancing the union effort. While the article is of course not an Aliquippa-based piece of writing, the *Press*'s decision not just to run it but to position it prominently marks the story as one strand of the paper's effort to reshape readers' identities by encouraging them to reposition their relations with others.

The most striking instance of this effort may appear in the journal's first issue in another front-page piece, one of that edition's two lead stories. By emphasizing the importance of the Aliquippa union's black constituency while treating an issue significant to all of the town's working-class readers, the article perhaps integrates black working-class readers' interests more thoroughly into the union agenda than would a piece explicitly targeting those interests. The story appears under the first of this edition's two banner headlines, "Union Wins First 15 Discharge Cases," and follows that with an article title and two subtitles: "Discharged Union Men All Put Back To Work"; "12 Men From Open Hearth Department, 1 Each From Cold Rolls, Restaurant And By-Products Plant, Win Jobs Back"; and "First Action Reinstates a Negro." While the article title is the largest of the three, the second subtitle is larger than the first and the only one printed entirely in capital letters. By putting the second subtitle in the context of the preceding two, the article already works to integrate black interests into a key Aliquippa union victory. By printing the second subheading in capital letters, the piece makes those interests a central part of the union's accomplishment in winning job reinstatement for its members. It fosters both black and white readers' awareness of their immediate collective interests as a cross-racial group. Thus it prompts them to shift their perception of self-other relationships related to their race and class identities by privileging the latter over the former.

The article's three opening paragraphs continue both the integration and foregrounding of black interests within union issues:

> Every one of the 15 union men who have been discharged from the mill here in Aliquippa since the strike and plant election last May has been put back to work, through the efforts of the union's officers and grievance committee.
>
> One man, a negro, was discharged from the cold rolls department of the tin mill, allegedly for fighting and insubordination, while the man he was fighting with, a non-union man, was given no penalty at first.
>
> Lodge President Paul Normile and Sub-Regional SWOC Director Joseph Timko took up the case with the management of the corporation immediately. The final settlement was that both men were penalized with the loss of two days work, the union man being paid for a third day's work which he missed while his case was pending settlement. This was the first grievance handled by the union after the election.

The story's move to integrate black workers' interests into union interests emerges powerfully in the grammatical structure of the second paragraph's opening sentence. By positioning the phrase "a negro" as an appositive—and thus grammatically subordinate—to the sentence's subject, "one man," the article's prose positions race as secondary to that subject's human status. As an appositive, the phrase provides identifying information that is, grammatically speaking, dispensable. Race, in the sentence's structure, is carefully positioned as unnecessary to the sense, to the basic meaning, of this unit of language and, by extension, to the basic meaning of the story.[9] Given Goodman's point that evaluation is largely a matter of rhetorical attitudes, the article's phrasing subtly but powerfully repositions racial identification as far less significant than class identification.[10]

This effort at integration emerges in the interplay among paragraphs as well. To begin, the first two of the three opening paragraphs are set in larger type than either the remainder of the story or most of the other front-page articles.[11] This layout decision positions the information conveyed in each paragraph—the newly won reinstatement and the specifics of one man's case—as equally important. But of course the order of the paragraphs subordinates the point of the second and its racial identification to the first paragraph's proclamation of a crucial union victory. The three paragraphs achieve this integration more fundamentally by following the subordinated mention of the worker's race with a description of the grievance incident, a description that replaces one kind of categorization, white versus black, with a very different kind, union versus nonunion. This move encourages readers' awareness of the power of class-based union identification, thus prompting them to shift their perception of their relations to other racial groups, thus promoting a contact style more focused on collective goals than on racial identity. That is, the *Press* fosters awareness of a revised set of categories and a shift in the perceptual and rhetorical habits of categorization. The final sentence of the third paragraph drives home the point that black grievances get top priority in the Aliquippa union's agenda. Thus these paragraphs work to heighten readers' awareness of a new set of possible identifications and alliances.

This work may well have changed the conditions of experience for many white and black Aliquippa readers. Given the racially divisive politics of 1930s America generally and of the steel firms particularly, as well as many southern and eastern European and Irish immigrants' efforts to define themselves as culturally white, it seems likely that many Aliquippa readers had not encountered assertions of black-white equality from white writers. I have no way to verify the accuracy of this speculation. But if accurate, the changed conditions of experience may have prompted some readers to reinterpret the evidence of their experiences. Such reorganizations are complex, and their direction (e.g., partial acceptance of equality, a politically correct public stance, or deepening racism) cannot be estimated without extensive empirical evidence. I suggest, though, that the *Union Press* works to foster readers' experiments with identification primarily in terms of class over race and especially in terms of union membership. The relevant articles exemplify Goodman's experimentation as a form of creative adjustment to new material. The stories respond to the exigencies of trying to forge an effective class politics and the newly viable hope for doing so by striving to promote a cross-racial, class-based identity.

This particular story amplifies its call for readers to revise their identifications with various groups in its fifth paragraph. "When asked about non-union men who had been discharged, Clifford Shorts, financial secretary and general grievance committeeman for Lodge 1211, said, 'Of course we have no record of non-union men discharged, for they have not brought their cases to us, but we have heard rumors of perhaps seven or eight such discharges. Presumably those seven or eight men are not in the mill any longer.'"

In the context of the story's trumpeting of union victory for twenty-six individual J & L employees, the Shorts quotation emphasizes that the group identification with material impact is union membership.[12] Nonunion employees appear, in Shorts's phrasing, not only outside the purview of official knowledge but materially vulnerable to losing their livelihoods at company whim. Through this positioning, the story urges readers to redefine their criteria for understanding group membership and thus seeks to prompt them to revise their identities. The piece drives home this lesson in its concluding paragraph: "'It is important to notice,' said President Paul Normile, 'that the very first man the union negotiated for was a colored man, as is one of the other fourteen men discharged. There is no discrimination whatsoever in union affairs between men of different races, nationalities and creeds. They're all alike: union steel workers.'"

These sentences, positioned as the article's coup de grace, emphasize explicitly that such categories as race and ethnicity are not only secondary but, in fact, irrelevant in terms of Aliquippa's grassroots movement. Instead, they claim, the only definitive category is union membership.[13] This claim heightens a new awareness of self-other relations and so encourages readers—black and white—to make a dramatic shift in perceiving their identities. By prompting them to undertake the intellectual work of redefining the categories through which they understand themselves, the piece pushes readers to invest emotional and intellectual energy in reimagining who they are, in reshaping their identities. It asks them to take up the intellectual project of remaking themselves.[14]

The final strands of the *Union Press*'s pedagogical strategy emerge in pieces that use shop and neighborhood micropolitics to teach readers rhetorical strategies for changing entrenched practices in mill culture, strategies that integrate action on individual incidents into broader union plans. This work happens especially in the paper's regular columns, which comment almost exclusively, and often satirically, on day-to-day plant and neighborhood events and on individuals' actions. With some exceptions, these columns often refrain from using names but include descriptions specific enough that local readers might well guess the identity of people mentioned. For instance, the September 29 "Guess Who?" column asks, "Who is the slick haired zig-zagger who no one talks to? The boys used to call him 'Snake Eyes,' but now it's just plain 'Stool,'" and "Who is the shop steward who keeps his record book so clean, but looks like Man Mountain Dean approaching the slackers? Net result: one more member in good standing." Such queries not only prompt readers to try to identify the person in question but, through their critiques or commendations, suggest that readers tailor their social interactions with the people described. As in the questions cited, the columns tend to move back and forth between lampooning actions that undermine Aliquippa's grassroots movement and commending practices that support it. In the first case, the columns' rhetorical moves model strategies readers can use to exert social pressure on the person satirized (as in the case of the "zig-zagger" who has already been shunned), while in the second they model rhetorical practices for socially supporting people who further the union's cause (e.g., by similarly pressuring slackers to pay up their union dues). At the same time, they offer social practices (such as recruitment) that readers can emulate.

Similarly, the columns and related stories convey neighborhood and shop floor information that readers otherwise might not learn to enable them to take up social interactions that further the grassroots effort. For instance, the story "Ask These Boys What They Think Of C.I.O. And What It Did For Them," just across from "Guess Who?" on the September 29 edition's second page, spends nearly all of its space listing names, departments, and, occasionally, gains, such as, "Eugene Ford, Strip Mill . . . Andrew Medjomorec, Cold Finishing Mill (6 1/2 cent raise)." The list concludes with the article's only full sentence: "If you are having such conditions existing on your job that are unfair to you, LET YOUR COMMITTEE MAN KNOW IMMEDIATELY." Through this structure, the piece works to push social interactions in several specific directions by modeling rhetorical moves that foster a contact style that integrates individual action with collective efforts. By trumpeting union accomplishments for particular individuals (and, in a few instances, departments), the piece prompts readers' awareness (or renewed awareness) of union successes. In encouraging this awareness, it models rhetorical moves that focus evaluation on the efficacy of collective power. Further, by urging readers to speak with people who have benefited from union activism, it fosters social and workplace conversations about the Aliquippa union's strength and effectiveness. The article positions the men listed to campaign in their work and social circles for people's support of the union. Thus the piece mobilizes Aliquippa's—and more specifically J & L's—social networks to nourish the grassroots movement's growth.

Between "Guess Who?" and "Ask These Boys," the column "The Spirits of 1843" pushes readers toward different kinds of social interactions. Like the other two pieces, it provides readers with local information they might not otherwise learn. One paragraph begins, "Guess who these birds are:" and lists various characters, such as "the dirty low down scab from the coal handling department who on certain nights spend[s] many hours with his friend's wife on the sly" and "the dirty oven foremen who make written reports of all conversations to the super." By assuming that readers have enough local knowledge to decipher the identities of the people it targets, the column spreads a kind of information generally circulated only through gossip. Such information, of course, can crucially structure social and work lives, as well as individuals' actions. By alerting the coal handlers and oven crewmembers to their co-worker's and supervisors' behavior, respectively, the piece seeks to prompt the targeted readers to intervene in what it portrays as unethical work and social situations. All of these pieces spotlight individuals' and groups' day-to-day actions to extend the *Press*'s pedagogy by providing readers with trenchant local information and, through their rhetorical modeling, prompting those readers to exert social pressures to change such day-to-day practices. In short, they not only provide readers with relevant information but instruct them in how to use that information to reshape entrenched practices in their local culture, both in town and on the shop floor.

The October 20 issue's "Seamless Sparks" column extends this instruction by teaching readers another way to intervene in local workplace practices.[15] In this case, it shows readers how they can mobilize the union structure to intervene in abusive actions.

> We wish to thank Johnny Klever of the tester crew for pointing out the reason why some of the union men on the tester weren't wearing their dues buttons. . . . It has been said that the spirit of the Seam-

less men is falling. . . . Keep it up boys!! Don't let anybody say that we will sacrifice the principles for which CIO stands. We all hate petty bossism and discrimination. As long as we have a contract with a Seniority clause in it like ours, those rotten things will not happen in J&L.

We aim to make this a column for the workers of the Seamless as well as to encourage other departments in sponsoring their own columns. So give us your news if you care to make this YOUR NEWS-PAPER. . . . Don't forget to help in investigat[ing] the UPSETTER'S CASE and THE OBSERVER'S NOTE. Tell us what you think of the case before we give you the results of the investigation. For the benefit of those who don't have any information on it, we might say that it deals with the boss's right in the contract. Can he, under contract, give his friends or another boss's relatives, the privileges which other deserving workmen should have? We say HELL NO! Furthermore, we will see that NO MORE of that goes on in the Seamless. Give us your help and that will be proven.

This excerpt spans the column and illustrates how the piece enacts its instruction through several connected methods. First, the subtle shifts in its use of "we," its most prevalent pronoun, works to fold readers into the initial "we" of the opening line, the "we" of the paper's staff, and vice versa. That first "we"'s boundaries dissolve into a "we" that encompasses staff and readers, the "we" who hate "petty bossism" and have a contract with a seniority clause.

While the grammatical boundaries of the final paragraph's uses of the pronoun are more solid, the column's content blurs them in another way. To begin, its example of the presumably pseudonymous Johnny Klever illustrates for readers a potential relation with the *Press*, a relation they might take up, namely one of liaison between newspaper and workplace. By tying union spirit in the Seamless department to the fight against "petty bossism" and moving from that topic directly into the description of the column's function and call for workers' contributions, the piece links such contributions to the *Press* with the union's efforts to better working conditions, not only in general but specifically in the Seamless department.

The concluding paragraph takes an even more localized tack, urging readers to contribute information and views as part of the fight against a specific case of the petty bossism condemned above. Thus the column asks readers to undertake specific rhetorical practices that, like those surrounding the pre-election issues' affidavits, translate their experience and interpretations into officially recognized knowledge, knowledge the union and the *Press* can use to reform the micropolitical practices in the Seamless department. The "we" who say "HELL NO!" and who promise to prevent future violations of the contract seems in grammatical terms to refer strictly to the newspaper's staff, but the column's instructional moves and earlier grammatical elisions combine to make these final "we"'s permeable, inclusive of readers as well as writers. This issue's "Seamless Sparks" pushes the paper's pedagogical project forward by teaching readers how to bring broad union positions to bear on local incidents—the day-to-day happenings in the shop, the building blocks of mill culture's practices. In effect, it instructs readers in rhetorical practices that foster a contact style tailored to integrate local actions with broader commitments.

The October 29 "Seamless Sparks" amplifies this kind of instruction, again urging readers to act as liaisons between workplace and newspaper. As in the October 20 issue, the column figures such endeavors as key to fighting bossism:

> A few weeks ago some inspectors petitioned for a raise. On inquiring for the reason of a certain inspector's signature not being on the line, we were told that hiis [*sic*] mother belongs to the same bridge club that Mrs.——— whose husband is ——— of the ——— department. That's good going old boy. But you're not fooling us. We're looking to see what breaks you will get that you don't deserve. . . . The policy of putting out production is throwing an awful scare into the "informer." Their kind of production doesn't bring results any longer. A few weeks ago we had a letter from our supervisor which warned us against certain activities. On asking for the proof of such actions we were of course, not justified. It's a darn good thing that the courts outside of Aliquippa don't render such Better Quality justice. Every accused person has a right to face witnesses testifying against him outside of Aliquippa. . . . Pittsburgh and Midland are doing a pretty good job in exposing the detrimental factors in their mills. Let's have the same fun at the expense of the informers. With the reputation of the Seamless we should do big things along these lines. Give your dope to your shop Stewards and don't forget to tell them to turn it into [*sic*] the newspaper editor or one of his assistants.

The early invocation of the old boy network signals the column's sustained attack on the patronage system gripping mill culture and, at the same time, prompts readers to look for individual cases of bossism. This example also sets the stage for the piece's focus on workers, rather than strictly management, complicit with such practices. By putting informers' and supervisors' actions in the context of an ideal of the American justice system, the column makes a double play. First, it heightens readers' awareness of the grassroots movement's fight to transform Aliquippa's own civil and judicial orders as a means to protect working-class (and other) residents from J & L's puppet government. That move is key in this preelection issue's effort to prompt readers to the polls the following week. Next, it uses both that reminder and new policies to picture the threat posed by company spies as dissipating in the face of grassroots power. The final section of the excerpt—also the column's concluding paragraph—makes readers and column extensions of one another: the *Press*'s columns mobilize pressure to transform mill practices, while readers energize those columns by contributing the shop and neighborhood details that produce such pressure. The paper thus models rhetorical moves that prompt readers' awareness of such details. It encourages readers to reinterpret local events and situations to evaluate their potential usefulness toward collective goals. The *Press*'s pedagogical, interactive relation with readers exerts grassroots sociopolitical pressure on department and neighborhood practices. In turn, that pressure promotes broader transformation by interweaving shop-floor and community activism with the union's strategies for recasting J & L, Aliquippa, and the steel industry. Thus it encourages a contact style that integrates individual action with collective efforts. It evokes the potential to link individual changes achieved through literate practices with collective endeavors, should a context support such coalitions.

7

Promoting Contact:
Literate Practices and Change

S THE Struggle, Digger, and Aliquippa cases suggest, the changes literate practices can promote depend on local and larger contexts. To consider what these three cases imply about how literate practices can support change, I return to my original questions about knowledge production. The limits of each of the three modes of knowledge production (empirical, theoretical, and experiential), as well as the limited generalizability of ethnographic knowledge, make it problematic to use these cases' implications to construct a model of how literate practices can support change.

Given the limits of each mode of knowledge production, we cannot generate definitive knowledge about most aspects of social behavior and identity formation. These kinds of development are idiosyncratic, uncertain, and uneven. Thus it is not feasible to construct a universally applicable model of how literate practices promote change. The danger in claims for generalizable knowledge is that they encourage us to approach a specific situation as if it were subject to universal laws. They encourage us to categorize and thus to miss the substantive differences in particular individuals and circumstances. Whether the mode of knowledge is empirical, theoretical, or experiential, that approach erases key aspects of experience, as in Spivak's examples of how post-colonial empirical researchers risk freezing subalterns into models for imitation, Marx misses readers' experience, and defenders of practices such as sati ignore ideology ("Can the Subaltern Speak?" "Limits and Openings").

The challenge is to learn about tendencies in individuals and systems and yet recognize that, because these tendencies provide at best a partial knowledge, the circumstances in any specific case can generate different results or warrant a different approach.[1] This challenge requires us to bring our existing knowledge from the various modes to each situation and yet approach it as a unique case, intending to learn from it and to adapt our understanding to its specifics. That is, we are best served by attuning our awareness to how each situation echoes and revises our prior knowledge. The question is how to do this yet still make productive use of existing knowledge.

We can do so by revising our uses of research findings. Rather than constructing universally applicable models, we can instead build heuristics, problem-solving tools designed to explore a situation or to improve performance in dealing with it. Instead of providing generalizable findings, heuristics offer questions and approaches for producing knowledge about a specific case. They can range from the simple (such as a series of questions, e.g., who? what? when? where? why? and how?) to the complex (a computer program designed to offer feedback on performance of a given task). Constructing a heuristic begins with the same steps used to construct a model. Here that entails charting patterns in when and how individuals and groups use literate practices to foster change. These patterns can be used to generate sets of questions or trial-and-error frames for exploring specific cases. This approach presupposes that studying new cases will reveal not only further patterns but also exceptions and their relative frequency, these exceptions' patterns, and complexities in all observed patterns.

This focus on exploratory tools rather than universal models does not free heuristics from the ideological and discursive grounds of all rational knowledge. But it orients them toward promoting expanded contact with the breadth of human experience by producing an interplay among empirical, theoretical, and experiential kinds of knowledge. It diminishes the risk of erasing key aspects of experience, a risk increased by claiming generalizable knowledge.

Supporting Change through Literate Practices

Parallels across the cases described here suggest specific ways in which literate practices can promote change. These parallels show comparable (and sometimes divergent) uses of literate practices made by the Diggers, the Aliquippa unionizers, and Struggle's participants and planners.

Taken together, the three cases suggest that the effects of ideologies and discursive structures result not strictly from the ideas or forms themselves but rather from the particular uses made of them. For instance, Diane invoked the rubric common sense to prompt Ian and Jody to undertake a disciplined reflection. Her use contrasts sharply with most academic critiques of common sense as an ideology promoting unreflective allegiance to the common wisdom. Through it, Diane encouraged the adolescents to increase their contact with their own internal experiences and so to expand their perceptions of external circumstances. Thus her use of the term supported reflection and broadened perception and explicitly countered the kind of knee-jerk response often associated with the rubric. Similarly, Winstanley drew on the long-established discourse of biblical exegesis to construct his argument for making the earth into a "common treasury." Other seventeenth-century Britons mobilized this discourse to argue for very different economic relations. Thus Winstanley's application of it highlights the importance of examining what conditions foster one use rather than another. The *Union Press*'s work within quasi-objectivist journalistic discourse is another example. Such discourse is often rightly seen in academic critiques as masking fundamental presuppositions that support an economically and culturally exploitative corporate order. Yet the *Press* draws on that discourse in pieces such as "Ask Questions" to instruct readers in analyzing the interests behind both local politics and media depictions. Thus it encourages us to explore what pedagogical function is served by any given use of a discourse.

Foucault argues that discursive systems structure knowledge production that coheres with centralizing, controlling, hierarchical forces (*Archaeology of Knowledge, History of Sexuality*). Similarly, Althusser holds that ideology must be overcome via rigorous critique. The cases of the Diggers, the Aliquippa unionizers, and Struggle's participants and planners show that people's varied uses of ideologies and discursive structures can support widely divergent social conditions and individual identities. They suggest that to understand how language shapes such phenomena, we cannot just analyze ideological forms or discursive structures. Rather, we must also consider in detail specific cases that illustrate various possible uses of ideologies and discourses. These cases turn our attention to the processes that shape people's applications of such materials.

The second parallel that emerges in these cases suggests that when language practices do support individual and communal change, they do so by expanding people's contact with unaware dimensions of their experience. This contact results from changed conditions of experience and in turn promotes change. For instance, Ian's post-Struggle interview shows that his interaction with his adult Struggle partner expanded his awareness of the risks his neighborhood posed for him. While he had heard his mother emphasize these risks, the Struggle program's structure changed the conditions of Ian's experience of that conversation. It placed him in a relatively equalized exchange with an unrelated adult, who embedded the conversation in an account of how taking such risks had seriously complicated her life. These conditions promoted Ian's expanded awareness, and in response to it, he reorganized his perception of his available options and shifted his habitual behavior. Thus he revised his relation with his environment. Similarly, my own experience with Struggle both broadened and deepened my contact with participants' investment in practices such as the socialization of schooling. That contact changed the conditions of my experience of reading critical theory and thus prompted me to reorganize my perception of its uses. As a result, I shifted from an emphasis on predefined large-scale social change to an emphasis on negotiating my goals with those of people most exploited by the present system.

The *Union Press* uses language practices to broaden contact with experience in paired articles such as "Text of Questionnaire" and "Ask Questions," which position readers to experience their own development of political and rhetorical competence and to recognize how new political conditions (such as the NRA) made such competence a relevant tool. Here, readers' conditions of experience are changed by the sense of competence produced by using the paired articles to carry out the analysis they invite. Further, by highlighting the new political conditions, the articles heighten readers' awareness of the national changes that have dramatically shifted all laborers' conditions of experience. Thus they expand readers' contact with their own potential for agency by showing what they can accomplish by undertaking the suggested analysis, and encourage readers to exercise such agency.

Winstanley's texts similarly work to broaden audiences' contact with their own agency, in this case by developing an argument for their right and ability to undertake the scriptural interpretation that others argued belonged strictly to university-educated clerics. They similarly promote audiences' sense of interpretive and argumentative competence, thus shifting the conditions in which audiences experience their own potential. And like the *Union Press*'s paired articles, they encourage contact with the revised conditions of experience produced by the era's ferment of religious and political change. Given the establishment of groups such as the one at St. George's Hill, greater contact with these conditions and with their own interpretive authority apparently encouraged some of Winstanley's audience to act socially and politically on that authority. Together, these cases suggest that to understand how language practices can promote change, we must examine how they relate to individuals' and groups' experiences, particularly how they inhibit or facilitate contact with unaware aspects of such experiences.

The third parallel suggests that such contact may be a prerequisite to substantively negotiating differences, which is in turn a prerequisite to building successful coalitions. The Digger and grassroots unionizing movements illustrate problems that can result from inadequate negotiation. In the Diggers' case, the group did not find ways to successfully manage their differences with surrounding landowners. As a result, their coalition dissolved under external pressures. Grassroots unionizers did not negotiate internal differences (e.g., those surrounding race and varying commitments to political change). As a result, their group was prey to co-optation by a national leadership that quickly allied itself with corporate and centralizing political interests. The local impetus toward substantive political change evaporated under this leadership.

Conversely, both groups' mobilizing strategies emphasized such negotiations of difference. The Diggers used lay preaching and scriptural interpretation to ground group discussion and debate as a means of developing collective plans. The *Union Press*'s "We Learn Union" and comparable articles show Aliquippa organizers using similar strategies by urging union members to learn parliamentary law so they could debate and resolve differences in democratically governed union meetings. Both of these approaches emphasize personal change as a prerequisite to negotiating with others. For instance, Winstanley urges readers to take up their interpretive authority and their collective agency by pursuing communal subsistence farming. This endeavor is a precursor to the group's efforts to persuade others to join the movement toward a more equitable society. The *Union Press* encourages readers to shift their own social relationships by educating themselves in buying union goods, reporting scabs and informers to the paper, and analyzing local and national events in light of their own experiences and their economic and political interests. It positions these activities as crucial to constructing the solidarity needed to wrest civic control of Aliquippa away from J & L.

Struggle's pedagogy took a comparable approach by focusing on individual and small-group change as a means of pursuing the goal of greater social equity. Participants also pursued this approach. For instance, Diane undertook it by following Struggle's call to consider how her rhetorical habits contributed to some of the conflicts between her and Ian. In working to establish a less demanding, more negotiated style of interaction with him, she focused on changing her own behaviors as a precursor to changing their relationship. The planning team's commitment to using more personal (rather than academic) rhetorical moves to introduce Struggle to participants similarly suggests an emphasis on modifying our own stance before asking participants to undertake new approaches. While the planning team's negotiating process did not take this approach, it did emphasize attempting to incorporate, or at least affirm, the agendas subordinated by the group's decisions.

Further, our negotiation process emphasized contact with differences. It succeeded, as in our negotiations over how to introduce Struggle, when we accomplished such contact. Similarly, I reached a point at which I needed to express my differences with my colleagues' religious beliefs. As my discomfort during services at First Allegheny grew, I decided to stop attending. I think my withdrawal evoked my colleagues' disappointment at a point when we had begun voicing our differences more explicitly on other topics as well. Yet these discussions also generated energy and renewed commitment to Struggle. To pursue generative contact with my colleagues and friends, I needed to assert and act on my different experience of church services. Thus the book's three collective endeavors support what Goodman and Wheeler argue: successful relationships require contact with differences, as well as similarities, to ground the negotiations necessary to building a common agenda.

But because the focus of such expanded contact is variable and unpredictable, these cases also imply that we cannot theorize in advance the direction change will take. Supporting language practices that foster contact does not guarantee change at all, much less the kinds of change we might prefer. Nonetheless, these three projects suggest that such contact and subsequent negotiations perhaps till the ground for any substantive change. Given that such individual changes helped form collective endeavors in the two cases where the context supported such efforts, these projects also suggest that promoting individual self-revisions can potentially contribute to social change. Further, the historical legacy of both larger movements implies that even when such efforts fail or only partially succeed, they may still encourage subsequent attempts. Given these circumstances, academics committed to social change may need to put our goals up for negotiation if we want to foster such change.

In a fourth parallel, the three cases show several patterns in how people use language practices as heuristics for growth. Of these patterns, three revise key aspects of Gestalt's model of how language practices support change. The first pattern shows that a revised version of Wheeler's joining-and-analyzing increased people's awareness of their own rhetorical habits and encouraged them to experiment with alternative rhetorical strategies. For instance, Struggle's introductory and training materials presented (and modeled) a version of joining-and-analyzing that asked participants to undertake such examinations of rhetorical moves through projection and reconsideration of exchanges, rather than through explicit conversation about them. An example of Struggle participants' use of such implicit joining-and-analyzing appears in such instances as Janine's application of rhetorical moves modeled by her teacher, Mr. Fine, to define a career goal that incorporated her own talents, as well as presumptions based on family experience. As Wheeler's model suggests, her use of this joining-and-analyzing increased Janine's proprioception of her own interests as well as her perception of the range of potential directions.

Similarly, Diane undertook such joining-and-analysis when she described how Struggle prompted her to shift her rhetorical habits from demanding to advising. She developed awareness of her existing style through her use of Struggle's encouragement to attend to rhetorical moves during her work with her adolescent Struggle partner. In turn, in her subsequent interactions with her son, she drew on that awareness to revise her contact style. I also undertook such implicit joining-and-analyzing in my retrospective examination of my Struggle interactions with colleagues and participants. Through that work, I developed greater awareness that by accenting critical literacy's and pedagogy's emphasis on limited agency in the face of powerful social and discursive forces, I was ignoring many Struggle participants' need for a sense of hope and agency.

Winstanley's texts also encourage poorer audiences to engage in an implicit joining-and-analyzing. His work urges audiences to consider the range of interpretive moves they undertake and to extend that range by establishing their own authority to construct—and act on—a worldview. He argues that only by undertaking the rhetorical moves to ground interpretive authority in their own experiences, thus reconfiguring their relationship to clerical authority, can the poor begin to change their material conditions. Thus his texts position audiences to increase their contact with their own potential agency. Similarly, in such articles as "We Learn Union," the *Union Press* also implicitly draws readers' attention to their existing rhetorical habits by encouraging them to learn new rhetorical strategies. By contrasting a nondemocratic union meeting with a democratic meeting that uses parliamentary procedures, the article directs readers' attention to the rhetorical strategies that produce each kind of meeting. The piece supports an internal joining-and-analyzing although it does not explicitly advocate (or model) such work. While the two historical cases show less direct attention to fostering an internal version of joining-and-analyzing, they do make such moves. In conjunction with Struggle's extensive emphasis on such work in its introductory and training materials and with evidence that Struggle's participants undertook that work and expanded their awareness accordingly, the historical cases suggest that this pattern is one significant way people use language practices as heuristics that support change.

The second pattern in how people use language practices as heuristics for growth supports existing theory and research in composition studies. It suggests that people take up proffered rhetorical moves when those moves provide a directly relevant means to pursue prior established goals. For instance, Winstanley's texts, like other religiously radical texts of the era, prompt audiences to take up biblical exegesis to accomplish prior goals of renewing dissolving social practices such as collective ownership and use of commonly owned village farm and pasture land. Similarly, the *Union Press* urges readers to take up the rhetorical moves of parliamentary law and of racial equity by appealing to their strong investment in improving their working conditions and establishing democratic control of their community. Likewise, Struggle persuaded Diane to undertake a more negotiatory approach to parenting Ian by providing a direct means she could use to pursue her long-held goal of helping him succeed in school.

In no case did organizers attempt to introduce rhetorical practices that were not directly relevant to audiences' pursuit of a strongly established prior goal. The new strategies proffered sometimes encourage audiences to shift existing investments, as when Winstanley urges the poor to stop selling their labor and subsist on communal farming, when the Aliquippa journal asks readers to shift racist and anti-intellectual attitudes, and when Struggle asked participants to forgo more directive or confrontational approaches to parenting. This counsel is proffered in the context of helping audiences to pursue larger goals, which they never challenge directly. Of course, these three cases do not demonstrate that new rhetorical practices cannot be successfully introduced without direct relevance to learners' prior goals. But the strong pattern they illustrate does imply that this approach may have much greater potential to succeed.

The third pattern suggests that the features defining particular language uses as contact-producing or alienating are matters of function rather than form. Specifically, the language practices that Goodman defines as aesthetic or plastic language uses can include material typically excluded from definitions of aesthetic language, namely, clichés and truisms. In contrast with "'empirical,' 'operational,' and 'instrumental'" language practices, Goodman poses "contactful speech," which he describes as poetic because it is "partly creative of the actuality, and the creative use of words plastically destroys and remolds the words" (*Gestalt Therapy* 331). He concludes that empty (or alienated) language practices can be made to encourage contact "only by learning the structure of poetry and humane letters, and finally by making poetry and making the common speech poetic" (331). While my three cases support the theory that contact-producing speech is partly creative of the actuality and that it remolds words' meanings, they show that such speech can include material typically excluded from definitions of the poetic.

Certainly, Struggle participants used the program's central metaphor of a table of advisers to prompt new approaches to issues, as when Joanne used it to consider how she would reply to her mother's urging to go out and meet a man. Further, participants sometimes developed their own metaphors to heighten contact with a relationship or issue, as when Ian compared his mother to a gate that opened when he was moving forward but not "when I need to go backwards." The image conveys the complexity of his feelings toward his mother in nonconfrontational, noncritical language, thus encouraging Ian to make contact with his experience of various aspects of their relationship. But participants also expanded their contact with the kinds of clichéd, formulaic language Goodman's definition implies cannot support contact. For instance, by quoting her mother's truisms, such as, "You are too hard on yourself" and "Look at where you are and what you have accomplished," Diane recontacted experience ignored in all other sections of her Struggle text—her own achievements. Similarly, Diane used such truisms as "think before you jump into it" in advising Ian and her teen Struggle partner, Jody. Rather than promoting alienation, as Goodman's theory might suggest, Diane's gloss demonstrated these sayings' tendency to heighten contact, even if that contact meant behaving problematically "with a conscience" rather than thoughtlessly.

Winstanley uses formulaic biblical images such as Jacob as a figure for the poor, Esau as a figure for the rich, and Israel as an image of both the poor living in community and the prophesied millennial order. Like many of Winstanley's rhetorical moves, this repetition of formulaic metaphors works to promote poorer audiences' contact with potential collective agency. Using clichéd images such as scab, slacker, and stool pigeon, the *Union Press* encourages readers to expand their contact with how they can integrate local action based in typical social pressures into broader union efforts. While Goodman's definition of poetic language does not explicitly exclude such clichéd images, his use of the terms *human letters* and *the structure of poetry* invokes a literary critical approach that typically excludes such images and language. My three cases suggest that if language practices that support contact are defined as aesthetic or poetic, aesthetic language must include formulaic language as well. That is, function rather than form determines whether or not a given language use fosters contact.

The final pattern supports arguments for explicit instruction and scaffolding rather than arguments for spontaneous, natural development of new rhetorical strategies in response to expanded awareness. It thus revises Good-man's theory that expanded contact prompts spontaneous experiments with new rhetorical practices. In some instances, Struggle participants experiment spontaneously with new rhetorical patterns when they recognize how their existing patterns interfere with their goals. Diane's shift from demanding to advising in working with her teen Struggle partner and with her son is one example. But all three cases suggest that building a structure of new rhetorical practices is facilitated by explicit instruction in new rhetorical moves, as well as by modeling and scaffolding.

For instance, Struggle's training materials integrate its metaphor of a table of advisers with subsequent questions on goals, challenges, and ideas about what advisers might say regarding those issues. This structure enables partici-pants such as Janine to draw on a formulation provided by her teacher, Mr. Fine, to reconsider her career goals not only during Struggle but, as her inter-view illustrates, in the year following as well.

Similarly, Winstanley's texts model key rhetorical moves he encourages audiences to undertake, such as interpreting scripture; telescoping biblical his-tory with ancient English history and contemporary events; analyzing social, political, and economic practices; and constructing accounts of personal and group experiences. The *Union Press* instructs readers in a complex, cumulative series of rhetorical moves by modeling and scaffolding them. For instance, the paired stories on affidavits charging police brutality construct an interplay among various textual elements to demonstrate a series of moves for trans-forming experience into evidence. They use modeling, explicit naming, and exhortation. This pattern suggests that while people spontaneously experi-ment with new rhetorical strategies given the motivation to do so, complex, cumulative systems of rhetorical moves can be more readily learned through modeling, scaffolding, and direct encouragement.

Exploring Literate Practices in Specific Contexts

Using the above parallels, I propose a heuristic for investigating how a community or a group of learners uses—and might extend—particular liter-ate practices. The group might be an existing community (like Aliquippa), a forming community (like the St. George's Hill Diggers), or a group brought together for instruction (like Struggle). Of course, as these examples suggest, required composition courses differ even from the book's most similar case, Struggle, because participation in that program was entirely voluntary, while most students' participation in such courses is required.[2] This partial fit suggests that while the heuristic I offer is relevant to such courses, it may need to be adapted for use in these contexts.

Based on the parallels, I developed the following sets of heuristic questions relevant to each. By applying these questions to specific situations (and adapting them as appropriate), researchers and teachers can bring to bear existing knowledge in investigating their local situations while also attuning themselves to how those situations both support and revise that knowledge.

What specific ideologies or discursive patterns do group members use frequently? What uses do they make of these materials, and what tendencies emerge? What kinds of individual, social, and systemic relationships do these various uses support?

Which language practices encourage expanded contact with previously unaware experience (of self or others)? Under what conditions does such contact occur most often? Do particular forms of language use encourage different kinds of results with different individuals or subgroups or under different circumstances? What patterns emerge? Under what conditions do specific language practices promote or discourage contact? When contact occurs, what kinds of changes result? Do some instances of contact foster group members' sense of agency? Given that contact with changed conditions of experience seems to promote change in rhetorical habits, how might one structure opportunities for such contact—and such changed conditions—into learning situations?

How often are differences negotiated, avoided, and escalated into conflict? How does each outcome affect individual and group dynamics? What kinds of language practices does the group use in each case? Which most effectively promote and facilitate negotiation? How do they encourage, discourage, or moderate contact with differences? What role do differing levels of contact play in negotiations? Does the group successfully negotiate common goals? How do successes and failures affect individual and group dynamics? What language practices support or discourage this work, under what conditions, and with which individuals and subgroups? What direction do resulting changes tend to take? What kinds of personal, social, and systemic relationships do they support? Does the context seem to support coalitions or links with budding or established collective efforts? Might individuals' existing and developing literate practices contribute to forming such coalitions, and if so, how?

What language practices encourage group members to increase awareness of their own rhetorical habits and encourage them to experiment with alternative rhetorical strategies? How does increased awareness affect individual and group dynamics? For example, how do habitual language-use practices change? What other kinds of new awareness result? Do communication patterns and interactional dynamics in specific relationships change, and if so, how?

What are group members' prior established goals? What new rhetorical strategies might most effectively help members pursue those goals? If the circumstances mandate instruction in predefined rhetorical strategies or literate practices, how might those practices be directly linked to group members' goals? In what circumstances do group members most readily engage with and undertake new practices? In what circumstances does learning new practices encourage group members to shift existing investments? Which investments are most likely to shift and in what direction(s)?

When do group members experiment spontaneously with new rhetorical strategies or literate practices (either when they make greater contact with their existing strategies or under other circumstances)? What form and direction do such experiments take? What various kinds of results do they produce in individual and social dynamics and learning processes? What kinds of direct instruction, modeling, and scaffolding most effectively build on the group's established goals, literate practices, and rhetorical habits? How do group members respond to each of these pedagogical approaches? Which facilitate development of greater competence in existing practices or acquisition of new practices? Under what conditions and with which subgroups or individuals is such facilitation effective or ineffective? What patterns emerge in group members' responses to each approach? What, if any, changes in the approaches might be inferred from those responses? What kinds and levels of competence develop, if any? What patterns emerge in direction, level, and number of competencies? How effectively, if at all, do group members develop cumulative competencies?

Using the Heuristic

To demonstrate how composition instructors and literacy researchers might use the heuristic, I illustrate a brief application of one set of its questions. The application is based not on formal data collection but on sporadic, informal observation of my own teaching and so has limited validity. To recognize patterns, especially those that do not fit my theoretical frame or other presuppositions, I would need to do formal, systematic data collection. In addition, I would need to do a much more specific, developed analysis than I can present here. Still, this illustration suggests the heuristic's relevance and potential applications.

Most of the observations used here I made to draft an article that compares my contributions to the interactional dynamics in two different intermediate writing courses.[3] In one course, my rhetorical choices in course design and classroom interactions helped produce a dynamic of resistance. In the other, I modified both kinds of rhetorical moves and saw a more negotiatory dynamic emerge. While this narrative suggests the difference resulted strictly from my changes, that is not the case, as my answers to specific heuristic questions show. I used the heuristic's second set of questions because my limited set of observations fits those questions best, and I include brief answers based on my observations.

Which language practices encourage expanded contact with previously unaware experience (of self or others)? In the second (and more negotiatory) intermediate course, a few weeks into the semester, several students complained about the seeming irrelevance of homework assignments. I responded by taking an explicitly persuasive stance, supplementing my original explanations of how the homework comprised steps toward their upcoming paper assignment by further illustrating the homework's relevance rather than merely insisting on it. At that point, students shifted their rhetorical approach, quickly acknowledging that they saw the homework's relevance but explaining that they each had a test or other substantial academic assignment due at nearly the same time the paper was due. I suggested one week's extension on the paper on condition that they complete all homework assignments on time. They agreed, appearing distinctly relieved. I think the shift in their approach (from protesting the assignments to explaining their dilemma) suggests greater awareness of the possibility that they could negotiate with me to devise a solution we all found acceptable.

Under what conditions does such contact seem to occur most often? The second version of the course was structured to allow students more latitude in choosing their research and writing topics. This suggests that structuring wider space for students to make choices about their topics may promote awareness of the potential for negotiation with an instructor. In the exchange about homework, students' willingness to approach me with their concerns seemed to result in part from the fact that several of them shared this concern. This implies that students in this course (as opposed to a more advanced course) may be most likely to approach me about a dilemma when they have collectively generated the energy to initiate a potentially confrontational interaction.

Do particular forms of language use encourage different kinds of results with different individuals or groups or under different circumstances? Several particular forms of language practices characterized the second course, in contrast with the first. One form was embodied in my choice of texts. The first course used explicitly critical texts dealing with race issues related to our city's local history. These texts, I realized in retrospect, functioned rhetorically to present a direct challenge to many students' identities and communities. In the second version of the course, I chose different texts and designed assignments to indirectly raise critical issues so as to avoid rhetorical moves that might put students on the defensive. Further, I attempted to undertake more extended persuasion in direct response to students' concerns, when expressed, rather than merely reiterating the rationale for an assignment.

What patterns emerge? The contrasting dynamics of resistance and negotiation in the two versions of intermediate writing suggest it is useful to take an indirect approach to critical work in my university's intermediate writing course. Similarly, they imply it is useful for instructors to use persuasive rhetorical moves to signal a flexible, negotiatory stance.

Under what conditions do specific language practices promote or discourage contact? I have limited material from which to answer this question. But in one case, I believe a student perceived my stance early in the second course as inflexible and resistant to negotiation. He wanted to move from his original group to another group, and I insisted he discuss it with his original group members before pursuing the move. Based on his later expressions of frustration (and what I perceived as resistance), I think he read my response as rigid or felt it posed too high a hurdle for him to achieve his objective. When I approached this student's group with persuasive conversation at later points in the semester, I think he remained skeptical because of his earlier interaction with me. These conditions suggest that perceived teacher rigidity early in the course might undermine later persuasive rhetorical moves designed to signal a flexible stance.

When contact occurs, what kinds of changes result? In their initial response to the successful negotiation (several weeks into the semester), the students involved immediately appeared more relaxed and open. As the course went on, they seemed to develop more willingness to do assignments and, particularly, to pursue a cumulative series of steps. Some (though not all) of the students involved appeared to develop markedly stronger investments in the assignments themselves.

Do some instances of contact foster group members' sense of agency? For students such as the one who perceived my stance as rigid, I think our contact encouraged alienation rather than agency. Some students appeared to treat their projects as academic exercises rather than as opportunities to use academic work to pursue their own interests. Thus I believe they did not experience our contact as inviting negotiation or agency. On the other hand, students such as those who negotiated the extension with me seemed to perceive such an invitation. Some of these students also negotiated with me about the content and format of their major projects, which suggests the contact encouraged their sense of agency.

Given that contact with changed conditions of experience seems to promote change in rhetorical habits, how might one structure opportunities for such contact—and such changed conditions—into learning situations? On the basis of my interpretation of this partial, informal data, I plan to restructure my next intermediate writing course to try to further encourage students to negotiate with each other and with me. I intend to design the course partly around a revised version of Wheeler's method of contracting for the experiment. Students will contract for assignments and grading criteria. Such emphasis on learning and negotiating with students' goals is one way of structuring the opportunity for students to make contact with changed conditions of experience in relation to most of their course work. For instance, as constructivist pedagogy requires, it immerses students in "situations of real language use, i.e., situations where language is being used for communicative purposes, not where the language event is primarily about teaching or evaluating students' language proficiency" (Edelsky 5). By making the process of negotiating assignments and grading criteria the focus of course design, I will shape the course around such situations of real language use.[4]

I will observe whether and how these changed conditions promote negotiatory rhetorical strategies. If they do, I will also observe whether and how those strategies facilitate students' investment in the course work. Wheeler argues that contracting for the experiment in Gestalt therapeutic sessions offers clients the chance to become more aware of their contact styles, to experiment with new rhetorical moves, and to revise their contact styles. In Gestalt terms, such expanded contact with one's own interactional style is a prerequisite to change. Wheeler contends that because there are real, but safe, stakes for the client in contracting for the experiment, that process encourages such contact. I will examine whether contracting for assignments and grading criteria produce such real but safe stakes for students and whether those stakes promote expanded contact, rhetorical experimentation, and revisions in rhetorical habits and other literate practices.

• • •

This plan draws from all three modes of knowledge production: empirical (though unsystematic) observations, theoretical models (Gestalt theory, critical literacy and pedagogical theory, and constructivist pedagogical theory), and experiential knowledge (my felt sense of students' varying attitudes and our interactional dynamics). Another teacher or researcher applying this heuristic would make different use of the observations I present (and of course might generate quite different observations as well). Such differences could result from a focus on different empirical circumstances, varying theoretical models, and divergent experiential knowledge.

Thus the heuristic I offer responds not only to differences in local situations but to differences in the researcher's or teacher's use of it. While this flexibility precludes generalizable findings (as intended), it increases our potential to generate more nuanced, complex understandings of how literate practices can promote change. It provides an approach both systematic enough and flexible enough to generate rich, multiplex data. That is, its systematic design grounds further observations in questions generated by previously documented patterns in how literate practices promote change. Its flexible structure ensures it can accommodate data generated from a range of theoretical models, empirical focuses, and experiential knowledge. Further, it ensures that teachers and researchers can approach each learning situation in a way that integrates all three modes of knowledge production to increase contact with that situation's specifics. In other words, it works to increase awareness of human experience rather than to erase such experience. I offer it in hopes other literacy researchers and composition teachers will find it useful and adapt it as they see fit.

Notes

Chapter 1: CONCEIVING CHANGE: MODELS, METHODS, AND LITERATE PRACTICES

1. Following Heath and others, I define literate practices broadly to include not just functional literacy but all activities related to reading and writing, for example, listening to an oral presentation of a text, reflecting, discussing, observing, and so forth.

2. See Spivak's "Limits and Openings" and Foucault's *Archaeology of Knowledge*, but more especially his *History of Sexuality* and the essays in *Power/Knowledge*, particularly "Truth and Power" and "Two Lectures."

3. Descriptions of Inform projects and documents appear in Flower and in Peck, Flower, and Higgins.

4. However, Heath's and Paul Willis's texts are excellent examples of ethnographies that explicitly consider such possibilities.

5. Both Marcus's essay and Marcus and Fischer's book note Willis's text as a leading example of such work.

6. Clifford points out that while Derek Freeman critiques Mead's depiction of Samoans as unduly idealist, Freeman's ethnography is itself unduly pessimistic.

Chapter 2: CONTACT STYLE

The epigraphs are from the following sources: Derrida's *Of Grammatology* 67; Perls, Hefferline, and Goodman's *Gestalt Therapy* 230; and Lao-tzu's *Te-Tao Ching*, chapter 49, *Te*, ll. 9–10 (p. 18 in Robert G. Hendricks's edition). For background on the *Te-Tao Ching* as an earlier version of the *Tao-Te Ching* and on Lao-tzu as the name for an anonymous (probably composite) author, see the introductory sections of Hendricks's translation. I use the final epigraph partly because Taoism and Zen Buddhism substantially influenced Paul Goodman and the development of Gestalt theory. In quoted material, emphasis is in the original text unless otherwise noted. Bracketed inserts are my additions unless otherwise noted.

1. Thomas Newkirk makes a similar argument regarding qualitative researchers' inevitable use of "culturally grounded narratives" (135).

2. Spivak glosses Derrida's argument in her "Translator's Preface," explaining that he undertakes a Nietzschean play with opposites to subvert the will to power inherent in his philosophical discourse, a will inherent in any discourse (xxviii).

3. For an example of such an integrated, ad hoc approach, see chapter 7's suggestions for action in Paul Willis's Marxist ethnography *Learning to Labor* (185–93).

4. Goodman held a Ph.D. in English literature from the University of Chicago. His works encompassed "psychotherapy, community planning, linguistics, literary theory, philosophy, sociology, politics, education, media criticism, as well as poems, plays, and fiction" (Stoehr 2). A few of his best-known works include *Growing Up Absurd*, *The Empire City*, and *Making Do*. (See Wheeler 67–68.)

5. Gordon Wheeler refers to Goodman as the primary author of volume 2 (67). As I cite primarily that volume of *Gestalt Therapy* here, I treat it as Goodman's work. In his 1994 introduction to Goodman's *Crazy Hope and Finite Experience*, Stoehr describes this book as "still the primary text of the new synthesis in psychotherapy that has become an international movement" (1–2).

6. In *The Feeling of What Happens*, neurobiologist Antonio Damasio stresses the visceral aspects that shape perception. He demonstrates that knowing is grounded in perceptual processes that are fundamentally physiological and emotional. Damasio's research shows that "there is no such thing as *pure* perception of an object without a sensory channel, for instance, vision. The concurrent [emotional and physiological] changes . . . are *not* an optional accompaniment. To perceive an object, visually or otherwise, the organism requires both specialized sensory signals *and* signals from the adjustment of the body, which are necessary for perception to occur" (147). Damasio argues that reason is grounded in emotion and that all perception is individual and subjective because it is fundamentally based in physiological and emotional responses to the objects perceived.

7. Since its development in the late 1960s and early 1970s, Pribram's model has become one of the competing scientific explanations of human consciousness, and it continues to inspire much research in relevant fields, from physiology to psychology to philosophy. In *Brain and Perception*, Pribram cites the following texts on "the holographic hypothesis of brain function in perception as developed in my laboratory": Barrett's "Cerebral Cortex," "Vibrating Strings," "Uncertainty Relations," "Structural Information," and "Sensory Systems"; his own "Some Dimensions of Remembering," *Languages of the Brain*, and "Localization and Distribution"; and Pribram, Nuwer, and Baron. Citations of Bohm's work in *Brain and Perception* include two of Bohm's own works ("Mind and Matter" and "Quantum Theory"), as well as Bohm and Hiley and Bohm, Hiley, and Stuart (xv).

8. To avoid the awkwardness of including both genders in each use of indefinite pronouns and generic nouns, I alternate between the two.

9. For examples of Goodman and his coauthors' exploration of such verbal reformulations, see *Gestalt Therapy* 211–24, especially 216–18.

10. As I use the term heuristic here, heuristic status does not mean a person is necessarily conscious of or reflexive about the discovery and feedback generated by his language practices. Rather, it means he experiments with language practices to achieve meaning and completion through the experience those practices enable. Such meaning and completion allow people to take in discovery and feedback. In alienating experiences, people block proprioception and perception and thus block the awareness required to assimilate such discovery.

11. I believe Goodman refers to Wilhelm Reich's concept of character-armor. (See, e.g., *Gestalt Therapy* x, 218, 364–46. No specific text by Reich is cited.)

12. Goodman's definition of a cause as "not itself an existing thing but a principle of explanation for some present problem" grounds Wheeler's claim. That is, Goodman implies that causes are, by definition, relational, part of experimental attempts to grasp and solve problems (*Gestalt Therapy* 351). In his introduction, Wheeler apologizes for using "his" as the standard pronoun for designating personal and collective references. He describes the decision as the best option among other cumbersome and unacceptable choices (14).

13. Wheeler cites Erving and Miriam Polster's *Gestalt Therapy Integrated* and J. Piaget's *Intelligence*. *Perlsian autonomy* refers to Frederick Perls's notion of a self that excludes considerations of social relationships (see, e.g., Wheeler 48).

14. In *Crazy Hope and Finite Experience*, a collection of several of Goodman's essays interspersed with some of his poetry, he says that "much serious writing . . . is written for no particular audience; and fiction and poetry for an 'ideal' audience. Nevertheless, the writer is always under an obligation to make it 'clear.' . . . In most cases, the writer is not thinking of a reader at all; he makes it 'clear' as a contract with *language*" (125). In the same volume, Goodman emphasizes that his own literary writing allows him to make contact with his experience and so to move through it (98–102). Clearly, Goodman's definition of aesthetics differs from those that center on the aesthetic object and its structure or formal characteristics. It is perhaps closest to the definition used by reader responses theorists such as Wolfgang Iser, who understand the aesthetic as an experience.

15. In "A Pedagogy of Multiliteracies: Designing Social Futures," the New London Group suggests, "We can instantiate a vision through pedagogy that creates in microcosm a transformed set of relationships and possibilities for social futures; a vision that is lived in schools" (19).

Chapter 3: A PASSION FOR THE POSSIBLE

1. Because Wayne and my other Struggle colleagues chose to use their real names rather than pseudonyms, I use the real names of organizations involved as well. Three Struggle participants (Diane, Ian, and Joanne) also requested I use their real names. To mask the identities of other participants, I changed some details of their identities, in addition to using pseudonyms. I use pseudonyms for family members and others referred to by Struggle participants.

2. Struggle began moving into work with community organizations as I was preparing to leave Pittsburgh to take a full-time academic position. Thus while this work was directly relevant to my interests, I was not able to participate in it.

3. I focus especially on Diane and Ian for intersecting practical and theoretical reasons. In practical terms, my role as a Struggle facilitator provided much more opportunity to collect data on Ian's work than on that of any other adolescent participant. Because Diane and Ian are mother and son, their Struggle work focused on their relationship with each other to a significant extent, so examining that relationship was especially revealing. I had more access to their Struggle endeavors than I did with any other pair of participants not only because of my work with Ian but because Joyce wrote about her work with Diane and because Diane's post-Struggle interview was especially rich (see chapter 5).

4. This instance is particularly telling given the local African American community's

emphasis on respect for elders, who were usually addressed by a Mr. or Ms. before their first names by younger interlocutors. Joyce was, at the time, old enough to be these young men's mother.

5. I originally represented speech patterns as I heard them in actual conversations. But when I discussed this manuscript with one Struggle participant, she said she would be comfortable with my depiction as long as I agreed to change her speech to standard English. To respect her request and achieve consistency, I changed nearly all speech to standard English, though I kept teens' language closer to the original to preserve the difference between their language and adults'.

6. The cycle of experience is often presented graphically as a circle and includes the following steps: awareness, energy/action, contact, resolution/closure, withdrawal, and new awareness. See Zinker for a description and diagrams (63–88, esp. 64).

7. He used other metaphors as well, for instance, describing Maureen's mother as a tree.

8. Bateson, a cultural anthropologist, also conducted research in psychology and biology. Over a fifty-year career, he did anthropological fieldwork in Bali, research on alcoholism and schizophrenia at the Palo Alto Veterans Administration Hospital, studies of porpoises to investigate prelinguistic mammalian communication, and work with larger ecological systems. Across these contexts, Bateson explored metaphor as a crucial basis of human perception and interaction (see esp. 177–93, 244–70, 271–78, 279–308, 309–37, 364–78, 432–45, 446–53).

9. See Fischer and Abedi; Harrison; Marcus and Fischer; Mortensen and Kirsch; Ruby; Schaafsma.

10. I believe this was the post-Struggle dinner held approximately a month after the project's completion.

Chapter 4: NEW HEAVENS AND NEW EARTH

For sources, I rely primarily on left-wing historians because mainstream historians have tended to ignore the Levellers and Diggers. Most of these left-wing histories situate the groups' projects in relation to a leftist vision of history (e.g., Aylmer, Berens, Brailsford, Frank, Petegorsky, Robertson, Sabine, and Wolfe). While sharing many of these historians' ideals, I do not entirely share their sense of history, and I have tried to move toward a different model by using a Gestalt analytic frame.

1. Historians and literary critics argue that using terms related to class (for instance, middle class) anachronistically imposes an inapplicable set of social relations onto seventeenth-century social strata. They prefer the use of the seventeenth-century terms upper, middling, and lower sorts. Although this convention may be unfamiliar to many readers, I've chosen to follow it to avoid historical inaccuracy.

2. Hayes argues that Winstanley's texts are written to be read silently, in private. He contrasts them with sermons, which he describes as "static reaffirmation[s] of existing ideas and institutions" (134). I found Hayes's book insightful and helpful in formulating my readings of Winstanley's work, but I disagree with his characterization of sermons and, by extension, of texts written for oral as well as silent reading. The inflammatory effects of John Ball–style preaching in 1381 are just one example of how texts written for oral presentation can perform social critique and mobilize audiences into action.

3. For a reading of Dewey's work (particularly *Democracy and Education*) as a kind of historical progressivism, see Robert Nisbet's *History of the Idea of Progress* (303–4).

4. This bracketed insertion is Sabine's rather than mine.

Chapter 5: WHERE WE'RE AT

1. Diane and Ian were interviewed separately on the same day and had only a few minutes to speak between the interviews.

2. On the uses of ethnography's representations for colonizing and similar exploitative purposes, see Harrison; Marcus and Fischer; and the introduction and many of the essays in Ruby. On the psychic and other risks ethnography poses to subjects, see Cheri L. Williams.

3. This argument is developed more fully in relation to teaching in Gorzelsky, "Making Contact" and "Redefining Resistance." It is developed in relation to ethnography in Gorzelsky, "Shifting Figures."

Chapter 6: To Feel That You Are a Citizen

1. Bell, who wrote the novel *Out of this Furnace*, was a Pittsburgher whose family members worked in the city's steel mills.

2. The columns "Seamless Sparks," "Nib Nabs," and "Spirits of 1843" are all clearly written by people with intimate knowledge of local residents and daily events.

3. Kaplan gives a history of U.S. journalism's shift from partisanship to an objectivist ethic between 1865 and 1920. He argues that the decisive, culminating moment in this shift came with the 1896 elections and subsequent political reforms, which encouraged newspapers to disown their prior partisan stances (17). I do not believe the *Union Press* takes the kind of partisan approach adopted by most nineteenth-century papers (see Kaplan, ch. 1–3). For instance, it does not publish daily lists of candidates it endorses but rather articles that encourage voters to think about upcoming local elections in terms of particular questions and issues. Similarly, its articles tend not so much to argue for a particular political platform as to urge readers to undertake the kinds of self-education directly relevant to understanding local politics in terms of union interests. Thus the paper integrates partisan strategies (such as a clear commitment to the union position and local Democratic Party) into a quasi-objectivist stance that frequently adopts an impartial analytic voice.

4. While Mahoney's piece suggests that Aliquippa schools had adopted some version of progressive education, it is not clear how or how extensively progressive methods came into practice in Aliquippa or whether those methods in fact served as a cover for J & L's avowed intention to educate not professionals but "good workmen in the mill." According to Mahoney, Dr. Vanderslice, the Aliquippa superintendent hired by J & L, remarked that he would have to "unlearn much he had learned" (4).

5. For a useful discussion of a literary construction of a generalized, fictional ideal reader, see "The Reader in Hard Times" (166–74, esp. 173–74), in Raymond Williams.

6. I was unable to find an explicit explanation of the column's name. U.S. ironworkers did not begin to organize until the late 1860s. The major labor-related incidents in 1843 in the United States and British Isles were the Rebecca Riots in Wales, 1839–1843. They emerged from the Chartist movement, which sought universal male suffrage and related

political rights for British laborers pursuing better working and living conditions. While the movement's petitions to Parliament failed in the late 1830s, Welsh iron and coal workers, many of whom were Irish immigrants, repeatedly rose against employers and local authorities through 1843. Even when the rebellions were finally suppressed and leaders tried, petitions from thousands of British citizens and strikes by Welsh coal miners pressured the courts to lighten sentences (see Peter Williams). Given the immigration of Welsh and Irish ironworkers and coal miners to the United States and their tendency to seek similar employment, as well as Aliquippans' explicitly political goals, I think the column may be named for this movement.

7. It seems likely that the National Citizens' Committee evolved out of the Johnstown [Pa.] Citizens' Committee, which cooperated with local mayor David Shields during the June 1937 strike against Bethlehem Steel in an antistrike campaign and employed Bethlehem Steel funds to purchase tear gas for use against strikers. See Filippelli (505–6).

8. Casebeer says that the Honor Roll eventually reached fifty-four members (666).

9. I am grateful to Kathryne Lindberg for pointing out that the use of the phrase "one man" echoes the slogan "I am a man," used by labor activists but even more prominently by black activists. Thus while the phrase "a negro" is grammatically unnecessary, its juxtaposition with the phrase "one man" folds black identity into a cross-racial labor coalition.

10. Of course, the sentence includes a second appositive: "the man he was fighting with, a non-union man." Arguably, that appositive makes union identification secondary to the initial description of the man as a member of the fight. The sentence could be restructured as follows: "while the non-union man he was fighting was given no penalty at first." But given the accumulated phrases, I think that rewording would deemphasize union membership. Thus in the second case, the appositive structure foregrounds the appositive's description, in contrast with the first case, where the appositive deemphasizes its description.

11. Except for the final line of the second paragraph, at which point the story narrows from two columns to one.

12. In addition to the twelve men mentioned in the article's second subtitle, the story notes that fourteen others were subsequently discharged and later reinstated.

13. I am grateful to Francis Shor for pointing out that such union efforts to foster cross-racial coalitions often feminized their antagonists, thus promoting patriarchal gender relations. While I do not see that ethos in the materials I analyze in this chapter, the question of whether the Aliquippa movement used it elsewhere warrants inquiry. Paul Willis documents similar use of sexist ideology to constitute class identity among young working-class males in his ethnography of schooling in a 1970s British industrial center (see esp. 43–49).

14. Much current literary criticism points out the dangers of a humanist approach to race that positions racial difference as unimportant or, essentially, nonexistent. See, for example, Spivak's "Can the Subaltern Speak?" and Patricia Williams. While I believe strongly in those arguments' importance, my point here is that this attempt by the *Union Press* to integrate blacks' interests into union interests and to prompt both black and white readers to identify themselves primarily as union members functions as a pedagogy that encourages readers to reposition their identities.

15. The column is named for a particular J & L mill department referred to as the Seamless.

Chapter 7: Promoting Contact: Literate Practices and Change

1. For a discussion of other compositionists' approach to this problem, see Bruce Horner's analysis of David Bartholomae's work (esp. 125–26 and 194).

2. As Horner notes, various composition theorists argue that because they bring people together for temporary, instrumental purposes, classrooms do not constitute organic communities or even incipient communities (44–47).

3. See Gorzelsky, "Redefining Resistance." At my university, intermediate writing is the course most students take to fulfill a sophomore/junior-level general writing requirement.

4. Ira Shor's *When Students Have Power* explains that he negotiated grading contracts, project topics, and some other course elements with students in his sophomore/junior-level writing course on utopias. I see my experiment as echoing the spirit of Shor's work because he emphasizes that such negotiations teach students democratic practices. But rather than focusing on the contracting process itself, Shor's book details how he drew on students' agendas to help them develop rhetorical skills and literate practices related to social critique and activism. In contrast, I plan to focus more on the contracting process itself as potential forum for developing stronger and increased competencies. This approach makes negotiation a more central aspect of the course's work and, by foregrounding situations of real language use, more closely parallels constructivist pedagogy's emphases.

Works Cited

Abel, I. W. "Comment." Clark, Gottlieb, and Kennedy 103–8.

Althusser, Louis. "On the Materialist Dialectic." *For Marx*. Trans. Ben Brewster. New York: Pantheon, 1969. 163–218.

"And Why." *Union Press* 20 Oct. 1937: 3. Beaver Valley Labor History Society archives, University of Pittsburgh.

Angelou, Maya. *On the Pulse of the Morning*. New York: Random, 1993.

"Ask Questions." Union Press 6 Oct. 1937: 1. Beaver Valley Labor History Society archives, University of Pittsburgh.

"Ask These Boys What They Think Of C.I.O. And What It Did For Them." Union Press 29 Sept. 1937: 2. Beaver Valley Labor History Society archives, University of Pittsburgh.

Aylmer, G. E., ed. *The Levellers in the English Revolution*. Ithaca: Cornell UP, 1975.

Barrett, T. W. "Comparing the Efficiency of Sensory Systems: A Biophysical Approach." *Journal of Biological Physics* 1.3 (1972): 175–92.

———. "The Cerebral Cortex as a Diffractive Medium." *Mathematical Biosciences* 4 (1969): 311–50.

———. "On Vibrating Strings and Information Theory." *Journal of Sound and Vibration* 203 (1972): 407–12.

———. Structural Information Theory." *Journal of the Acoustical Society of America* 54.4 (1973): 1092–98.

———. "Uncertainty Relations in Interaural Parameters of Acoustical Simulation: An Evoked Potential Study of the Auditory Cortex in the Anesthetized Cat." *Behavioral Biology* 8.3 (1973): 299–323.

Baskins, Joyce. "Good Cop, Bad Cop." Letter. *Pittsburgh Post-Gazette* 21 July 1996: E1.

Bateson, Gregory. Steps to an Ecology of Mind. U of Chicago P, 2000.

Bell, Thomas. Out of this Furnace. 1941. Pittsburgh: U of Pittsburgh P, 1976.

Berens, Lewis H. *The Digger Movement in the Days of the Commonwealth as Revealed in the Writings of Gerrard Winstanley, The Digger Mystic and Rationalist, Communist and Social Reformer*. London: Simpkin, 1906.

Berlin, James. Rhetorics, Poetics, and Cultures: Refiguring College English Studies. Urbana: NCTE, 1996.

Bohm, D. J. "A New Theory of the Relationship of Mind and Matter." *Journal of the American Society for Physical Research* 80 (1986): 113–35.

————. "Quantum Theory as an Indication of a New Order in Physics." *Foundations of Physics. Part A* 1.4 (1971–73): 354–81.

Bohm, D. J., and B. J. Hiley. "On the Intuitive Understanding of Non-Locality as Implied by Quantum Theory." *Foundations of Physics* 5 (1975): 93–109.

Bohm, D.J., B. J. Hiley, and A. E. G. Stuart. "On a New Mode of Description in Physics." *International Journal of Theoretical Physics* 3.3 (1970): 171–83.

Brailsford, H. N. *The Levellers and the English Revolution.* Ed. Christopher Hill. Stanford: Stanford UP, 1961.

Brody, David L. "The Origins of Modern Steel Unionism: The SWOC Era." Clark, Gottlieb, and Kennedy 13–29.

Brooks, Robert R. R. *As Steel Goes, . . . : Unionism in a Basic Industry.* New Haven: Yale UP, 1940.

Burton, Vicki Tolar. "John Wesley and the Liberty to Speak: The Rhetorical and Literacy Practices of Early Methodism." *College Composition and Communication* 53.1 (2001): 65–91.

Casebeer, Kenneth. "Aliquippa: The Company Town and Contested Power in the Construction of Law." *Buffalo Law Review* 43.3 (1995): 617–87.

Cintron, Ralph. *Angels' Town:* Chero *Ways, Gang Life, and Rhetorics of the Everyday.* Boston: Beacon, 1997.

"City Bows to U.S. on Police Reforms." *Pittsburgh Post-Gazette* 27 Feb. 1997.

Clark, Paul F., Peter Gottlieb, and Donald Kennedy, eds. *Forging a Union of Steel: Philip Murray, SWOC, and the United Steelworkers.* Ithaca: Industrial and Labor Relations Press, New York State School of Industrial and Labor Relations, Cornell UP, 1987.

Clifford, James. "On Ethnographic Allegory." Clifford and Marcus 98–121.

Clifford, James, and George E. Marcus. *Writing Culture: The Poetics and Politics of Ethnography.* Berkeley: U of California P, 1986.

Cohn, Norman. *The Pursuit of the Millennium: Revolutionary Messianism in Medieval and Reformation Europe and Its Bearing on Modern Totalitarian Movements.* 2nd ed. New York: Harper, 1961.

Cozzicolli, Mary. Interview. n.d. Beaver Valley Labor History Society archives, University of Pittsburgh.

"Crime: Prison Population Increased 1% in 2000." *Facts on File: World News Digest* 16 Aug. 2000. 20 Jan. 2003. <http://www.2facts.com>.

Cushman, Ellen. "The Rhetorician as Agent of Social Change." *College Composition and Communication* 471 (February 1996): 7–28.

————. *The Struggle and the Tools: Oral and Literate Strategies in an Inner City Community.* Albany: SUNY P, 1998.

Cushman, Ellen, Eugene R. Kintgen, Barry M. Kroll, and Mike Rose, eds. *Literacy: A Critical Sourcebook.* Boston: Bedford, 2001.

Damasio, Antonio R. *The Feeling of What Happens: Body and Emotion in the Making of Consciousness.* New York: Harcourt, 1999.

Davin, Eric Leif. "The Littlest New Deal: How Democracy and the Union Came to Western Pennsylvania." Unpublished paper. U of Pittsburgh. n.d.

"Democrats Challenge School Policies." *Union Press* 6 Oct. 1937: 1+. Beaver Valley Labor History Society archives, University of Pittsburgh.

Derrida, Jacques. *Of Grammatology.* Trans. Gayatri Chakravorty Spivak. Baltimore: Johns Hopkins UP, 1974.

Dewey, John. *Democracy and Education: An Introduction to the Philosophy of Education.* New York: Macmillan, 1916.

Dickerson, Dennis C. *Out of the Crucible: Black Steelworkers in Western Pennsylvania, 1875–1980.* SUNY Series in Afro-American Studies. Ed. John Howard and Robert Smith. Albany: SUNY P, 1986.

"Discharged Union Men All Put Back To Work." *Union Press* 11 Aug. 1937: 1. Beaver Valley Labor History Society archives, University of Pittsburgh.

Durst, Russel K. *Collision Course: Conflict, Negotiation, and Learning in College Composition.* Urbana: NCTE, 1999.

Dyson, Anne Haas. "Coach Bombay's Kids Learn to Write: Children's Appropriation of Media Material for School Literacy." Cushman et al. 325–57.

Edelsky, Carole, ed. *Making Justice Our Project: Teaching Working toward Critical Whole Language Practice.* Urbana: NCTE, 1999.

"Editor'[s] Note." *Union Press* 29 Oct. 1937: 1. Beaver Valley Labor History Society archives, University of Pittsburgh.

Erickson, Frederick. "School Literacy, Reasoning, and Civility: An Anthropologist's Perspective." Kintgen, Kroll, and Rose 205–26.

Farr, Marcia. *"En Los Dos Idiomas*: Literacy Practices Among Chicago Mexicanos." Cushman et al. 467–87.

Filippelli, Ronald L., ed. *Labor Conflict in the United States: An Encyclopedia.* New York: Garland, 1990.

Fischer, Michael M. J., and Mehdi Abedi. *Debating Muslims: Cultural Dialogues in Postmodernity and Tradition.* Madison: U of Wisconsin P, 1990.

Fitch, John A. *The Steel Workers.* 1910. Introd. Roy Lubove. Pittsburgh Series in Social and Labor History. Ed. Maurine Weiner Greenwald. Pittsburgh: U of Pittsburgh P, 1989.

"Five-Day Work Week In Slack Is Guaranteed to Senior Employees." *Union Press* 29 Sept. 1937: 1. Beaver Valley Labor History Society archives, University of Pittsburgh.

Flower, Linda. "Negotiating the Meaning of Difference." *Written Communication* 13.1 (1996): 44–92.

Foucault, Michel. *The Archaeology of Knowledge.* Trans. A. M. Sheridan Smith. New York: Pantheon, 1972.

———. *The History of Sexuality*, vol. 1. Trans. Robert Hurley. New York: Random, 1990.

———. Power/Knowledge: Selected Interviews and Other Writings 1972-77. Trans. Colin Gordon, Leo Marshall, John Mepham, and Kate Soper. New York: Pantheon, 1980.

———. "Truth and Power." Foucault, Power/Knowledge 109–33.

———. "Two Lectures." Foucault, *Power/Knowledge* 78–108.

Frank, Joseph. *The Levellers: A History of the Writings of Three Seventeenth-Century Social Democrats: John Lilburne, Richard Overton, William Walwyn.* Cambridge: Harvard UP, 1955.

Freeman, Derek. *Margaret Mead and Samoa: The Making and Unmaking of an Anthropological Myth*. Cambridge: Harvard UP, 1983.

Gee, James Paul. "Literacy, Discourse, and Linguistics: Introduction" Cushman et al. 525–37.

———. "What Is Literacy?" Cushman et al. 537–44.

Gere, Anne Ruggles. "Kitchen Tables and Rented Rooms: The Extracurriculum of Composition." Cushman et al. 275–89.

Goodman, Paul. *Crazy Hope and Finite Experience*. Ed. Taylor Stoehr. A Gestalt Institute of Cleveland Pub. San Francisco: Jossey-Bass, 1994.

———. *The Empire City*. New York: Bobbs Merrill, 1942.

———. *Growing Up Absurd: Problems of Youth in the Organized Society*. New York: Random, 1960.

———. *Making Do*. New York: Random, 1959.

Goody, Jack, and Ian Watt. "The Consequences of Literacy." Kintgen, Kroll, and Rose 3–27.

Gorzelsky, Gwen. "Letter from a Displaced Roadviller." Unpublished essay, 1995.

———. "Making Contact: Experience, Representation, and Difference." *JAC* 23.2 (2003): 397–427.

———. "Redefining Resistance: Rereading Critical Pedagogy." *Reader* 48 (2003): 51–86.

———. "Shifting Figures: Rhetorical Ethnography." *Ethnography Unbound: From Theory Shock to Critical Praxis*. Ed. Stephen G. Brown and Sidney I. Dobrin. Albany: SUNY P, 2004. 73–97.

Graff, Harvey J. "The Legacies of Literacy." Kintgen, Kroll, and Rose 82–94.

"Guess Who?" *Union Press* 29 Sept. 1937: 2. Beaver Valley Labor History Society archives, University of Pittsburgh.

Harrison, Faye V., ed. *Decolonizing Anthropology: Moving Further toward an Anthropology for Liberation*. Washington: American Anthropological Assn., 1991.

Hayes, T. Wilson. *Winstanley the Digger: A Literary Analysis of Radical Ideas in the English Revolution*. Cambridge: Harvard UP, 1979.

Heath, Shirley Brice. *Ways with Words*. Cambridge, Eng.: Cambridge UP, 1983.

Hendricks, Robert G., ed. and trans. *Lao-tzu Te-Tao Ching*. Trans. based on the Ma-Wang-Tui Texts. New York: Ballantine, 1989.

hooks, bell. "Representing Whiteness in the Black Imagination." *Black Looks: Race and Representation*. Boston: South End, 1992.

Horner, Bruce. *Terms of Work for Composition: A Materialist Critique*. Albany: SUNY P, 2000.

"How to Settle Your Grievance Under Contract." *Union Press* 11 Aug. 1937: 1. Beaver Valley Labor History Society archives, University of Pittsburgh.

Iser, Wolfgang. *The Act of Reading: A Theory of Aesthetic Response*. Baltimore: Johns Hopkins UP, 1978.

Kaplan, Richard L. *Politics and the American Press: The Rise of Objectivity, 1865–1920*. Cambridge, Eng.: Cambridge UP, 2002.

Kintgen, Eugene R., Barry M. Kroll, and Mike Rose, eds. *Perspectives on Literacy*. Carbondale: Southern Illinois UP, 1988.

Kromer. "The Spirits of 1843." *Union Press* 29 Oct. 1937: 2. Beaver Valley Labor History Society archives, University of Pittsburgh.

Kromerich, Frank. Interview. 13 Sept. 1978. Beaver Valley Labor History Society archives, University of Pittsburgh.

"Ladies Only." *Union Press* 20 Oct. 1937: 3. Beaver Valley Labor History Society archives, University of Pittsburgh.

"Lay-Offs." *Union Press* 20 Oct. 1937: 3. Beaver Valley Labor History Society archives, University of Pittsburgh.

Lindquist, Julie. *A Place to Stand: Politics and Persuasion in a Working-Class Bar.* Oxford: Oxford UP, 2002.

Linebaugh, Peter, and Marcus Rediker. *The Many-Headed Hydra: Sailors, Slaves, Commoners, and the Hidden History of the Revolutionary Atlantic.* Boston: Beacon, 2000.

Long, Elenore. "The Rhetoric of Literate Social Action: Mentors Negotiating Intercultural Images of Liberacy." Diss. Carnegie Mellon U, 1994.

Lu, Min-Zhan. "Redefining the Literate Self: The Politics of Critical Affirmation." *College Composition and Communication* 51.2 (1999): 172–94.

Lu, Min-Zhan, and Bruce Horner. "The Problematic of Experience: Redefining Critical Work in Ethnography and Pedagogy." *College English* 60.3 (1998): 257–77.

Lynd, Staughton. "The Possibility of Radicalism in the Early 1930s: The Case of Steel." *Workers' Struggles, Past and Present: A "Radical America" Reader.* Ed. James Green. Philadelphia: Temple UP, 1983.

Lytle, Susan L. "Living Literacy: Rethinking Development in Adulthood." Cushman et al. 376–401.

Mahoney, Bertha Winter. "Erie Daily Times Exposes Inept School System in Aliquippa." *Union Press* 6 Oct. 1937: 1+. Beaver Valley Labor History Society archives, University of Pittsburgh.

"Man Beaten and Injured by Policeman." *Union Press* 29 Oct. 1937: 1. Beaver Valley Labor History Society archives, University of Pittsburgh.

Manning, Brian. *The English People and the English Revolution 1640–1649.* London: Heinemann, 1976.

Marcus, George E. "Contemporary Problems of Ethnography in the Modern World System." Clifford and Marcus 165–93.

Marcus, George E., and Michael M. J. Fischer. *Anthropology as Cultural Critique: An Experimental Moment in the Human Sciences.* Chicago: U of Chicago P, 1986.

Masthead. *Union Press* 13 Oct. 1937: 3. Beaver Valley Labor History Society archives, University of Pittsburgh.

Mead, Margaret. *Coming of Age in Samoa.* New York: Morrow, 1923.

Meyerhuber, Carl I. Jr. *Less than Forever: The Rise and Decline of Union Solidarity in Western Pennsylvania, 1914–1948.* Selinsgrove: Susquehanna UP, 1987.

Miller, Susan. *Assuming the Positions: Cultural Pedagogy and the Politics of Commonplace Writing.* Pittsburgh Series in Composition, Literacy, and Culture. Pittsburgh: U of Pittsburgh P, 1998.

Montini, Ormond. 2 August 1978. Beaver Valley Labor History Society archives, University of Pittsburgh.

Mortensen, Peter, and Gesa E. Kirsch, eds. *Ethics and Representation in Qualitative Studies of Literacy*. Urbana: NCTE, 1996.

"Mr. Vanderslice Resigns." *Union Press* 20 Oct. 1937: 3. Beaver Valley Labor History Society archives, University of Pittsburgh.

Muselin, Pete. "The Steel Fist in a Pennsylvania Company Town." *It Did Happen Here: Recollections of Political Repression in America*. Ed. Bud and Ruth Schultz. Berkeley: U of Californa P, 1989. 65–75.

"Negro Problems Discussed." *Union Press* 29 Sept. 1937: 1. Beaver Valley Labor History Society archives, University of Pittsburgh.

New London Group. "A Pedagogy of Multiliteracies: Designing Social Futures." *Multiliteracies: Literacy Learning and the Design of Social Futures*. Ed. Bill Cope and Mary Kalantzis for The New London Group. New York: Routledge, 2000. 9–37.

Newkirk, Thomas. "The Narrative Roots of the Case Study." *Methods and Methodology in Composition Research*. Ed. Gesa Kirsch and Patricia A. Sullivan. Carbondale: Southern Illinois UP, 1992. 130–52.

Nisbet, Robert. *History of the Idea of Progress*. New York: Basic, 1980.

Nyden, Philip W. *Steelworkers Rank-and-File: The Political Economy of a Union Reform Movement*. New York: Praeger, 1984.

Ogbu, John U. "Literacy and Schooling in Subordinate Cultures: The Case of Black Americans." Kintgen, Kroll, and Rose 227–42.

"Old Council Condemned/Affidavits, Pictures Prove Brutality/Kiefer Blames Burgess Sohn." *Union Press* 29 Oct. 1937: 1+. Beaver Valley Labor History Society archives, University of Pittsburgh.

"One-Third Organized." *Union Press* 13 Oct. 1937: 3. Beaver Valley Labor History Society archives, University of Pittsburgh.

Ong, Walter J. "Some Psychodynamics of Orality." Kintgen, Kroll, and Rose 28–43.

Passaro, Vince. "Black Letters on a White Page." *Harper's* July 1997: 70–75.

Peck, Wayne Campbell. "Community Advocacy: Composing for Action (Literacy)." Diss. Carnegie Mellon U, 1991.

Peck, Wayne Campbell, Linda Flower, and Lorraine Higgins. "Community Literacy." *College Composition and Communication* 46.2 (1995): 199–222.

Perls, Frederick, Ralph E. Hefferline, and Paul Goodman. *Gestalt Therapy: Excitement and Growth in the Human Personality*. New York: Dell, 1961.

Petegorsky, David W. *Left-Wing Democracy in the English Civil War: A Study of the Social Philosophy of Gerrard Winstanley*. London: V. Gollancz, 1940.

Piaget, J. *Intelligence*. New York: Basic, 1947.

Polster, Erving, and Miriam Polster. *Gestalt Therapy Integrated*. New York: Brunner, 1973.

Powers, George. *The Cradle of Steel Unionism: Monongahela Valley, Pa*. East Chicago: Figueroa, 1972.

Pribram, Karl H. *Brain and Perception: Holonomy and Structure in Figural Processing*. Hillsdale: Erlbaum, 1991.

———. "Some Dimensions of Remembering: Steps toward a Neuropsychological Model of Memory." *Macromolecules and Behavior*. Ed. J. Gaito. New York: Academic, 1966. 165–87.

———. *Languages of the Brain: Experimental Paradoxes and Principles in Neuropsychology*. Englewood Cliffs: Prentice-Hall, 1971.

———. "Localization and Distribution of Function in the Brain." *Neuropsychology after Lashley*. Ed. J. Orbach. New York: Erlbaum, 1982. 273–96.

Pribram, K. H., M. Nuwer, and R. Baron. "The Holographic Hypothesis of Memory Structure in Brain Function and Perception." *Contemporary Developments in Mathematical Psychology*. Ed. R. C. Atkinson, D. H. Krantz, R. C. Luce, and P. Suppes. San Francisco: Freeman, 1974. 416–67.

"Protesting the Protesters: Gammage Rally Protesters Meet Police Supporters." *Pittsburgh Post-Gazette* 13 Nov. 1995. NewsLibrary. newsbank media services.

Purcell-Gates, Victoria. "A World Without Print." Cushman et al. 402–17.

"Remember . . ." *Union Press* 11 Aug. 1937: 1. Beaver Valley Labor History Society archives, University of Pittsburgh.

Resnick, Daniel P., and Lauren B. Resnick. "The Nature of Literacy: A Historical Exploration." Kintgen, Kroll, and Rose 190–202.

Robertson, D. B. *The Religious Foundations of Leveller Democracy*. New York: King's Crown, 1951.

Royster, Jacqueline Jones. *Traces of a Stream: Literacy and Social Change among African-American Women*. Pittsburgh Series in Composition, Literacy, and Culture. Pittsburgh: U of Pittsburgh P, 2000.

Ruby, Jay, ed. *A Crack in the Mirror: Reflexive Perspectives in Anthropology*. Philadelphia: U of Pennsylvania P, 1982.

Sabine, George H., ed. *The Works of Gerrard Winstanley with an Appendix of Documents Relating to the Digger Movement*. Ithaca: Cornell UP, 1941.

Schaafsma, David. *Eating on the Street: Teaching Literacy in a Multicultural Society*. Pittsburgh: U of Pittsburgh P, 1993.

Scribner, Sylvia, and Michael Cole. "Unpackaging Literacy." Kintgen, Kroll, and Rose 57–70.

"Seamless Sparks." *Union Press* 20 Oct. 1937: 3. Beaver Valley Labor History Society archives, University of Pittsburgh.

"Seamless Sparks." *Union Press* 29 Oct. 1937: 4. Beaver Valley Labor History Society archives, University of Pittsburgh.

Seitz, David. "Review: Hard Lessons Learned since the First Generation of Critical Pedagogy." Rev. of *Teaching Composition as a Social Process*, by Bruce McComiskey, *Mutuality in the Rhetoric and Composition Classroom*, by David Wallace and Helen Rothschild Ewald, and *Collision Course: Conflict, Negotiation, and Learning in College Composition*, by Russell K. Durst. *College English* 64 (2002): 503–12.

Shor, Ira. *Empowering Education: Critical Teaching for Social Change*. Chicago: U of Chicago P, 1992.

———. *When Students Have Power: Negotiating Authority in a Critical Pedagogy.* Chicago: U of Chicago P, 1996.

"The Spirits of 1843." *Union Press* 13 Oct. 1937: 2. Beaver Valley Labor History Society archives, University of Pittsburgh.

Spivak, Gayatri Chakravorty. "Can the Subaltern Speak?" *Marxism and the Interpretation of Culture.* Ed. Cary Nelson and Lawrence Grossberg. Urbana: U of Illinois P, 1988. 271–313.

———. "Limits and Openings of Marx in Derrida." *Outside in the Teaching Machine.* New York: Routledge, 1993. 97–120.

———. "Translator's Preface." Derrida ix–xc.

"State Law Now Prohibits Employment of Company Thugs as Deputy Sheriffs." *Union Press* 11 Aug. 1937: 1. Beaver Valley Labor History Society archives, University of Pittsburgh.

Steedman, Carolyn. *The Radical Soldier's Tale: John Pearman, 1819–1908.* History Workshop Series. Ed. Raphael Samuel. London: Routledge, 1988.

Stoehr, Taylor. Introduction. Goodman, *Crazy Hope* 1–25.

Street, Brian. "The New Literacy Studies." Cushman et al. 430–42.

Szwed, John F. "The Ethnography of Literacy." Kintgen, Kroll, and Rose 303–11.

"Text of Agreement." *Union Press* 29 Sept. 1937: 1. Beaver Valley Labor History Society archives, University of Pittsburgh.

"Text of Democrats' Statements and Affidavits." *Union Press* 29 Oct. 1937: 1+. Beaver Valley Labor History Society archives, University of Pittsburgh.

"Text of Questionnaire." *Union Press* 6 Oct. 1937: 1+. Beaver Valley Labor History Society archives, University of Pittsburgh.

Thompson, E. P. *The Making of the English Working Class.* New York: Pantheon, 1963.

"Timko and Carr Sign Agreement." *Union Press* 29 Sept. 1937: 1. Beaver Valley Labor History Society archives, University of Pittsburgh.

Trainor, Jennifer Seibel. "Critical Pedagogy's 'Other': Constructions of Whiteness in Education for Social Change." *College Composition and Communication* 53 (2002): 631–50.

Tuveson, Ernest Lee. *Millennium and Utopia: A Study in the Background of the Idea of Progress.* New York: Harper, 1964.

Tyler, Stephen A. "Post-Modern Ethnography: From Document of the Occult to Occult Document." Clifford and Marcus 122–40.

"Union Conducts Mass Meetings on [Political] Registration." *Union Press* 11 Aug. 1937: 1. Beaver Valley Labor History Society archives, University of Pittsburgh.

"The Union in Politics." *Union Press* 6 Oct. 1937: 3. Beaver Valley Labor History Society archives, University of Pittsburgh.

"Union Wins First 15 Discharge Cases." *Union Press* 11 Aug. 1937: 1. Beaver Valley Labor History Society archives, University of Pittsburgh.

"Vanderslice Resigns Position." *Union Press* 20 Oct. 1937: 1. Beaver Valley Labor History Society archives, University of Pittsburgh.

"We Beg To Suggest—." *Union Press* 29 Sept. 1937: 3. Beaver Valley Labor History Society archives, University of Pittsburgh.

"We Learn Union." *Union Press* 6 Oct. 1937: 3. Beaver Valley Labor History Society archives,

University of Pittsburgh.

"We Publish—." *Union Press* 13 Oct. 1937: 3. Beaver Valley Labor History Society archives, University of Pittsburgh.

"Welcome to the Struggle Project: Training Manual." Unpublished manual. Pittsburgh: Community Literacy Center, n.d.

Wheeler, Gordon. *Gestalt Reconsidered: A New Approach to Contact and Resistance.* New York: Gardner, 1991.

"Will All Those Who Wish to Work." *Union Press.* 11 August 1937: 1. Beaver Valley Labor History Society archives.

Williams, Cheri L. "Dealing with the Data: Ethical Issues in Case Study Research." Mortensen and Kirsch 40–57.

Williams, Patricia. *The Alchemy of Race and Rights.* Cambridge: Harvard UP, 1991.

Williams, Peter N. "The Great Rising." *A Brief History of Wales.* 2001. BritanniaTravels 17 May 2003 <http://www.britannia.com/wales/whist16.html>.

Williams, Raymond. *Writing in Society.* London: Verso, 1983.

Willis, Paul. *Learning to Labor: How Working Class Kids Get Working Class Jobs.* New York: Columbia UP, 1981.

Wolfe, Don M. *Leveller Manifestoes of the Puritan Revolution.* New York: Nelson, 1944.

Young, Margerite. "Ruffner Led Vigilante Committee." *Union Press* 20 Oct. 1937: 1+. Beaver Valley Labor History Society archives, University of Pittsburgh.

Zinker, Joseph C. *In Search of Good Form: Gestalt Therapy with Couples and Families.* San Francisco: Jossey Bass, 1994.

Index

abstractions, 11, 18, 33–34, 167; alienation and, 16–17, 20; experiences' relation to, 28, 49, 54, 133; reorganizing, 52–53, 95; Winstanley rejecting, 105, 111

academics, 140; coalition building by, 69, 71, 156–57; influence on social change by, 40–41; marginalized groups and, 14–15; oppression among, 11–12; unlearning privilege, 25–27

action, 36, 133, 190; and awareness, 28–32; changing, 30–31, 35, 40; collective *vs.* individual, 135–37, 173; perception and, 9, 18–19; planning for, 112–14; unionizers promoting, 167–68, 172–73, 189, 191, 193, 204–8; Winstanley promoting, 118, 123–26, 128

aesthetic language, 228n7; in Diggers' texts, 104–5, 127–28; facilitating contact, 61, 66; Goodman on, 150, 216–17, 227n14; in Struggle documents, 79–81, 217; uses of, 38–40, 65–66

affect, 24, 226n6; awareness of responses, 28, 31–32; roles of, 22, 37–38

African Americans, 74. *See also* Struggle program

agency, sense of: in Diane and Ian's relationship, 153–54; in Diggers' texts, 105, 107, 109, 133, 138–39; increasing, 10, 170, 175, 181; individual *vs.* group, 156, 158–59; need for, 4, 25, 94, 215; of the poor, 123–25; religion and, 133–35; rhetorical strategies to encourage, 21, 29–30, 167, 212–13, 222–23; steelworkers', 169–70; Winstanley promoting, 134–35, 137–38, 215

Agreement of the People (Levellers), 116, 129

alienation, 72, 75; and awareness, 20–21, 25; effects of language practices on, 15–17, 21, 148, 150, 216–17, 226n10

Aliquippa Gazette (newspaper), 162, 181–82, 198

Aliquippa (Woodlawn), Pa.: citizens reclaiming power in, 164–71, 174, 200, 207–8; education in, 174–75, 180–83, 229n4; effects of steel industry in, 161–62; effects of strike in, 198–99; effects of unions in, 174–75, 192–95; as Jones & Laughlin Steel Company town, 162–64, 177, 184, 200; politics in, 181–83, 186–87, 192–93; unionizing of, 160, 177–78, 197

Althusser, Louis, 2, 7, 211

Amalgamated Association of Iron, Steel, and Tin Workers of North America (AA of IS and TW of NA), 165, 171, 176–78, 194–96, 198

Ambridge, Pa., 161–62, 176

American Federation of Labor (AFL), 178; relations with other unions, 191, 195; and unionization of steel industry, 161–62, 175–76

Anabaptists, and Levellers, 118–19

Atallah, Albert, 178, 195

awareness, 7, 25, 34, 103, 228n6; of alternatives, 49, 52–53, 56, 105–6, 150; blocks to, 22, 168; of changed conditions, 173–74, 187; changing, 29–30, 32; diminished, 20, 28; of emotional responses, 28, 31–32; expansion of, 17, 27, 30–31; juxtaposition of, 178, 182, 184, 186–87, 191; of language practices, 50, 214, 219–20; proprioceptive, 17, 26, 51; role of language practices in expanding, 27, 42, 211–12, 218; of self-restraint, 21–22; Struggle program's focus on expanding, 54, 146–47, 150

Baskins, Joyce: paper on Struggle interactions by, 90–94; religion of, 63–64, 81–82, 89–90;